List of Testimonials

"Fascinating book that gets to the heart of how organizations are governed in China and how they differ from elsewhere."
Patrick Dunne, Chair of EY Foundation, Chair of ESSA, Author of Boards

"Zhang is a true expert on both Chinese culture and business. In this book she tackles Chinese corporate governance practices through thoughtful analysis supported by several case studies. Any investor or executive who invest in or compete against Chinese companies should read this book."
Jack McCullough, President of CFO Leadership Council, Author of Secrets of Rockstar CFOs, The Psychopathic CEO – An Executive Survival Guide

"Lyndsey does a masterful job of rendering an inherently complex topic into a highly accessible guide for businesses and investors. Lyndsey's astute analysis frames Chinese corporate governance within its proper historic, economic, societal, and political context. The extensive use of relevant case studies throughout the book brings additional clarity and helps tie a number of critical, seemingly independent, concepts into a coherent whole. As China continues its economic ascent, and as corporate governance practices gain additional scrutiny amid the rise of ESG investing, investors and businesses alike can't afford to ignore this seminal book."
Nawar Alsaadi, FSA, SIPC, Senior Portfolio Manager, ESG Investing, Canada Post, Author of The Bull of Heaven, Clock Zero

"Lyndsey Zhang offers her unique experience of being a Chinese American with a corporate career in both countries, to help the reader better understand China's rapidly changing (corporate) culture, regulatory developments, and business practices.

Having done quite some business in China myself, I wished I could have benefitted from Lyndsey's invaluable -practical but academically substantiated - insights, when I needed them so badly.

For anybody who is interested in doing business in China, no matter at which level or in which role, this book is a Must Read.

I have no doubt that *Corporate Governance in China Seen Through a Practitioner's Lens* will fast become a standard work, both in the academic as well as in the business world."

Rosa Zeegers, Partner at Newport LLC.

"Lyndsey's initiative and effort in enhancing the understanding of the corporate governance issues of Chinese companies is impressive and impactful. Specifically, she approaches and unpacks this complex topic with a broad array of experts and their respective perspectives via lively dialogues and concrete examples. I think her work will continue to contribute positively to raising corporate governance awareness and improving ESG practices among the Chinese companies and a broader stakeholder network."

Vivian Lin Thurston, CFA, Partner and Portfolio Manager at William Blair Investment Management, co-managing various Emerging Markets and Chinese equity strategies.

"Lyndsey has a talent of combining hard-core research with her extensive personal experience to provide very insightful knowledge of the evolving Chinese business culture and how it influences governing itself. Anyone trying to decide whether to enter the Chinese market needs to understand this. Those who are already in the Chinese market but are struggling will benefit by incorporating this information to re-evaluate their current market strategy. Of course, those who invest in Chinese companies who value the "G" of ESG need to read this as well."

Jerry Strub, CEO & Founder of Strategic Growth Consulting, Inc.

Corporate Governance in China Seen Through a Practitioner's Lens is an important book for several reasons, and it is quite frankly much more than just a practical guide for businesses and investors "Through a Practitioner's Lens". It sheds light on a topic quite unknown and often misunderstood in the West, it does it in a knowledgeable and clearly accessible way, and it does it from the perspective of an author very familiar with both the Chinese and the American corporate world. The result is a hands-on and not theoretical analysis of corporate governance in China, not just for what it is now, but looking at its roots and very recent developments. The Chinese corporate world is often explained or described from a Eurocentric or US-centric point of view, or from a strictly Chinese perspective that does not help the reader. One of the most important elements of this book, besides being extremely up to date, is Lyndsey Zhang's capacity of taking both perspectives into account. Her exhaustive analysis of corporate governance in China will clarify most questions.
Andrea Fiano, Editor of Global Finance Magazine

"Following mainland China's opening approximately forty years ago, Western businesses have learned to operate and participate in China's fantastic economic growth, essentially functioning as the world's factory. Since the last decade, China is coming of age with the goal to provide further development to its people and find a new place in the world.
Lyndsey's book describes China's master plan and the mega trends at play that impact businesses and mindsets. If not their acceptance, it will help Western corporate leaders build understanding and set strategies for their investments and relationships with this essential country. For this reason, *Corporate Governance in China Seen Through a Practitioner's Lens* is a must read."
Christine Raynaud, Former Director of the European Chamber of Commerce in Hong Kong and business owner in China

"Lyndsey Zhang is a consummate professional. With great insight, experience and passion, Lyndsey has taken on a subject –Corporate Governance in China- that would overwhelm and confound many, and yet she brings all her knowledge and communication skills to make the topic of understanding Chinese corporate governance very readable, understandable and especially interesting. It has been my pleasure to know Lyndsey for several years and to observe her vigorous work ethic, enthusiasm for new challenges and dedication to excellence in her work. These core traits of Lyndsey show through in this latest effort of hers, to compile the definitive and comprehensive guide to *Corporate Governance in China Seen Through a Practitioner's Lens*.

Anyone involved in business that touches China, internally or externally, by ownership or investment, should read Lyndsey's book, and in doing so will certainly gain the knowledge Lyndsey set out to provide, as a clear guide to the intricacies and evolution of Corporate Governance in China. Excellent effort Lyndsey, and thoroughly and thoughtfully presented!"

Anthony Nasharr, Shareholder of Polsinelli PC

"Combining a Chinese and American academic background as well as business experience in both countries, Lyndsey Zhang explores in this well documented volume the key issue of corporate governance in China. In addition to broad ESG issues, she addresses some of the hottest topics surrounding governance in corporate China. The book offers an historical vision of how governance evolved, from China's development journey to its regulatory reforms. It also explores a variety of more specific topics such as, inter alia, the involvement of the Party in business and economic matters, the country's 14th Five-Year Plan, its Social Credit System, the Variable Interest Vehicle Structure (VIE) or the Belt and Road Initiative. The author shares her own personal insights and assessment of developments in China, illustrating them with a wide array of iconic case studies. This approach contributes to bringing a sense of reality to the book, while making its reading quite lively. Highlighting the uniqueness of China -its demographic characteristics, the size of its economy, its thousand years of history, culture, and values – Lyndsey Zhang recognizes how complex (and sometimes confusing) Chinese business practices or Government policies can be for the global business community outside China. At the same time, she contends that Western growth and business models are not necessarily fitted to the needs and constraints of emerging markets. On the contrary, she argues, the

"China model" developed in recent decades points to the need for a diversified approach. Applying a "Western lens" to emerging markets may not be the proper way to measure their true economic and social performance. While the author does not provide definite answers to all of these complex (and sometimes sensitive) issues, her fresh perspective invites the reader to think deeper, and at times reconsider some of their basic assumptions. Regardless of one's opinion on some of the hot topics addressed, this book, written in a lively style, constitutes a very interesting and enriching reading for the business community, students and anyone who wants to better understand corporate governance in China."
Professor Anne Miroux, Faculty Fellow, Emerging Markets Institute, Cornell S.C. Johnson College of Business, Cornell University

Corporate Governance in China Seen Through a Practitioner's Lens

Lyndsey Zhang

© 2021 Lyndsey Zhang

This book is sold subject to the condition that it shall not, by way of trade or otherwise, be lent, resold, hired out, or otherwise circulated without the publisher's prior consent in any form of binding or cover other than that in which it is published and without a similar condition including this condition being imposed on the subsequent publisher.

The moral right of Lyndsey Zhang has been asserted
First published in Great Britain in 2021 by Governance Publishing and Information Services Ltd

ISBN 978-1-9162569-3-4

www.governance.co.uk

Designed and typeset in 12pt Dante MT by Geoff Fisher

Book cover designed by Doudou Lv at CENOZOIC

Author photo by Yong Wu

Printed by CPI Group (UK) CR0 4YY

Dedication

Dedicated to the memory of my mother Lanfen Ding (1949 - 2005). Her encouragement of resilience and persistence and her passion about education and sharing have always been inspiring.

Also dedicated to my father Liuzhou Zhang, his unconditional support made me fearless on the journey to chase my dreams.

About the Author

Lyndsey Zhang has extensive experiences working for western and Chinese multinational companies in automation manufacture, clean energy, renewable energy and high-tech sectors. She held CFO and VP of Strategy positions in Chinese companies and served on the board of directors as both executive and non-executive directors. Leading these Chinese companies' global expansion including fundraising on Hong Kong stock exchanges, cross-border mergers and acquisitions in European countries, and post-acquisition integration in the US, have positioned her to understand the opportunities and challenges for both Chinese multinationals and their global partners.

As an advocate of good corporate governance and ESG practice, Lyndsey hosts the Boardroom&Beyond podcast Corporate Governance Around the World, and ESG In Action shows, and regularly publishes articles in the UK's Governance and the US's Global Finance.

Lyndsey has been a licensed CPA in the state of Illinois since 2007, and a certified Independent Board Director from Harvard University since 2019. She received her Master of Science in Accountancy from Illinois State University, and Bachelor of Science in Economics from Xiamen University in China. Lyndsey is now a PhD researcher at Henley Business School at the University of Reading for corporate governance and ESG research.

Living in Chicago with her husband, Lyndsey is a long-time yoga practitioner and runner, who believes in finding the right methodology, keeping practice, and never giving up can make most impossible possible.

Contents

Acknowledgements   xv

Foreword by Professor Andrew Kakabadse   xix

Introduction   xxiii
The inspiration for this book
What this book offers
For whom this book is intended

Chapter 1 - A Brief Overview of Corporate Governance Development in China

1.1. The Status of CG Development in China   1
    1.1.1. The Shanghai Stock Exchange (SSE) and Shenzhen Stock Exchange (SZSE)   1
    1.1.2. The China Securities Regulatory Commission (CSRC)   4
    1.1.3. The Chinese Government's Intervention   6
    1.1.4. China's CG Code   8

1.2. A Close Look at Chinese Companies' Governance Models   8
    1.2.1. Two-Tier Boards (German vs China)   9
    1.2.2. "Owned by the People"   9
    1.2.3. Creative Governance Models of China's Non-SOEs   10

1.3. Major CG Differences between China and the US   16
    1.3.1. Governmental Influence   16
    1.3.2. The Power of SOEs in China   17
    1.3.3. CEO Nomination, Succession Planning and Compensation   18

1.4. Major CG Differences between China and Japan   19
1.4.1. Controlling Structure   19
1.4.2. Stakeholder Relationships   19

Case Study 1.1. Alibaba's Controlling Structure   11
Case Study 1.2. Alibaba's Succession Planning   12
Case Study 1.3. Huawei's Rotating CEO/Chairman System   12
Case Study 1.4. Huawei's "Superfluid" Organizational Structure   13

Chapter 2 – The Ownership and Controlling Structure

2.1. Chinese SOEs and their Key CG Matters   23
2.1.1. The "China Puzzle"   23
2.1.2. Key CG Matters of Chinese SOEs   25

2.2. Founder Controlling Structure and its Sustainability   27
2.2.1. Dictatorship and Voting Rights   28
2.2.2. Long-Term Value Creation   29
2.2.3. The Founder's Commitment   30
2.2.4. Sustainability Considerations   31

2.3. VIE Structure Loophole and the Government's Approach to Fix it   35
2.3.1. What is a VIE Structure?   36
2.3.2. Brief History of China's VIE Structure   37
2.3.3. The Chinese Regulator's Oversight of the VIE Structure   39

Case Study 2.1. Alibaba's Voting Arrangements with Softbank and Yahoo   28
Case Study 2.2. Alibaba Founder's Commitments to Alleviate Investors' Concerns   30
Case Study 2.3. Pinduoduo Founder's Retirement – Trend of a New Succession Plan Model   32
Case Study 2.4. Sina.com VIE Structure - A Potential Investor's Intriguing Story   38

Chapter 3 – An Overview of China's SOE and CG Regulation Reform

3.1. Timetable of China's SOE and CG Regulation Reform Milestones   44

3.2. History is Not Repeatable – China's SOE Reform   48
    3.2.1. Stage One (1978 – 1984): Autonomy and Incentive   48
    3.2.2. Stage Two (1985 – 1992): "Neither This Nor That" - Separating SOEs' Ownership and Operating Rights Based on Public Ownership   50
    3.2.3. Stage Three (1993 – 2002): SOE Corporatization - the beginning of China's CG Development   51
    3.2.4. Stage Four (2003 – 2012): State-Owned Asset Management System Reform   54
    3.2.5. Stage Five (2013 – present): Extensive SOE reform   55

3.3. China's CG Reform   58
    3.3.1. Chinese Companies' CG Improvement Parallels Regulatory Development   59
    3.3.2. China's CG Reform Trends   61

Case Study 3.1. The Establishment of Haier – Collective Ownership Structure (SOE Reform Stage One)   49
Case Study 3.2. Haier's Opportunity for IPO and International Growth (SOF Reform Stage Two & Three)   52
Case Study 3.3. Haier's Rendanheyi Model (SOE Reform Stage Four & Five)   56
Case Study 3.4. Lenovo's CG model   60

Chapter 4 – Key CG Risks of Chinese Companies

4.1. Insider Share Pledging Risk   65
    4.1.1. CEO Share Pledging Motivations   65
    4.1.2. Risk Mitigation of Insider Share Pledging   66
    4.1.3. CEO Share Pledging Landscape in the US   68
    4.1.4. Chinese Companies' Founders & CEOs' Share Pledge   69

4.2. VIE Structure Risks   71
    4.2.1. Legal Uncertainty   72
    4.2.2. Investors' Fragile Ownership   73
    4.2.3. How do Chinese Companies Handle VIE Structure Risks?   74

4.3. The Founder Controlling Company's Key Person Risk   75

4.4. Party Committee and Party Involvement – Risk or Support?   77

4.5. Other Risks   78

    Case Study 4.1. Luckin Coffee Scandal and Founder Pledge   69
    Case Study 4.2. Alibaba Alipay Ownership Transfer Case - VIE Structure and its Risk to Shareholders   73
    Case Study 4.3. JD.com Founder's Poor Reputation Impacts Company's Stock Price   75

Chapter 5 – What is Driving China's CG Development?

5.1. Pros and Cons of Chinese Companies' CG Practices   83
    5.1.1. Government Influence   83
    5.1.2. Creativity and Quick Reaction Capacity   84
    5.1.3. The Vernal Years   85

5.2. Key Domestic Drivers   87
    5.2.1. Global Branding Challenges   88
    5.2.2. Leadership Transfer Challenges –Founder Generation Retirement   90
    5.2.3. China's Continuous Regulation Reform and Enhancement of Regulation Enforcement   93

5.3. Main International Drivers   98
    5.3.1. US Scrutiny of US-listed Chinese Companies   98
    5.3.2. The Increase of Foreign Investments in Chinese Companies   100

Case Study 5.1. Corporate Governance Weakness of Haier's
　　　　Rendanheyi Model　　　　　　　　　　　　　　　　89
　　Case Study 5.2. Wahaha's Corporate Governance Weakness
　　　　Revealed Through its Leadership Transfer　　　　　91
　　Case Study 5.3. Ant Group IPO Incident　　　　　　　　94

Chapter 6 – Chinese CSR and ESG Evaluation Systems

6.1. Corporate Social Responsibility in China　　　　　104
　　6.1.1. CSR History and Development in China　　　　104
　　6.1.2. Chinese Government's Influence in CSR
　　　　　Development　　　　　　　　　　　　　　　106

**6.2. Chinese CSR Evaluation Systems and ESG Rating
　　Systems**　　　　　　　　　　　　　　　　　　　　107
　　6.2.1. Chinese CSR Evaluation Systems　　　　　　108
　　6.2.2. Chinese ESG Rating Systems　　　　　　　　108

6.3. MSCI ESG Rating Systems and MSCI China ESG Index　111
　　6.3.1. MSCI Global Sustainability Indexes　　　　　111
　　6.3.2. MSCI China ESG Leader Index　　　　　　　114

6.4. China's ESG Evaluation System's Future Development　116
　　6.4.1. Non-Government Advocate Organizations　　116
　　6.4.2. The Necessity to Develop a Chinese ESG Evaluation System　117
　　6.4.3. The Context for China's ESG Evaluation System
　　　　　Development　　　　　　　　　　　　　　　118

Chapter 7 – China's ESG Revolution in the Post-COVID-19 Era

7.1. ESG Movements in China　　　　　　　　　　　　124
　　7.1.1. Regulation Reforms　　　　　　　　　　　　124
　　7.1.2. Transforming to Green Finance　　　　　　　125
　　7.1.3. Carbon Emission Control　　　　　　　　　127

7.2. Major Drivers of China's ESG Revolution   128
    7.2.1. Policy Makers and Regulators   128
    7.2.2. Domestic Asset Owners, Asset Management Firms and Investors   130
    7.2.3. Chinese Corporations   133

7.3. Challenges and Opportunities in China's ESG Revolution   137
    7.3.1. Moving up the Value Chain   137
    7.3.2. Trend of Business Mindset Change   139

Case Study 7.1. Ping An Insurance Group ESG Adoption in the Post COVID-19 Era   131
Case Study 7.2. Xiaomi ESG integration in the Post COVID-19 Era   134
Case Study 7.3. VIPKid's Social Impact Strategy   139

Chapter 8 – Trends to Watch

8.1. China's 14th Five Year Plan (FYP)   144
    8.1.1. The Three Development Features of the 14th FYP   145
    8.1.2. How will the 14th FYP Reshape China's ESG Landscape?   146

8.2. China's Social Credit System (SoCS)   147
    8.2.1. The Tradition Version of China's SoCS   148
    8.2.2. Punishments and Rewards of China's SoCS   149
    8.2.3. China's SoCS Impact on ESG Revolution   151

8.3. China's Commitment to a Higher Standard Regulation System   153
    8.3.1. Intellectual Property Protection   154
    8.3.2. Anti-Trust Law Enforcement   156
    8.3.3. Minority Shareholders' Interest Protection   157

8.4. The Rise of Social Entrepreneurship in China   160

Case Study 8.1. Feilo Acoustics Co Ltd Minority Shareholders Interest Protection   158
Case Study 8.2. ByteDance Founder CEO Zhang Yiming's Resignation   160

Chapter 9 – Future Trends of Regional Agreements and Partnerships

9.1. Regional Comprehensive Economic Partnership	165
9.1.1. What We Should Know About RCEP	166
9.1.2. Opportunities and Challenges for China as RCEP's Leading Country	168
9.2. China's Belt and Road Initiative and Feedback	170
9.2.1. Positive Economic and Social Impacts	170
9.2.2. Challenges for BRI's Future Development	171
9.3. China-Africa Collaboration	173
9.3.1. Impacts and Challenges	173
9.3.2. Major Problems of Chinese Multinationals' Overseas Operations	176
9.3.3. Major Problems in Host Countries and Solutions in Home Countries	179
Case Study 9.1. SinoHydro-Ghana Bui Dam Hydroelectricity Project – Calling for Regulation Improvements for Multinational Companies' Home and Host Countries	174

Chapter 10 – China's RMB Internationalization and the Future of Hong Kong

10.1. China's RMB Internationalization	184
10.1.1. The Importance of RMB Internationalization	184
10.1.2. The Progress of RMB Internationalization	186
10.1.3 Chinese Digital Currency	192
10.1.4. What's Next?	193
10.2. The Future of Hong Kong	194
10.2.1. International Financial Center Roles	194

    10.2.2. An Important RMB Offshore Center   198
    10.2.3. Potential of Guangdong Hong Kong Macau GBA   198

CHAPTER 11- Conclusion

"Stay low profile, work high profile"   202
Mutual Understanding   203
A Mindset Change of Regulation Compliance and Social Impact   206
Continuous Evolving of Chinese Companies' CG Models   207

Appendix I: List of Further Reading   209
Appendix II: List of Acronyms   211
Appendix III: References by Chapter   215
Appendix IV: List of Interviewees   246

Index   249

Acknowledgements

Writing this book has been a valuable learning, thinking and growing journey. I want to thank all those below who have helped me allow this book to become a reality!

To Patrick Dunne, the Chair of ESSA (Education Sub-Saharan Africa) and various education organizations: Thank you for your multitude of advice before I first started planning for this book, and for your generosity in spending time carefully reviewing the less-polished version of the entire manuscript while offering insightful comments that improved it greatly.

To Christine Raynaud, a former director of the European Chamber of Commerce in Hong Kong and business owner in China: for sharing your own experiences partnering with Chinese companies during your ten years of living in Hong Kong, for offering penetrating comments for this book, given your profound understanding of Chinese culture and Chinese companies' opportunities and challenges based on forty years of experience advising Western and Asian multinationals - including Chinese companies.

To Andrea Fiano, Anthony Nasharr, Vivian Lin Thurston, Jerry Strub, Rosa Zeegers, Marie-Josée Privyk, Jack McCullough, and Nawar Alsaadi: For reading the manuscript draft and offering your thoughtful and candid comments to improve the manuscript for future readers. Special thanks to Nawar Alsaadi, you made the last push as a trustworthy friend when I was hesitant to start this book.

To the more than twenty people who participated in formal interviews (published on the Boardroom&Beyond podcast platform) and informal discussions, for sharing your stories and opinions regarding corporate governance, corporate cultures, and business practices in different parts of the world, including China. Many of your stories were helpful comparisons needed for readers to understand corporate governance in China.

To Doudou Lv at CENOZOIC for the sharp selection of Chinese elements for the book cover and the book cover design. To Yong Wu and Wei Zhang for the wonderful author photo, and for encouraging my writing and publishing with your friendship and much practical support. To David Warren, for being my sounding board of this book's ideas at its early stage of development. – Thank you!

To my publisher Lesley Stephenson at Governance Publishing and Information Services Ltd: For your vision identifying the demand of understanding China Corporate Governance practice in the global business community due to your decades of experience publishing and witnessing the world-wide evolution of corporate governance; for being the first global corporate governance magazine publisher to publish my China Corporate Governance articles; for encouraging me to start this book and also deciding to publish it; and for making it possible to publish this only eight weeks after the final manuscript's delivery, thus allowing for timely world-wide availability so readers will be able to acquire an initial understanding of China's economic environment of fast-paced regulation updates concurrent with business practice reactions, which has and will influence Chinese companies' corporate governance developments.

And to my editor Dan Covic: For your tireless assistance and enthusiastic hard work that always made the manuscripts available ahead of schedule in order for them to be reviewed; and for making the manuscript stronger.

More importantly, this book would not exist without the inspiration, encouragement, advice, and suggestions from people who have devoted decades of their lives researching and studying corporate governance and related topics, and then generously shared their wisdom and offered support during my journey.

To Professor Andrew Kakabadse: Your research and books on corporate governance, leadership, and government policies have been inspiring while your personal advice has guided me during my thought process development regarding global views on China corporate governance matters (*every conversation with you made me a little smarter!*). Your feedback and endorsement of this book gave me the confidence that was so important for a new author. Thanks also to my good friend Fabio Oliveira for introducing me to Professor Kakabadse.

To Professor Lourdes Casanova and Professor Anne Miroux: Your research and books on emerging market multinationals and Chinese multinationals opened my mind and enhanced my interest to study the meaningfulness of Chinese companies' corporate governance in emerging markets and the world. Conversations with both of you when I first started writing the China Corporate Governance articles helped plant the seeds for this book. Special thanks to Professor Anne Miroux for reviewing the manuscript.

To my mentor Michele Wucker: Your books have enlightened me with the understanding of how to convert an individual's voice in order to powerfully provide influential messages; Your generous advice was mercifully given to seemingly "millions" of questions - some of which I did not know who or how to ask, while some would have become future questions unless you shared your wisdom.

To Professor Bob Tricker and Professor Gregg Li: Your 2019 book *Understanding Corporate Governance in China* epitomized the direction of my research. Regular exchanges with both of you were the most significant factors that encouraged my two-year journey of researching corporate governance development in China. Special thanks to Professor Li for regularly sharing with me news about various China corporate governance and ESG developments that kept me close to the fast pace of development changes in China.

To all my colleagues, business partners, mentors and friends with whom I worked and met during my five years of employment with three Chinese multinational companies: Sharing your experiences, knowledge, advice, opinions, and personal/professional networks made those five years an unforgettable and profound life-changing journey filled with exciting interactive experiences and fathomless understanding of Chinese companies' corporate cultures, business operations, stakeholder management and governance practices. Despite not listing your names for various reasons, your support, friendships and contributions are divinely treasured within my heart, and were relied upon as the primary foundation of my research of China's corporate governance. - Thank you!

Finally, to my father Liuzhou Zhang, for encouraging me to pursue my dreams since my childhood; and to my husband, Dong Jiang, for understanding this endless curiosity-seeking adventure and always being my audience. This journey wouldn't have been possible without both of your unconditional support!

Foreword

It was with great pleasure when Lyndsey invited me for an interview as part of her research for this book. With my years of research in corporate governance (CG), leadership, and government policy, she was interested in learning my opinions regarding a new international business order with the rise of the emerging world led by China, the future of the China – US relationship and its impact on the world, and how China can lead. Our conversation was as enjoyable as every other we had over the past several months, given her endless questions and passion for researching China's CG development trend and for helping bridge the understanding gap of CG practice between China and the West.

CG, including its progress in China, has been evolving across the world due to perpetual changes in the global business landscape. China's effective control of the pandemic and its quick recovery from COVID-19 made the country's markets more attractive that resulted from their proven success and increasing returns from domestic output. Regardless of the increased tension between the US and China, the trend toward further investment and engagement in Chinese markets has been led by world-class investors such as Blackrock, who was the first foreign institution receiving a license to operate a wholly-owned subsidiary in the country. The need to understand China's CG has become both important and urgent, although concurrent with some doubts of the effectiveness and trustworthiness of a high-standards institutional system to which the Chinese Government has committed.

The unique path China has been taking for its economic development over the past several decades, given its different political system and traditionally restrained culture, has been the subject of considerable research and interminable study that has been mainly confined to the academic world. Lyndsey's dual background and first-hand experience working for Chinese multinationals has enriched her understanding of China's CG practice that frequently differs from those of Western companies. Lyndsey's work includes insightful comparisons between China's CG and other prominent CG models, and case studies of a number of Chinese companies and their paths toward development in the modern world. The case studies and her examination of these companies' behaviors are undoubtedly credible since they are seen through a practitioner's lens that will assist readers to understand the uniqueness of the "China model" and help readers to connect their own experiences for more rational decisions.

China has been ascending the international hierarchy and will indisputably become a superpower. The question is, *can* China become a leader and *how*? A country who leads is expected to conform to a few basic criteria and China is compelled to demonstrate their compliance. Specifically, a sophisticated and trustworthy institutional system that supports and encourages fair competition and sufficient investor protection of its domestic market with built-in prevention of systematic risks is necessary; a transparent process regarding how the government operates across different levels since that is the foundation of CG development in a country; and a healthy global partnership network that enables the country to contribute and influence global growth. While China continues to work on improving its global position, the following questions are also essential: Will diversity of thought be further encouraged that allows different voices and opinions to be heard? Can the Chinese Government handle today's international relationships and crises diplomatically?

The fact that China has become a global leader in AI, biotech, and space exploration, as well as an economic titan allowing its citizens the privileges of improved consumer lifestyles, leisure travel and a high demand for tertiary education, has confirmed a truth – *the Western models are not singularly successful options; the "China model" also works*. While the Western models have been extraordinarily efficacious, let us not forget that China is feeding 20% of the world's population with land size similar to that of the US, where coal has been that country's dominant energy source for decades, which means it has to pursue its own path and overcome much more challenging and different hurdles to build a trustworthy society and to achieve its carbon neutrality goals. Therefore, measurements to evaluate China's approach must be adjusted accordingly.

In addition, will the rise of the "China model", the critics of Chinese companies' overseas operations, as well as China's quick reaction to the COVID-19 pandemic cause the three reconsiderations respectively? First, diversified economic models that are more suitable for emerging market countries with their inherent social and economic conditions; second, a brand new global collaboration that will help prevent bad business behaviors in developing countries and help these countries to improve their regulation systems simultaneously; third, the trend of studying through an ideological lens regarding the advanced characteristics of emerging economic models? Although the emerging markets models may be obscured, causing faulty judgment of seemingly obvious risky behaviors according to the Western standards, these models were actually proved to be more resilient under a crisis such as COVID-19 as they were developed from an environment with many uncertainties. Global business outlook adjustments resulting from the emergence of Asian and African countries' innovation and a blossoming workforce, in contrast with advanced countries' well-structured, stable, although ageing societies, are revelations that the modern world will indeed benefit from the growth of emerging market countries. Perhaps understanding China's CG development can also lead to a different mindset regarding the underlying context of a future global society that demands exhaustive collaboration.

Understanding is the "magic" that will bolster societies to continue moving forward. As humans, understanding enables us to solve problems, explore other parts of the universe that may be unknown, and that placing "civilians in space" is no longer a dream. As a unified, global society, understanding empowers us to share resources, freely exchange knowledge, and to partnership while focusing on a mutually-shared planet. Understanding is a journey that includes searching, thinking, comparing, judging, and finding solutions. Through sharing her personal journey as she searched for answers regarding Chinese companies' CG development and their impact on the rest of the world, Lyndsey is trying to help us understand the process with an open mind.

Andrew Kakabadse
Professor of Governance and Leadership at the Henley Business School

Introduction

The inspiration for this book

The idea of writing about Chinese companies' corporate governance (CG) and business practices was inspired by my exchanges with two CG gurus, Professor Bob Tricker and Professor Gregg Li. After reading *Understanding Corporate Governance in China* co-authored by these two professors, I was deeply enlightened by how they linked Chinese culture, the Chinese regulatory system, and the country's ever-changing economic environment to Chinese companies' CG practices and China's CG development journey. I then connected with both authors and was encouraged by both of them to write and publish.

Prior to that time, I had worked for three Chinese multinational companies, experienced many confusing moments when navigating these corporate systems and struggled to comprehend their organizational behavior, while being amazed by these companies' fast growth and aggressive expansion in the global market. These three companies employed different ownership structures and CG models (private company, State-Owned Enterprise (SOE) and overseas-listed company), which exposed me to many topics related to their CG practices and China's regulation reform at the time, and my front line experience with these subjects later became a valuable foundation of my research.

However, beginning to write this book did not happen until I spent a couple of years studying the history of CG and its evolving journey in different parts of the world, and also upon reviewing China's regulatory reform since the country opened its door in 1978. I also collected and examined a number of Chinese companies' CG models and business practices that reflected special time periods of China's regulatory reform which serve as documentation of the reform journey.

China's quick recovery from the COVID-19 pandemic, the country's sustained GDP growth over the past decades, and progressive opening of its financial markets attracted and enabled global investors to invest directly in its capital market. In addition, with the global growth of

Chinese multinationals, an increasing number of professionals from advanced and emerging market countries have started to join Chinese companies' boards of directors or as executives. As a result, investors and business leaders from many countries are now interested in learning about Chinese companies' CG and business practices.

However, with China's one-party political system and its unique economic reform approach of "feeling the stones while crossing the river", its constant attempts at correcting and altering regulatory measures and companies' business practices, systematically studying the country's CG journey has not been easy. Somewhat complicating matters is China's rapid economic growth within the global market which amplified the social and economic panic caused by periodic occurrences of some Chinese companies' corporate fraudulent behavior, with the following questions regarding Chinese companies' CG practice raised in the global market:

- How do Chinese SOEs govern their business? What are the Party's roles in SOEs? Are all Chinese companies controlled by the Chinese government?
- Will Chinese companies improve their CG practices? What are the drivers for their improvement?
- What are the main reasons for Chinese companies' financial fraud? What are other risks of Chinese companies' CG practices for investors and business partners?
- And, **HOW**, do we step out from the "navigating in the dark" feeling when working with Chinese companies?

While conducting the research for this book and pulling together the various strands of knowledge on the topic, I was able to connect the dots collected during my five years experience with the Chinese companies I worked for, and have learned a great deal to answer these questions. In addition, with the worldwide Environmental, Social and Governance (ESG) movement accelerated by the COVID-19 pandemic and the increase in the global public opinion war led by US – China tension, I found the topics below are equally important to understand China's CG development and future trends:

- What is China's take on the worldwide ESG movement? How will Chinese companies' CG practices evolve in the future?
- What is China's Social Credit System? How will the system work for foreign companies' operations in China and for foreigners working in China?
- What is the status of China's currency's the renminbi (RMB) - internationalization? Will China's digital currency accelerate its RMB internationalization?
- What is the future of Hong Kong?

Although most of these topics are still evolving and subject to considerable academic and professional research, I believe the highlights of these topics and the relationship between them and China's CG development are an indispensable part of the book too.

Therefore, I have included them all in this book. I really hope that you find the book both useful and enjoyable!

What this book offers

To help readers easily understand Chinese companies' CG practices and development along with China's regulatory reform over the past several decades, this book presents and analyzes several iconic business case scenarios that introduce and explain China's CG development, uniqueness, challenges, and future development trends. It also points out the key CG risks that global businesses, investors, and other professionals should be aware of when making business and personal financial decisions. Relevant concepts such as corporate social responsibility (CSR) and ESG and their importance to Chinese companies, the process of China's metamorphosis from a CSR standards-taker to a leader, how the global ESG movement has impacted and rapidly evolved in China over the past few years, and the impact of China's ESG development on global business will be discussed. The book also reviews China's 14th Five-Year Plan that focuses and emphasizes the country's determination for transferring its development model from high-speed to high-quality, and the government's commitment toward its 2060 carbon neutrality goals together with higher-standard ESG compliance and regulation reform that will likely catapult the country into an influential superpower in the post-COVID-19 era and certainly the leader in Asian-Pacific growth. Also presented are methods the Chinese government and the country's companies are considering while pursuing global economic opportunities and how those will evolve in the always intricate international business climate.

The case studies within this book were carefully selected to reflect on the impact these companies' CG structures and practices have experienced from certain milestones or special events in the different stages during China's economic and regulatory reforms, and to evaluate the current trends of Chinese companies' CG development and ESG improvement.

As a Chinese American who spent nearly half of my life in each country, I am fortunate to understand both cultures and their influence on organizational governance models and business practices. While the US is an advanced country with an established and well-structured business order containing a comprehensive regulatory system, China is the most rapidly growing emerging markets country and is steadily modernizing its business environment to align with international standards. Therefore, I hope this book can serve the following purposes:

1. **To assist the global business community's understanding of Chinese companies' CG practices and economic development journey**

    Twenty years ago, when I was a graduate student in a US business school, I learned how Western multinational companies expanded their businesses in developing countries when confronted with the challenges of duplicating a Western-style operation overseas. Since then, I have observed China become the world's second-largest economy as it increased the number of companies in the global marketplace. Owing to numerous overseas acquisitions in the 2010s, some have taken leading roles in different business sectors, enabling Chinese multinationals to establish their own governance models resulting in demonstrable success. Understanding Chinese companies' CG models and business practices will help businesses and investors make better decisions when collaborating with Chinese partners or while growing their businesses in China.

However, Chinese companies' CG models and business practices are invariably influenced by Chinese culture, its regulatory system, and a unique economic reform strategy. China's corporate atmosphere - including CG development - changes very quickly, which complicates evaluating and learning CG systematically. Some Chinese CG hot topics, such as the Variable Interest Entity (VIE) structure, government intervention, and Party Committee involvement, have been mysterious to the global business community, and it may be difficult to understand these topics without reviewing these companies' business practices which are simultaneously intertwined with them. After two years of researching a number of companies, I believe examining a few case studies is the most productive approach to explain China's regulatory reform, as well as the reasons for China's CG implementation and development that have been instrumental in the country's economic growth since 1978. Also briefly discussed are three incidents that occurred in 2021 after I began writing this book. These examples demonstrate the quickly evolving nature of Chinese companies' business practices since the beginning of 2021. For example, in March, the founder of Pingduoduo retired and handed the company's board chairman position to his business partner, the CEO of the company, which is indicative of the current trend of Chinese companies' future succession planning. In May, the first class-action lawsuit (filed by 315 shareholders) against the first Chinese publicly traded company ruled in favor of the shareholders, marking the initial successfully litigated case in Chinese post-1949 history that protected minority shareholders' interests. Also in May, the 38-year-old founder and CEO of TikTok's parent company, ByteDance, announced he would resign by the end of the year to better focus his energy on the company's long-term strategy while concentrating on the social good of the company, revealing the modern business mindset of the current generation's attitude toward social entrepreneurship in China.

2. **To shorten the learning time for Western business leaders and investors**

   I was born and raised in China, received my education in both China and the US, and have held executive positions in companies in both countries. Despite my dual background, I have also struggled and been as intrigued as many Westerners currently are when I worked for Chinese multinationals from 2014 to 2019. I can only image how tough this learning process will be for Westerners and professionals from other emerging countries. I desire that my colleagues in the rest of the world benefit from my knowledge and experience so that they may learn to understand Chinese corporate practices much more quickly than I did.

3. **To help understand the necessity of diversity in global economic growth models**

   Because of the success of advanced countries' economic models in the modern era, we often believe that the need exists to apply these models to emerging market countries. This approach may have realized some success forty years ago when Western multinational companies expanded into Asia and other developing countries and imposed their home model on these countries. However, the increasing economic influence of emerging markets countries, continuing improvements of their regulatory systems, and most importantly, the distinct cultures and environments impacting their economic status contradicts the "one-size-fits-all" model. Many Chinese companies have succeeded while using their own models (some are quite creative) over the past few decades, consistently announcing that what is suitable for advanced countries may not be advantageous for emerging markets, and raising demands for alternative models of economic growth, CG development, ESG adoption and evaluation for emerging market countries. However, developing the models for emerging market countries requires understanding, respect, and collaboration among these countries, advanced market countries, and international organizations.

For whom this book is intended

This book will be of interest to global investors who want to invest in Chinese companies as well as learning how to evaluate Chinese companies' CG risks. It will also be useful to corporate chairpersons, board directors, executives of multinational companies, and individuals seeking to obtain board director or executive roles in Chinese multinational corporations. Those with CG, ESG, law, merger and acquisition (M&A) interests, strategic and accounting experts from international consulting firms, and other inquisitive individuals will undoubtedly benefit. The book will also benefit business school students who are pursuing a Master of Business Administration degree (MBA) or other master's-level business, law, accounting, auditing, or corporate secretary programs degrees (or similar programs), as well as scholars or researchers of CG, emerging markets, Chinese multinationals, Chinese economic reform, or other academic topics.

Chapter 1

A Brief Overview of Corporate Governance Development in China

"I often feel I am navigating in the dark while working with Chinese companies."

In October 2014, I first heard the phrase "navigating in the dark" during my initial conversation with Chris (not his real name), an attorney from Germany, who had been living in Shanghai for several years to help his firm expand its business in China.

In September 2014, I moved back to China for a job opportunity at a manufacturing company in Ningbo, a fast-growing city 200 km from Shanghai. After living and working in North America for over a decade, I was impressed by Chinese companies' international growth in the early 2010s, and very excited about a new VP of Strategy position, as I would be responsible for the company's first overseas acquisition project in Germany, and lead its global growth strategy including seeking more acquisition opportunities. What a thrilling opportunity compared to my former director of finance position that included so many mundane routines!

I met with Chris one month later while I was searching for German attorney firms to build an external team for the acquisition project. Chris spoke fluent Chinese. His firm offered legal services to Chinese companies on various topics including mergers and acquisitions in Germany and other European countries. During the "golden" period of China's foreign investments that began in 2010, Chris, as well as many other Chinese-speaking European professionals, moved to China to grow their businesses. I was so impressed by Chris' Chinese, and he was excited to talk with someone with a Western background. However, and despite Chris' confusion and frustration while working with Chinese companies, I was very ambitious and also confident about my future career due to my dual background.

Within the following five years, I worked for three Chinese companies and lived in mainland China, Hong Kong, and the West Coast of the US. The three Chinese multinationals were governed by entirely different models and ownership structures, and of course, disparate company cultures. I also had numerous opportunities to participate in various roadshows, conferences and meetings with investors, banks, third-party service providers, and local government officials. The phrase "navigating in the dark" flashed across my mind many times when I found myself struggling to understand the business interactions among these parties and the decisions that were made by its top leaders. I started to better understand the meaning implied by the phrase and Chris' plight as a Westerner working in China. I also realized my disconnection with China during its growth period while I was pursuing the American dream on the other side of the world.

Why does working with Chinese companies seem like "navigating in the dark"? This very question led to my two-year research and study project regarding Chinese companies' corporate governance (CG) practices, so I thought this should be the ideal place to start this book.

There are many definitions of CG; the one below, I believe, best suits China's CG:

"Corporate Governance is about power and responsibility." - *Political Power and Corporate Control: The New Global Politics of Corporate Governance* by Peter Alexis Gourevitch and James J Shinn.

In other words, CG is how power is deployed and allocated in an organization, which includes the board, executives, and middle management. Power allocation cannot be separated from the influences and interventions of important stakeholders such as government and regulators. With China's unique one-party political structure, the way power is executed in Chinese companies involves both uniqueness and similarities compared to and contrasted with advanced countries.

To understand Chinese companies CG practices, let us start from the beginning of China's CG development.

1.1 The Status of CG Development in China

The reopening of the Shanghai Stock Exchange (SSE) in 1990, the establishment of the Shenzhen Stock Exchange (SZSE) in 1991, as well as the establishment of CSRC as the new stock market regulating authority in 1992, are the landmarks of China's modern CG journey.

1.1.1. SSE and SZSE

The history of SSE can be traced to June 1866 when the securities trading market in Shanghai listed its first shares, while the name of "Shanghai Stock Exchange (SSE)" was given in 1904. With its coastal location in the Yangtze River Delta, Shanghai became China's industry, trading and financial center in the late 1800s and early 1900s. The SSE began in the middle 1800s, and progressed during the turbulent period of the early 1900s as part of Shanghai's prosperity. However, the SSE ceased operations from 1949 to 1990 due to China's communist revolution in 1949 and for three decades thereafter due to internal restructuring.

China's economic reform in 1978 marked the beginning of the country's modern economy. With the policy of reform and re-emergence in August 1979, the Chinese government officially pronounced four southern coast cities as special economic zones: Shenzhen, Zhuhai, Shantou, and Xiamen. Geographically next to Hong Kong, Shenzhen soon became the dominant leader of the four. Although Shanghai was not part of these zones, the city's important role in China's economy never changed.

The first step in China's economic reform started with business ownership structure transformation. In addition to State Ownership, which was almost the only business type formally allowed in China from 1949 to 1978, other business ownership structures, such as township ownership, collective ownership, and private ownership, all began thriving after the 1978 economic reform. The capital demands of these entities triggered increasing non-official fund-raising transactions, which led to the first wave of a stock-issuing trial period in the mid-1980s in two stock exchange pilot cities, Shanghai and Shenzhen.

Before we delve into a brief history of China's stock exchanges, I should explain the three different stock types: A-Shares are traded in Chinese currency RMB for equity shares of China-based companies listed on the SSE and SZSE; B-shares are equity shares of China-based companies listed on the SSE and SZSE. B-shares are traded in USD on the SSE and in Hong Kong Dollar (HKD) on the SZSE; H-shares are traded in HKD for equity shares of China-based companies listed on the Hong Kong Stock Exchange (HKEX).

The purchase of company bonds and stocks proliferated in the Shanghai stock market beginning in 1984, when the People's Republic of China's first joint-stock listed company, Feilo Acoustics Co Ltd (SSE Code: 600651) issued A-shares to the public of a combined value of RMB 500,000 ($78,000) in November. In December 1990, the Shanghai Vacuum Electron Devices Co Ltd (SSE Code: 600602) became the first company to issue B-shares, raising RMB100 million ($15 million) on the SSE, which, at that time, was paid by an equivalent USD currency amount of the company's B-share sales. Those transactions also marked China's first foreign stock execution since the 1949 communist revolution. And Shanghai Vacuum Electron Devices Co, Ltd also became the first foreign joint venture in China with foreign investors on the B-share market.

Stock trials in Shenzhen also began in the mid-1980s. The Shenzhen Development Bank was the city's first company to issue stock to the public in May 1987, followed by many other companies, including Vanke (SZSE Code: 000002), a trading company during that time which later became one of China's leading residential real estate developers.

Stock exchanges quickly emerged in both Shanghai and Shenzhen trial stock markets in the late 1980s with an increasing number of transactions which was concurrent with a continuous rise in stock prices. Chinese investors began to experience the power of the stock market after decades.

After a few years of trials, the SSE officially began operations in December 1990. The SZSE officially began in April 1991.

1.1.2 The China Securities Regulatory Commission (CSRC)

The CSRC is the equivalent government authority to the Securities and Exchange Commission (SEC) in the US. The establishment of the CSRC is a beneficial accomplishment of the Chinese security market and also a perfect example of the nation's economic reform strategy (a Chinese proverb *"cross the river by feeling the stones"* exemplifies this effort).

The official operations of the SSE and SZSE stirred modern China's first stock market fanaticism, especially in Shenzhen, the leading city of China's first four economic special zones, besides Hong Kong. The SZSE building was crowded daily with people who were supposed to be at work. Hefty and quick profits at the SZSE from stock transactions attracted sizeable daily commuters from Hong Kong. Back then, all transactions were manually recorded. Arguments and fights often occurred between stockholders when share prices tumbled after transaction losses. A memorable incident known as "Shenzhen 8.10" resulted in additional regulations of the market imposed by the government, its impetus promulgated by the media's fascination with that incident.

Having opened its stock market in 1991, it took over a year for Shenzhen to receive permission for the public stock offering. Led by Shenzhen city authorities, the Initial Public Offering (IPO) plan was announced on August 7th, 1992 declaring that the SZSE would be selling five million stock subscription rights on the 9th and 10th of the month. 10 percent of the rights would win the lottery, and each lottery ticket would be granted for 1,000 stocks at the IPO price. Each buyer was able to purchase a maximum of ten stock subscription rights, providing they had ten citizen's identity cards [1]. 1.2 million people from Shenzhen and other cities in China flooded the 320 box offices in the city the day of the announcement. With the expectation of quick profits at the market, people gathered while possessing cards from family, friends, and neighbors, overwhelming the lines in front of the box offices beginning on August 8th, two days before the offices' opening.

The box offices opened at 9:00am on August 9th, and five million rights were sold within one hour. Many people waited in the line overnight but unfortunately were unable to purchase any of those rights. Anger and complaining permeated the city on the 10th. Shenzhen authorities were subsequently forced to issue an additional 500,000 rights

---

[1] During the 1990s in China, the concept of privacy and the risk of having other people use your own ID was very weak. In this case, one can borrow identity cards from family members or friends in order to buy more stock subscription rights, which was allowed by the authority too.

under emergency order to squash the public outcry. After this incident, the SZSE stopped issuing new stocks for one year. The "Shenzhen 8.10" fiasco compelled government regulators to realize the necessity of professional regulatory guidance for the stock market's operation. The CSRC was then established as the government authority to regulate the market. Before the CSRC, the People's Bank of China, the central bank of China, was the only authority in charge of the stock markets.

I also had my first taste of China's first stock market wave during my freshman year at the university. In the Chinese university system, the academic year schedule is September to July with a winter (Chinese New Year) break between January and February. I started my university education at Xiamen University in September of 1991. Toward the end of my freshman year in June 1992, four companies from Xiamen were planning IPOs at the SZSE. On June 19th of that year, the city authorities announced to the media that those companies would sell stock subscription rights. In the evening of June 20th, I was invited by a schoolmate from the university's finance department to join the waiting line of a box office located near the university to buy stock subscription rights. The box office opened the following morning and each person in the line was allowed to purchase five rights. It was revealed that professors from the university's finance department were paying their students a small premium to buy the rights for their professors. We purchased those rights that morning and observed throngs of people also waiting in the lines who were willing to pay RMB 100 for each right that we bought for RMB 5. Of course, many of us sold our stocks rights at the "market" and made the first "decent" profit of our student lives. As a result, some professors never got their rights back from the students. In my late teens, I made my first side income of RMB 475 after selling my five rights. Just to put that in context, in my freshman year, the cost of monthly meal and school supplies were RMB 150.

1.1.3. The Chinese Government's Intervention

Whenever I speak with my Western colleagues about doing business in China, their biggest concern is always the Chinese government's intervention. In the early stages of China's modern economy under the State planning model, the country started its economic reform without systematic regulatory guidance, so economic reform was moving toward a path of trial, correction, retrial, re-correction. I must emphasize the necessity of government intervention to control excessive speculation, in order to prevent a potential crash during the modern economy's infancy. Below are a few examples of the government's intervention in the market, particularly during the 2008 global financial crisis, to support my argument.

- In March 1994, the CSRC suspended permission for the issuance of IPOs for a short period of time due to extreme stock index fluctuations stirred by the early IPO booming wave that began in 1992.

- In December 1996, both the SSE and SZSE set a ten percent daily stock price change cap in both directions. The 10% cap system has remained in force since then.

- In May 2005, the CSRC suspended the permission to issue IPOs due to fear of the market being flooded as a result of regulations that were issued in July 2001, and ordered listed companies to sell some State shares by IPOs to raise funds for the national pension fund. The IPOs resumed sales in May 2006.

- In October 2008, the CSRC suspended IPOs again after attempting to prevent market crashes due to the global financial crisis. In November 2008, the government announced a two-year stimulus plan with a RMB 4 trillion ($650 billion) infusion into the market. The CSRC resumed IPOs in June 2009 after when the market was revived.

The Chinese government's interventions appeared in many business activities other than the stock market. Considering China's economic success today, these interventions should get some credit for successfully guarding and protecting the country's economy throughout the infancy and early growth period over the past few decades.

1.1.4. China's CG Code

The CSRC issued the first Chinese CG Code in 2002. The 2002 Code established principles and frameworks of basic shareholder rights, information disclosures, voting mechanisms in shareholders' meetings, and primary functions and features of boards of directors and supervisory boards.

The first revision of China's CG Code was issued in 2018. The new Code focused on improving Chinese regulations to encourage innovation with key changes in: establishing ESG requirements on green development and targeted poverty alleviation; encouraging institutional investors to play active roles in Chinese companies' CG practice; encouraging cash dividend distributions to actively reward shareholders; strengthening audit committee functions; promoting board diversity; and restricting controlling shareholders' power. The new Code became an important landmark in China's CG development. However, the provisions in the new Code requiring the Communist Party's participation in Chinese companies without providing details of the Party's unique position have become one of global investors' biggest concerns regarding Chinese companies' CG practice.

More information regarding Chinese CG regulation reforms will be discussed in Chapter 3 of this book.

1.2. A Close Look at Chinese Companies' Governance Models

Unlike US companies' corporate boards which are predominantly controlled by independent, outside directors, Chinese companies' CG structure combines elements from both the US model and the German-style two-tier board model, according to *Understand Corporate Governance in China* by Tricker & Li (2019). Chinese-listed companies and SOEs normally have boards of directors with some independent, external directors, and boards of supervisors consisting of employee and shareholder representatives. The chairperson and most shareholder representatives on the boards of supervisors are assigned by the State-Owned Assets Supervision and Administration Commission (SASAC). China's two-tier board is meant to be a mechanism for the Chinese government to assign its people to the company. With China's flexible CG regulation system, although many private companies have created different CG models, all listed China SOEs and most unlisted SOEs maintain a two-tier board structure.

1.2.1. Two-Tier Boards (German vs China)

The German Two-Tier board structure, by definition, is a dual-board system with a supervisory board and an executive board. Half of the supervisory board members are elected by shareholders and the other half represents employees. The supervisory board approves major business decisions and oversees and appoints members of the executive board, while the executive board oversees the company and makes operational decisions and guidance. Although China's SOE two-tier board structure was originally based on the German-style boards, the functions are not exactly the same. I only started to understand the differences during my experience leading the German acquisition project in 2014.

The German company was a 200-year-old manufacturer with world-class technology and a top brand-name in the industry. Unexpectedly, the most difficult negotiable component with the shareholders during the acquisition process was not regarding purchase price, but on post-acquisition human capital arrangements with the company's union and labor representatives on the board of supervisors. From a Chinese company's standpoint, having employee representatives on a company supervisory board is customary, but the fact that the share purchase agreement would not be signed without the consent from union and labor representatives shocked everyone on the acquisition team, including the founder and chairman of the 30-year-old Chinese company. Obviously, although the Chinese companies' two-tier board structure is identical to German companies, the understanding and application of board functions are quite different.

1.2.2. "Owned by the People"

In addition to two-tier boards, unions are quite common in most Chinese SOEs and private companies. The Chinese companies' unions are responsible for company events and some employee benefits, in contrast to the human resource function in Western companies. And of course, employee representatives of Chinese companies' boards of supervisors never have the power to stop an acquisition deal like their counterparts of the German company.

Perhaps the original idea of having employee representatives on China's two-tier board structure was from a concept that Chinese SOEs are "owned by the people". However, even in China's State-planned economy, "owned by the people" is a very ambiguous concept, which does not equate to "employee ownership" at all. In addition, the concept has led to the overconsumption of SOE assets by various parties.

While the State-planned economy has been replaced with a quasi-free market model, many people still misunderstand the concept of "owned by the people" today. However, the participation of union and employee representatives on companies' boards of supervisors in China compared with the German model has clearly defined the contrasting roles of union and employee representatives in Chinese companies' CG.

1.2.3. Creative Governance Models of China's Non-SOEs

Like most countries with emerging markets, China's CG development started under the tutelage of Western countries, then moved into a self-development phase and has become a fluid-learning system. With few restrictions or legal guidance, Chinese companies have created many new, different, and often innovative governance models. Leading companies like Alibaba and Huawei have demonstrated the advantage of their unique governance models, reaping steady success and slowly gaining recognition from the global business community.

Alibaba's Partnership Governance Structure. With Alibaba's first IPO at the New York Stock Exchange (NYSE) in 2014, institutional investors were concerned about the company's extreme insider-controlled governance model that limits investors' influence on business operations. What does Alibaba's governance structure look like? Let us delve into our Case Study 1.1. for some details.

Case Study 1.1. Alibaba's Controlling Structure

> Alibaba designed Alibaba Partnership to ensure the mission, culture, and value of its business for the long term. Alibaba Partnership is a dynamic group with a fluctuating number of members (30 before the 2014 NYSE IPO and 37 members in 2019). Alibaba Partnership holds one class of shares and controls over half of the candidates for directors. A five-member Partnership Committee within the Partnership is the core controlling group that determines the nomination of directors and future partners and the annual cash bonus pool for all partners.
>
> Alibaba's governance structure has multiple layers of takeover protection: (1) A super-majority provision: any change to Alibaba Partnership's nomination requires 95% voting approval at the shareholders meeting; (2) Proxy voting agreements: Alibaba reached agreements with its biggest strategic partners, Softbank and Yahoo, to ensure that voting power of these two shareholders will not escape the control cycle; (3) A staggered board structure: at each annual shareholders meeting, only one-third of the directors can be replaced.

In Western countries, the takeover protection governance structure has been outdated since the mid-2010s, and many companies have reversed the structure. The number of S&P 1500 companies with staggered board structures have declined from 900 in 2004 to 477 in 2014, according to data summarized in David Larcker and Brian Tayan's book *Corporate Governance Matters* (2016). If we consider two elements simultaneously: the number of S&P 1500 companies which had takeover protection governance structures before 2010, and the short history of Chinese companies' global growth - it is not difficult to assert that a takeover protection governance structure is a popular protocol for early-stage companies. Whether the protection structure in Chinese companies will fade over time along with the maturity of these companies remains to be seen. The answer will depend on the results obtained over the next few decades.

Regardless of the trouble Alibaba and its founder, Jack Ma, have experienced since late 2020, the company has demonstrated considerable CG development. While recognizing Alibaba's creative governance model, we should not neglect to consider another unique success that also resulted from this model – Alibaba's Succession Planning (please see Case Study 1.2 below).

Case Study 1.2. Alibaba's Succession Planning

> Alibaba has a transparent and thoughtful succession plan. The company began succession planning almost since its inception in the early 2000s. Daniel Zhang, Jack Ma's successor, has been with Alibaba since 2007 and served as Alibaba Group CEO since 2015. Given his finance background, Daniel was highly praised by Ma for his analytical mind and an intuitive grasp of innovation and creative business models. Zhang was also well-known for successfully running Alibaba's e-commerce platforms, Taobao and Tmall, where he created the magic of Alibaba's Single Day shopping event. His contribution to Alibaba paved the way for him to take over the leadership role from Jack Ma. In 2018, when Ma announced his retirement and Zhang stepped up as chairman, the leadership transfer was highly praised by Western financial media outlets. The smooth transfer of power ensured the continuity of Alibaba's core values.

In a September 2018 Forbes article named *"What Jack Ma Taught Us About Good Corporate Governance This Week"*, high praise was given to Alibaba's Partnership structure as "the most powerful thing that will drive Alibaba for generations". The Partnership allows Jack Ma's lifelong membership of the Alibaba Partnership, and plays an important role in Alibaba's succession planning. "Alibaba is a leader in terms of governance and its succession planning" the article concludes.

Huawei's governance model is new and creative in a different way, having evolved from a perfectionist culture with leaders who are unafraid to make bold reforms (see Case Studies 1.3. and 1.4).

Case Study 1.3. Huawei's Rotating CEO/Chairman System

> In 2011, Huawei implemented a rotating CEO system with the three CEOs and deputy chairman taking turns as the CEO for six months at

a time. The functioning CEO oversees Huawei's operations and crisis management and chairs the meetings of the Executive Committee. The three rotating CEOs are from different company departments, and during each of their turns as CEO, are also responsible for their daily responsibilities. The rotating CEO system then incorporated the chairman's position into the rotation in 2018.

Huawei's rotating CEO/chairman system was designed by its founder, Ren Zhengfei, to build an effective and mechanical governance structure to serve Huawei's long-term sustainability. The idea was inspired by two animal kingdom stories: (1) A buffalo herd story from "Flight of the Buffalo" by James A Belasco and Ralph C. Stayer (buffalo herds is also known as alfalfa). In this book, the authors uses Buffalo herds' story (Buffalo herds follow chief buffalos, and once the chief buffalo is killed the entire herd will end up in chaos and die) to inspire and encourage organizations for a new leadership structure with employee empowerment; and (2) "The Flight Pattern of Migratory Birds" which explains the rotation of bird flock leaders to ensure the success of a long migration. The allegories of these stories describe Ren's desire for Huawei's journey to be like the one of migratory birds. He also applied the US presidential term-limit concept to the company's leadership arrangement plan.

Case Study 1.4. Huawei's "Superfluid" Organizational Structure

In addition to the rotating CEO/Chairman structure, Ren Zhengfei designed a superfluid organizational structure to maximize its customer-centric business strategy. This organizational structure placed all of Huawei's most talented experts in a human resource pool, enabling the team to be deployed worldwide at any time. This organizational innovation is the foundation and driving force of Huawei's commitment to serving ever-changing customer needs. In order to understand how this organization's innovative structure enabled Huawei's success, consideration also needs to be given to those who function within it. Below are three key components that demonstrate some pros and cons of this structure:

1. ***The "Superfluid" Organizational Structure***
   The Vodafone Spain project is a good example of how Huawei utilizes its "superfluid" organizational structure as a competitive strategy. In 2006, Vodafone was having difficulty delivering a reliable mobile phone signal for Spain's newly completed high-speed rail network. Huawei rapidly assembled a team of professionals with expert knowledge and abundant ancillary resources to develop and test a high-speed packet access network expansion solution. The project was successfully completed within two months. Huawei's quick resolution enabled Vodafone to serve all of the major cities in Spain. Vodafone Senior managers highly praised Huawei's efficiency which resulted in Huawei sharing significant market share with Vodafone Spain. During the same time, Huawei's competitors, Ericsson and Nokia, were still preparing initial proposals.

2. ***The concept of rotating middle and senior managers every three years to expose them to multiple responsibilities and encourage a superfluid culture.***
   As one of the biggest Chinese multinationals, the rotating positions for these managers can be hosted all over the world. Employees' families, though, are not included. There is nothing comparable to that in Western companies. Most employees rotating to overseas positions are able to visit their families only during the Chinese New Year celebration. Huawei might appear to be extreme with the three-year rotating term, but the same policy applies to most Chinese companies' overseas employees. Rotating employees are comfortable with the company's business operations, which helps building Huawei's corporate culture at overseas subsidiaries, and facilitates co-operation between headquarters and its subsidiaries.

3. ***Two surgical organizational restructures in Huawei's 30-year history.***
   During a 1996 annual review, all Huawei marketing managers were asked to submit a work plan report and a resignation letter. The company would either approve the report or accept the resignation. In 2007, Huawei conducted a resignation and rehiring exercise to

optimize its organizational structure and requested 7,000 employees resign. 6,581 were subsequently rehired for more suitable employment positions.

Huawei's organizational restructures in 1996 and 2007 brought a sense of urgency, energized its employees, and established the tone of Huawei's corporate culture that promotes dedication, encourages competition, and recognizes employee contributions. According to Tian Tao and Wu Chunbo's "The Huawei Story" (2014), an executive of Motorola China once commented of Huawei's dramatic organizational restructures, "Only Huawei dared to do it, and it had succeeded."

Regardless of its success, Chinese and foreign medias criticized the experiment.

Huawei's "superfluid" organizational structure demonstrated its efficiency with many projects such as with Vodafone Spain. However, the rotating system did not consider employees and their families' quality of life. In addition, with rotating employees filling most management positions, very few management positions remained for non-Chinese employees in overseas countries. Moreover, Huawei's dramatic organizational restructure caused many people to lose their jobs. With today's ESG movement, employees' well-being and workforce equity around the world are very important factors for evaluating a company's social performance. Multinationals like Huawei need to reconsider their strategy when trying to strengthen their industry- leading positions in the global market.

Since Huawei's chief financial officer Meng Wanzhou's arrest in Canada in December 2018 (resulting in a US ban on technology imports over the past few years), Huawei entered a new stage of its corporate journey. Although there are many uncertainties in Huawei's future, the company's performance is a testament to China's economic reform. Huawei's success is not coincidental, since some strategies such as the surgical organizational restructuring was concurrent with the unique stage of China's economic reform at the time when the strategies were executed. I will explain more in later chapters.

In addition to the differences between German two-tier boards and the Chinese ones, the following comparisons will be helpful to understand China's CG structure and some practices.

1.3. Major CG Differences Between China and the US

Despite the fact that China's CG development is a few decades behind those in Western countries, many aspects of Chinese companies' CG practices will improve over time due to the maturity of those companies and the entire Chinese economic system. There are some differences that will likely never be reconciled due to the profound influences of Chinese culture, China's one-party system, and more importantly, China's economic growth that has been realized due to its particular economic development path.

1.3.1. Governmental Influence

As we discussed in the early portion of this chapter, Chinese companies' two-tier board structure, with the chairperson and most shareholder representatives on the board of supervisors purposely assigned by the SASAC, is designed for Chinese government officials to appoint its members to the company. Additionally, according to the CG code of 2018, Party Committees are required for Chinese-listed companies. Although there are no delineated responsibilities of Party Committees within these companies, the Party's influence is fundamental and imperative. In addition to listed companies, many private Chinese companies have voluntarily established Party Committees to remain "politically-correct and connected". Just like the US companies' reactions to their Black Lives Matter and climate change movements, what's the harm with being allied to a Government's political strategy?

Although the Chinese government's influence has been one of the top concerns of global investors, the Chinese government's effective control of the COVID-19 pandemic, and the country's ability to recover quickly, enhanced its global reputation. As China attempts to further position itself as the global economic leader, the government's influence in Chinese companies will likely remain the same, if not greater.

1.3.2. The Power of SOEs in China

According to a 2019 Organization for Economic Cooperation and Development (OECD) report, US and Chinese companies are positioned at opposite ends of the spectrum of two investor categories when it comes to investor ownership, while other Western countries are in the middle of the spectrum. On average, institutional investors own 72% of the shares of US companies, 38% of European companies, 9% of Chinese companies and 41% as a global average. However, public sector investors (including State and local governments) own 38% of shares in Chinese companies, 9% of European companies, and 3% of shares in US companies, with a 14% global average. Obviously, institutional investors are the driving force in global CG development today, but their minimal ownership in Chinese companies raises questions regarding Chinese companies' motivation to improve their CG. With that said, it is important to understand the progress Chinese companies have made thus far. The diversified ownership structure (consisting of five investor categories—private and public sector corporations, strategic individuals, institutional investors and other free-float), forty years of reduced SOE from 100% to its present amount, and various attractive initiatives such as the opening of the country's stock exchanges to foreign investors have contributed to a considerable financial windfall. Corporate ownership diversification has been the primary focus of SOE reform since its second stage in the 1990s, according to *Corporate Governance and Financial Reform in China's Transition Economy* by Jing Leng (2009). With China's continuous effort to reform SOEs and open its stock markets to the rest of the world, the country's corporate ownership structure is likely to gradually appear more diversified and balanced in each category to better facilitate the next phase of economic growth. Based on strategies and goals of China's 14th Five-Year Plan released in late 2020, SOEs will continue to drive China's economic development in the coming decades. Details regarding China's 14th Five-Year Plan will be discussed in Chapter 8.

1.3.3. CEO Nomination, Succession Planning and Compensation

The US companies' boards of directors make decisions regarding the CEO's recruitment, succession planning and compensation. Because US companies tend to tie a significant portion of CEOs' compensation packages to company performance, CEOs tend to be highly motivated. According to data from June 2013 to May 2014, 47.4% of compensation packages for CEOs of the top 100 US companies are related to company stock price, according to *Corporate Governance Matters* by David Larcker and Bryan Tayan (2016). In China, CEOs and most executives of Chinese SOEs are selected by the Chinese government and can be rotated to other SOEs by government authorities, not the board. These SOE executives rank in a hierarchy within the Chinese government. Moreover, their primary job is not increasing business value but by ensuring that SOEs remain in compliance with the law. Unlike US CEOs' attractive compensation packages with stock options, Chinese SOE CEOs' compensation have to align with government officials of the same rank, and stock options are not in the picture. According to 2019 Fortune Global 500 rankings, 23 of the top 25 Chinese companies are SOEs, which means that a majority of China's top CEOs are not incentivized to maximize company performance. Given that a CEO is not just the head of a company, but its most important leader, the differences in how CEOs are selected and motivated in each country accounts for the many differences in their governance and operation.

Obviously, there are other differences in CG practices between US and Chinese companies, including information transparency and disclosure, decision-making processes, shareholder voting rights, etc. However, these and other differences emerge from the three primary differences noted above. As China's economy continues to grow in the global market, it is reasonable to expect Chinese CG practices to continue to evolve, improve and close the gap with Western countries. While Chinese SOEs may remain dominant in the nation's economy, with SOEs increasing in number (as well as the percentage rate of shareholders), and given the SOEs' growing commitment to international regulations concerning climate change and ESG standards, the CG practice and business mindset of SOEs will gradually reflect international standards. As a result, the entire landscape of Chinese CG development will change, facilitating rapid adoption of improved CG practices and ESG performance.

1.4. Major CG Differences between China and Japan

Before China's rise over the past couple of decades, the most influential economy in Asia was Japan. Although Japanese multinationals have not been as active in the global market as they were a couple decades ago, its CG model was once considered one of the three most prevalent models in contemporary corporations, together with the Anglo-US model[2] and German model. Therefore, it is worth mentioning below the two major CG differences between China and Japan.

1.4.1. Controlling Structure

The controlling structure is common in companies from both China and Japan. However, different controlling parties affects the controlling structures in both countries.

With most Japanese companies being governed by power concentrated among a limited number of Japanese corporations and banks that have deep-rooted inter-relationships, a lack of corporate transparency is the biggest concern of the Japanese CG model.

Chinese companies' controlling parties are the Chinese government for SOEs and the founders for private companies. Although some successful Chinese companies have become shareholders of newer companies (for example, Tencent is the largest shareholder of Meituan), the relationship between these two giant tech companies has not caused any detrimental CG concerns for investors or regulators.

1.4.2. Stakeholder Relationships

The Japanese CG Model is well known for the loyalty – "keiretsu" in

---

[2] The Anglo-US model was established in the UK and US, under which shareholders and boards of directors are the controlling parties and management needs to obtain authority from the board. Independent board directors are widely used in corporate boards with the Anglo-US model.

Japanese - between internal (employer and employees) and external stakeholders (customers and suppliers). The influential professor and philosopher at the Darden School of Business, University of Virginia, Edward Freeman , who has conducted considerable research of the "Stakeholder Theory"concludes that stakeholders' interest considerations are a natural characteristic of Japanese corporations that includes a "built-in" loyalty cultural aspect.

Many Chinese citizens who are in their sixties today worked for only one SOE during their career, and most have opted for early retirement due to China's retirement program (most Chinese workers retire by the time they are sixty, if not earlier). Most younger generation Chinese do not have the same career options due to China's SOE reform and a plethora of job opportunities that are offered by new private companies. Also, the Chinese regulatory system and most Chinese companies both lack maturity, so considerable time is needed for growth and improvement in Chinese companies before a mechanism can be established for stakeholders' interest consideration.

Today, both Japan and China are working to improve their CG practices to comply with international standards. Japan took the lead role in Asia when the government released the second revision of its stewardship code in March 2020 as part of Japan's CG reform, while China is working to improve the standards of its entire institutional system to enable CG improvements. The two countries are also competing to be the Asian ESG leader. For instance, the Government Pension Investment Fund (GPIF) in Japan, the world's largest pension fund, has been committed to an ESG strategy since 2015 when it signed as a signatory to the United Nation's "Principle for Responsible Investment", while the Chinese government has been leading the ESG revolution with various initiatives and regulatory guidance (details regarding China's ESG movement will be discussed in chapters 6 and 7). Considering both countries' influential economies in Asia and worldwide, the competition between Japan and China is a healthy indication of CG practice improvements in the region.

Chapter 2
The Ownership and Controlling Structure

The company I worked for in Ningbo is a successful business according to the traditional manufacturing industry model. The Chairman/CEO was the founder, established the business in 1987, and has been running it since then. One of its subsidiary companies was listed on the SSE and his nephew is the CEO of the subsidiary. Acquiring this once German-owned company was the founder's 20-year dream since he admired its brand, technology, and product quality. Working closely with the founder/chairman for the acquisition deal, I had chance to get to know this hard-working entrepreneur and was deeply impressed by his obsession to be the leader of the technology industry, his plan to build a world-class brand, and his dream to implement a modern business model within his company.

Having lived in Ningbo for nearly one year, I was amazed by the number of joint research and development projects between the local government and private-owned companies, and the local government's support for these companies' overseas acquisitions. I also gained frontline experience of the vibrancy of Chinese companies' growth that made me very excited to be a part of that growth.

Upon completion of the acquisition deal, I moved to Hong Kong to join another company there, which was then a newly established subsidiary of an SOE located in a Chinese province[1]. Due to China's "going global" wave in the middle of the 2010s, the SOE was planning to develop this Hong Kong subsidiary as its overseas headquarters to achieve future global growth. My main responsibility was to assist the

---

[1] In China, Central SOEs are supervised by the central State-Owned Assets Supervision and Administration Commission (SASAC). Local SOEs including provincial-level SOEs and city-level SOEs are supervised by local SASACs.

company to establish its long-term business strategy and operations of this important subsidiary while simultaneously report to its chairman/CEO, who also held an executive position in the SOE. I had opportunities to attend meetings at the SOE's headquarters in mainland China, interact with the SOE's chairman, board directors and different levels of executive managers, and participate in meetings with government officials in both Hong Kong and mainland China as the representative of the Hong Kong company. These experiences exposed me to the inner-workings of the SOE's board structure, board functions, board decision-making process, SOE executives' responsibilities, and the most sensitive matter – the government's intervention with the SOE.

Although I did not understand CG practice until researching it years later, my experience with this Hong Kong company became a valuable foundation for my research, because of the complexity of an SOE's organizational structure and decision-making process, the dual roles of SOE board directors and executives, the important roles SOEs play in China's economic growth, and SOEs' influence on Chinese private companies' operations.

In this chapter, I will review the CG impact on the ownership and controlling structures of Chinese SOEs and private companies, the variable interest entity (VIE) structure, and the contractual controlling structure, which has remained in a legal grey area with on-going debate although they have been widely used by overseas-listed Chinese companies.

2.1. Chinese SOEs and their Key CG Matters

State-Owned Enterprises (SOEs) are an important element in most countries, including advanced and emerging market economies. In certain sectors like energy, minerals, infrastructure, utilities, and financial services, SOEs are the most prevalent due to many countries' strategic positions within these sectors and the amount of capital needed for these businesses.

SOEs dominate the Chinese economy and have been playing an increasingly important role in the nation's economy. According to some research data, in 2000, there was a total 27 SOEs in Fortune Global 500 (FG500) companies, nine (33.3%) of which were Chinese; in 2017, there were 102 SOEs in FG500 companies, 75 (73.3%) of which were Chinese. As China has been effectively promoting SOE reform over the past 40 years, statistics show that the total number of SOEs in China has decreased from 262,000 in 1997 to 110,000 in 2008, then increased to 173,000 in 2016, while the total asset value under SOEs management has continuously increased from RMB12 million in 1997 to RMB154 million in 2016. Like SOEs in many other countries with emerging markets, Chinese SOEs have been known for their inefficiency for many reasons.

Despite this, the Chinese economy has relied primarily on the outstanding growth of SOEs over the past 40 years even though most SOEs have been inefficient due to their low productivity. This phenomenon is known as the "China Puzzle".

2.1.1. The "China Puzzle"

China's fast economic growth along with its lagging regulation is contradictory to Western countries' growth philosophy. "China Puzzle" refers to this exact phenomenon.

Similar to questions raised worldwide regarding the effectiveness of capitalism during the COVID-19 pandemic, research on the "China Puzzle" anomaly might lead to challenging the law of finance-growth economic philosophy. China has been trying to prove that the law of finance-growth economic philosophy is not the only path for economic success by demonstrating its success in many different aspects.

To understand the "China Puzzle", we should first review the strengths and weaknesses of Chinese SOEs due to their controlling structure by the government:

Strengths. Why are SOEs so important for China's economy? How did Chinese SOEs support the rapid Chinese economy growth over the past decades? Below are three key strengths of Chinese SOEs:

- Government intervention enables SOEs to maximize their resource mobility. Most Chinese SOEs operate in essential and capital-intensive industries. The lump-sum investments needed by these businesses cannot be achieved through the capital market alone.
- SOEs are valuable to maintain social stability. Chinese SOEs have been a major source of retirement pensions. During economic downturns like COVID-19, SOEs can be utilized to hire excess labor and achieve social goals by sacrificing profit.
- SOEs are the Chinese government's device to control key elements of society.

Weaknesses. What are the weaknesses of SOEs that caused the low operative efficiency?

- Ambiguous ownership. Chinese SOEs are theoretically "owned by the people", which leads to non-recognition of SOEs' performance and profitability, opportunities of overconsumption of SOEs' assets, executives' enjoying on-the-job perks, and unmotivated employees in the SOEs.
- Heavy Social Burden. Chinese SOEs carry a heavy social burden because of their high financial cost due to a capital-intensive focus, heavy tax burdens in order to support governments' functioning, and obligation to hire redundant labor and offer pension and welfare to retirees on behalf of the State and local governments.
- No accountability. With SOEs' heavy social burden, soft budget targets, and lack of incentives for value creation, the main responsibility of SOEs executives is to solve social problems, not

create business value. CEOs are not incentivized by SOEs' operational performance as we discussed in chapter one. Therefore, the government cannot hold executives accountable for SOEs' low operation performance.
- Information asymmetry. Since most decisions are made by the State or local government, the complicated hierarchy of SOEs complicates the information transmission and decision-making process which breeds inefficiency.

The "China Puzzle" might not be able to eliminate SOE weaknesses, but it obviously maximizes SOEs strengths, offsetting weaknesses in order to facilitate China's economic growth. The Chinese government is well aware of these strengths and weaknesses and have been pursuing SOE reform since reopening the economy in 1978.

2.1.2. Key CG Matters of Chinese SOEs

Why is the Chinese SOE's controlling structure one of the biggest concerns of global investors? Let us review some key CG elements of Chinese SOEs:

Conflicts of Interest due to Controlling Ownership. Statistical data shows that Chinese central and local governments are the largest shareholders of companies' stocks. They possess approximately 40% of the equity in Chinese SOEs and have controlling rights as the majority owner through various direct and indirect ownership formalities. In addition, the government employs a pyramid structure consisting of "cross ownership[2]" among SOEs to effectively control a large number of corporations. Confoundingly, the pyramid- structure model is the primary reason for the exceedingly complicated ownership structures of most SOEs. I will discuss the details of the SOE ownership structure further in Chapter 4.

Moreover, the concentrated controlling structure creates conflicts of interest among controlling shareholders, minority shareholders, and executives, which is the so-called "agency problem" of SOEs. As the

---

[2] Cross ownership refers to different SOEs becoming shareholders of each other.

controlling shareholder, the Chinese government often requests SOEs to absorb excess labor to help reduce unemployment and to sponsor public projects, which become obstacles to the SOEs' operational improvement and investment return. Since most executives of SOEs are appointed by government authorities, those executives tend to overinvest in government projects and also consume excessive benefits.

However, regulators were previously aware of the conflict and are working on raising awareness to protect minority shareholders' interests and voting rights. In the 2018 CG code revision, provisions exist to encourage investors to participate in voting and to advocate for CG policies and practices that promote cash dividend distributions.

Ineffective boards independence and board functions. Since 2003, government regulations require that at least one-third of each company board must consist of independent directors. A relevant question, though, is whether independent directors play an effective monitoring and advising role in the SOEs. The generally agreed answer to this question is presently mixed.

A 2015 research project determined that independent directors are less likely to vote against any proposals from SOE boards. Another research venture in the same year showed a positive relationship between board independence and companies' performances in China after accounting discrepancies are resolved. However, many independent directors on SOE boards are professors and influential celebrities, who might not have requisite business experience to monitor and guide an SOEs' growth.

At the time this book was written, a new practice appeared within some local governments that authorities rotate former SOE executives to non-executive directors' roles. These non-executive directors are still enjoying government official rankings and their former executive experiences will improve boards' monitoring and advising functions, although they are not independent from SOEs. This new practice, together with Chinese SOEs further participation in the global business community and regulators commitment to build higher CG practice, may be a new trend of Chinese SOEs CG reform that will improve the effectiveness and professionalism of SOE boards' functions.

Information transparency issue. Lack of transparency has been one of the top concerns of China SOEs. Traditionally, SOEs' controlling shareholders intended to keep the information transferring environment opaque (especially negative information) mainly for political reasons, which created a company culture that people were not willing to share with outsiders primarily to avoid any unnecessary trouble.

With Chinese regulators' efforts to establish high-standard economic regulations, and to enforce audit firms' independence, public information disclosure requirements for companies will likely benchmark Western standards. Encouraging free conversation and business sharing practices requires business culture changes that will take some time. With a new development philosophy including openness and sharing initiated in China's 14th Five-Year Plan released in late 2020, the hope is that the new philosophy led by government will stir business mindset changes for SOEs' leaders who can drive SOEs' business culture changes.

2.2. Founder Controlling Structure and its Sustainability

The founder controlling structure is investors' paramount concern regarding privately-owned Chinese companies. The founder controlling structure often comes with dual-class shares, where one share class controls the company's voting power. However, the founder controlling structure is common in nearly all companies' early stages, including companies in more developed economies. American giant tech companies Facebook and Google both have founder controlling structures with dual-class shares. Perhaps the biggest difference is the institutional investor's common share percentage in Chinese companies versus their counterparts in the US. Data collected at the time this chapter was written explains the differences:

Table 2.1. Share Structure Contrasts with Alibaba and Facebook:

	Alibaba Group Holding Ltd (NYSE: BABA)	Facebook Inc. (NASDAQ: FB)
Mutual Fund Holders	18.58%	45.76%
Other Institutional Investors	19.54%	34.28%
Total Share Percentage by Institutional Investors	38.12%	80.04%

As I explained in Case Study 1.1. – Alibaba's Controlling Structure, for example, describes the authoritarian nature of its founder that detrimentally impacts potential investors' influence on company board governance, development, and decision-making. However, considering Alibaba's success over the past two decades, it is worth examining the advantages and disadvantages of Chinese companies' founder controlling structure.

2.2.1. Dictatorship and Voting Rights

As we see from Table 2.1., the institutional investors shared percentage in Alibaba (38.12%) is significantly less than Facebook's (80.04%). However, 38.12% is much greater than other Chinese companies that average 9%, as discussed in Chapter 1. In fact, the egregious controlled structure examples of companies like Alibaba are not indicative of only the investors' share and founders' voting power structures, but also its exclusive board nomination rights and voting power through voting arrangements with major shareholders.

Case Study 2.1. Alibaba's Voting Arrangements with Softbank and Yahoo

> In addition to the Alibaba Partnership that enables exclusive control over half of the company's board positions, Jack Ma and another founder, Joe Tsai, also signed a voting agreement with two additional major shareholders, Softbank and Yahoo. Below are three important aspects of the voting agreement:
>
> 1. Softbank has rights to nominate one director upon the condition it owns at least 15% of Alibaba's common shares;
> 2. An Alibaba Partnership and Softbank coalition agrees to support the nomination of each parties' director, provided Softbank owns at least 15% of Alibaba's common shares;
> 3. Softbank and Yahoo grant voting powers to Jack Ma and Joe Tsai through proxy agreements
>
> At the time of Alibaba's IPO in 2014, Softbank and Yahoo owned a

combined total of 56.5% of Alibaba's shares (Softbank 34.1%, Yahoo 22.4%), while Jack Ma and Joe Tsai owned 8.8% and 3.6%, respectively. However, the voting agreement detrimentally limited the influence of Softbank and Yahoo in Alibaba's boardroom. At the time this chapter was written, Softbank owned 25%, while Yahoo had sold the majority of its Alibaba shares.

Despite its autocratic rule, Alibaba was an investor's darling as the largest Chinese e-commerce company until the Chinese government's scrutiny was triggered by its suspension of Alibaba's affiliate company Ant Group's IPO plan in late 2020. Just like Facebook and Google, investors wanted a piece of these companies' growth, regardless of the controlled-structure limitations. Plus, as we all know, shareholder engagements from most institutional investors have never reached the level expected by the public, even with recent years' shareholder activism movements in the West. According to my interviews with institutional investors and proxy agencies in North America - with thousands of companies in their portfolios - many institutional investors simply do not have enough resources for the shareholder engagement they prefer, even with their American portfolio companies. And most of them rely heavily on proxy agency recommendations for their voting rights.

Of course, because of the language and culture barrier, it is difficult to communicate with Chinese companies' executives and to attend Chinese companies' AGMs. Shareholders' engagement with Chinese companies is still also at a minimal level. As long as the portfolio company financially performs well, however, why bother?

2.2.2. Long-Term Value Creation

During my recent interview with Professor Andrew Kakabadse, regarding board leadership, the professor raised concerns about the non-balance between compliance and stewardship of corporate board functions today. He also shared his opinions regarding the importance of boards' in-depth understanding and engagement of company business.

In founder controlling companies, the founder's commitment is an important measurement that rational investors believe creates value that offsets the disproportional controlled structure imbalance. Successful entrepreneurs usually possess great passion for their businesses so therefore are willing to devote all their effort to grow the company. A disproportionately controlled structure allows founders to actively participate in management, which ensure the continuity of company strategies even if the founder's share percentage is reduced over time.

In Alibaba's case, Jack Ma has identified Alibaba's core values – customers first, teamwork, embracing change, integrity, passion, and commitment, all of which are consistent with his personal values. Alibaba's investors expect that they will benefit from the current structure as long as Ma continuously moulds Alibaba in his entrepreneurial vision to build an online global empire. And with the Alibaba Partnership structure, his control and influence will remain during his lifetime, regardless of his retirement status.

2.2.3. The Founder's Commitment

If the founder controlling structure is a concern of global investors, how do companies like Alibaba reassure the market and persuade investors to continue funding them, given their extreme insider controlling system?

Case Study 2.2. Alibaba's Founder's Commitments Alleviate Investors' Concerns

> With the founder controlling structure, primary concerns raised by investors are conflicts of interest and related party transactions. To address these concerns, Jack Ma has promised to donate all of the personal distributions he receives to the company and charity from the following two self-dealt transactions:
>
> 1. The ownership transfer of Alipay[3] to Jack Ma's wholly owned

---

[3] Alipay is the mobile payment platform launched by Alibaba in 2004 as an escrow account to bridge the trust between online buyers and sellers, which became the main competitive advantage of Alibaba's e-commerce business, given the fact that credit cards were not widely used in the early 2000s. Alipay later became the core business of Ant Group. A case study of Ant Group will be examined in Chapter 5.

company Ant Financial Services in 2011 is a controversial example since the transfer appeared to be a self-dealing transaction. To address concerns raised by the Alipay transaction, Ma committed in Alibaba's first IPO prospectus to reduce his interest in Ant Financial Services to the degree that was commensurate with his interest in Alibaba Group, and agreed to refrain from capitalizing on proceeds of the company's share reduction.
2. As a major shareholder of Yunfeng Capital, which co-invested with Alibaba in Youku Tudou and Citic 21CN, Ma committed in Alibaba's first IPO prospectus to donate all his interest in Yunfeng Capital to the Alibaba Foundation, a charitable non-profit organization.

Obviously, in the first chapter of Alibaba's success, Jack Ma's individual charisma and his commitment of not taking economic benefit from his controlling interest of the businesses has played a large role in order to engage investors, build trust, and preserve faith in the market.

2.2.4. Sustainability Considerations

Sustainability concerns for a founder controlling structure is always connected to leadership transfer as part of succession planning. These two types of leadership transfers are prevalent in today's Chinese companies:

The Leadership Transfer Between Board Chair and Current Executives. Alibaba's succession planning is a splendid example. The company's smooth leadership transfer in 2018 demonstrated the necessity of transparency and long-term planning, elements that are now included in the best practices of corporate governance. Pinduoduo, a large e-commerce company in China, is an example of the trend of new succession planning models and the rise of social entrepreneurship that may inspire future generations of Chinese entrepreneurs.

Case Study 2.3. Pinduoduo Founder's Retirement – Trend of a New Succession Plan Model

The Shanghai-based company was founded in 2015 and has been listed in the NYSE since 2018. Pinduoduo is a platform focused on agricultural and low-price consumable products, with a next-day grocery pickup service that was launched during the pandemic. In 2020, Pinduoduo overtook Alibaba Group to become China's largest e-commerce platform of 788.4 million annual active buyers. The fast-growing e-commerce company reported 26.55 billion yuan ($4.08 billion) in the fourth quarter of 2020, which is 146% of the estimated 19.22 billion yuan that was initially anticipated.

Current CEO Chen Lei was appointed as chairman. Lei is a founding member of Pinduoduo and has been in the position since July 2020. The leadership transition plan between Pinduoduo's chairman and CEO is similar to Alibaba's from Jack Ma to Daniel Zhang in 2018. However, unlike Ma, who still controls Alibaba through Alibaba Partnership, the current CEO, Huang Zheng, will relinquish his super voting rights in the company upon retirement. Zheng will then explore his interest in food science upon retirement and recently donated $100 million to Zhejiang University to support biomedical science, agriculture and food research.

On March 17, 2020, Pinduoduo's stock price fell 8% when Huang Zheng announced his retirement. Experts, though, believe Zheng's retirement indicates Pinduoduo's confidence in future growth without the founder's influence, and significant changes in company operations are not anticipated.

As a result of Chen Lei's solid planning, a firm foundation exists in the company. Given Pinduoduo's accomplishments in rural product quality and continuous investments in agricultural technology and rural infrastructure, the company's future seems promising after Huang Zheng's retirement.

Although both Alibaba's and Pinduoduo's leadership transfers upon each founders' retirement were considered successful, the latter initiated the start of a new succession plan model for Chinese companies that is in line with the global trend in the rise of social entrepreneurship.

Important factors that contribute to the differences between these two companies' CG models and the two leaders' business mindsets are the 15-and 16-year age differences, respectively, between these two entrepreneurs and their companies: Jack Ma (currently 56 years old) founded Alibaba in 1999, and Huang Zheng (currently 41 years old) started Pinduoduo in 2015. The Chinese economy and China's regulation reform made fundamental improvements between 1999 and 2015 (In Chapter 3 I will review China's regulation reform). The 15 years age difference between these two founders distinguishes each founders' personal values and business vision. The 16 years age difference between these two companies defines their remarkable corporate cultures, CG practices and development paths, and probably the futures of these two giant e-commerce companies.

Generational Leadership Transfer within the Founder's Family. During my career and within my professional network, I have observed and experienced a few successful family businesses in the US and other Western countries. Although stable family ties are the strongest core for a business' success in most cases, an emotionally charged family relationship often causes unnecessary complications for the business' operation and decision-making process. However, CG of family-owned businesses carry an advanced "spirit" that publicly listed companies can learn from. Today, when corporations worldwide are asked to rethink their business sustainability and to look after stakeholders' interests, we often neglect to acknowledge that these are the natural characteristics of many successful family-owned businesses. In one of my podcast episodes, my friend, Fedor Heijl, a former second-generation family business owner of an automobile parts business in the Netherlands, shared his opinions regarding the success of a family-owned business: long-term value creation and stakeholders' consideration. Fedor successfully took over the business from his father with the ambition to build long-term value for the business, in order to carry over the family culture of the business, and to pass it to his children in the future. Fedor later sold the business when a great opportunity came. But it was a very hard decision with many emotional moments and a rational consideration of the growing opportunity for the business and employees to perpetuate the family's legacy.

Another friend, Ernest Gylfe, the fourth-generation owner of a knit products business in Finland, also shared very interesting stories of his family-owned business, and his opinion regarding leadership transition between generations. He poked fun at the pattern: the first generation starts the business, while the second grows the business, and the third sells the business! Dramatically, instead of selling the company, his father reinvented the business together with Ernest. Ernest is now in the process of refining its CG structure while also expanding it via overseas acquisitions. Ernest told me during our conversation that he considers himself of the second generation according to his definition of the generation difference.

Fedor's and Ernest's family-owned businesses are in different countries and industries, but both stories demonstrate that generational transition is the natural succession plan of family-owned businesses regardless of the geographic and product differences. Both stories also reveal business mentality differences between generations.

However, generational transition is a new topic and challenge for Chinese companies, considering that the most successful Chinese companies are only 30 to 40 years old. These companies were founded after 1980 and the majority of them are still controlled by the founders' generations, while a significant number of these companies are now, or will soon be, facing generational transfer disputes. The rapid growth of the Chinese economy over the past four decades made dramatic changes in China's business environment. Most second-generation owners of these businesses have an overseas education from countries with more developed economies, which builds business mindsets closer to international standards, and provides them with broader business perspectives.

A 2017 research article from *Frontiers of Business Research in China* revealed that Chinese business leaders receiving an education from developed countries have advanced knowledge and often promote corporate social responsibility. With ESG being part of business sustainability pondered by the brightest minds within the global business community, a 2018 research project conducted by KPMG concluded that a corporation's leader's attitude is the primary impetus of a company's ESG protocol. Will an overseas educational background of founder controlling companies' second generation eventually become the horsepower for these companies' long-term sustainability? The challenging leadership transition experiments some Chinese companies are going through at the moment will most likely lead to governance model changes. We will further discuss Chinese companies' leadership transition in Chapter 5.

2.3. VIE Structure Loophole and the Government's Approach to Fix it

Over the past three decades, the Variable Interest Entity (VIE) structure has been a widely used business practice for Chinese companies to access overseas capital. As of October 2018, 92% of Nasdaq-listed and 64% of NYSE-listed Chinese companies took advantage of the VIE structure. This practice has been an unsolved mystery in the global market. But because its impact on the market is not as visible as other hot Chinese business topics like related-party transactions and auditor independence, the VIE structure remains as powerful as it is hidden.

For many Chinese companies expanding their business within the global market, establishing a VIE structure becomes a "must have" set-up routine regardless of the necessity. I had the opportunity to participate in some of these orchestrations during my career from 2014 to 2017 when working for various Chinese companies to help their "going global" strategies. Establishing a VIE structure is not cheap; maintaining a VIE structure can be very costly. Because of my corporate finance background, I always care about a multinational company's tax structure whenever adding new entities to that organization. One VIE can cause a complex tax structure by adding a few new entities to the organization, but the implication is not that some Chinese companies have multiple VIEs in their organizations. All these complexities could lead to potential tax burdens for the entire internationalization operations. Eliminating these complexities afterwards, though, could be even more costly.

I remember that I could not understand why decision-makers of these companies never cast doubt on the complicated organizational structure caused by VIEs, which may or may not be utilized in the future. Despite the sizable amount of service fees for attorney firms and secretary services to maintain the structure during a VIE's lifetime, few individuals seem to consider the hidden dangers of potential future tax burdens and tax-planning complexities. Furthermore, I was constantly confronted with challenges when attempting to convince some company executives about the necessity to seriously consider global tax-structure planning before executing overseas acquisition transactions. I also wish that the same routine as the VIE structure would have been established as part of Chinese companies' overseas acquisition strategies, which would have saved these companies millions of tax dollars in their post-acquisition operations.

So, what is the beauty of VIE structures that made Chinese companies so obsessed with them? I discovered the answer after considerable research and study.

2.3.1. What is a VIE Structure?

A VIE structure is a unique business structure in which investors do not have direct ownership but have a controlling interest of the entity through special contracts. The contracts specify the service and purpose of the agreements and the percentage of profits allocated to each party, but do not provide direct voting rights to the controlling party. The VIE structure comprises the following (see Figure 2.1.)

In the case of overseas-listed Chinese companies, a VIE refers to a company that is incorporated in China and owned by individuals who are Chinese citizens (usually the founders). The Overseas Listed Offshore Entity (OLOE) is typically a shell company domiciled in the Cayman Islands. An OLOE often incorporates a Wholly Foreign Owned Enterprise (WFOE) in China that holds material assets and conducts operations on behalf of the overseas-listed company. An OLOE generates revenue mainly through its ownership of WFOE, the WFOE captures profits of the VIE through a series of contracts between the WFOE and the VIE. The contacts (loan agreements, technical services agreements) give WFOE the rights to the VIE's residual profit. Additionally, the VIE and its owners will sign a power of attorney or proxy agreement to grant the WFOE voting rights at the VIE shareholder meetings. Technically, OLOE shareholders do not own the VIE but have

Figure 2.1.: The Simplified VIE Structure

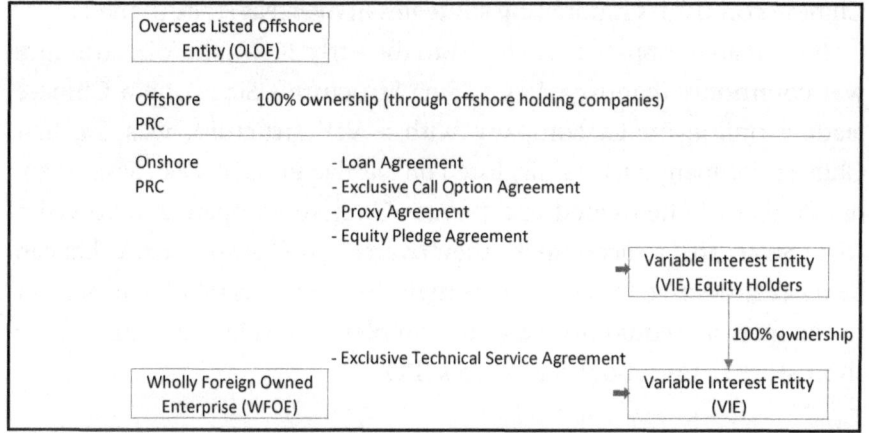

contractual rights to the VIE's profit and will be able to conduct voting rights through its WFOE. An OLOE can operate its business through more than one VIE. We often refer to the entire set of relationships as a "VIE structure".

2.3.2. Brief History of China's VIE Structure

The VIE structure emerged in China primarily for two reasons. First, the Chinese government has forbidden foreign investments in certain sectors, though regulators have increased the number of acceptable foreign investments over the years. Investments in industries like telecommunications, e-commerce, education, and media were still restricted as of June 2019. Second, Chinese authorities have complicated the approval process for overseas fundraising, making it extremely burdensome for private companies to access offshore capital. Of the eleven Chinese IPOs in the US between November 2019 and January 2020, six were structured as VIEs due to China's foreign investment restrictions and two were structured as VIEs for other reasons.

The prototype of the VIE structure was first designed in the 1990s to avoid the approval process and bypass foreign investment restrictions. In 1993, Ping An Insurance in Shenzhen used the early stage VIE structure to simplify its government approval process in order to obtain strategic investment from Morgan Stanley. Due to Ping An's success, the VIE prototype evolved to the current VIE structure, which enabled many Chinese companies fundraising strategies in overseas stock markets.

If we read newspaper articles from the early 2000s, the VIE structure was commonly mentioned as a "Sina Structure". Sina.com, a Chinese leading online media company with a VIE structure, was the first Chinese company successfully listed on Nasdaq in April 2000. Since then, hundreds of State-owned and private Chinese companies followed a "Sina Structure" to accomplish their overseas IPO ambitions. What can be more attractive for companies than the path to capital? The answer to the question could not be much simpler. Consider the entertaining short story below about Sina.com's IPO:

Case Study 2.4. Sina.com VIE Structure - A Potential Investor's Intriguing Story

This story was revealed by an anonymous investor who was offered an opportunity to invest in Sina Company (Sina) in 1999 before the creation of Sina.com and its IPO. After consulting his attorney, the investor declined the offer that could have made him a considerable amount of money. Below are the highlights of the attorney's opinions:

1. *Sina was incorporated in the Cayman Islands with the deliberate purpose to circumvent the regulatory restrictions of operating through domestic companies in China;*
2. *Sina did not own those domestic companies, but controlled them through a set of service and license agreements, share pledges, and loan agreements, etc.;*
3. *Sina's model was new and had not been sanctioned by Chinese regulations*
4. *Investing in Sina was an exorbitant risk*

Because of the attorney's advice, that investor rescinded Sina's offer. However, since 2000, many who did not consult attorneys or were willing to take the risk made personal fortunes from companies that utilized the "Sina Structure".

But if the VIE structure is a workaround solution to avoid regulations, are there any risks using the structure? Are Chinese regulators planning to fix this loophole? Answers to both questions are "Yes". Let us seek some understanding of Chinese regulators' actions on VIE structures. We will review VIE structure risks in Chapter 4.

2.3.3. The Chinese Regulator's Oversight of the VIE Structure

Like many other unique events during China's economic reform over the past three decades, the VIE structure was formed at a time when China's economic growth exploded and its desire and demand for global expansion accelerated rapidly while regulation development lagged behind. As the VIE structure has been considered, this regulation loophole needs to be closed by regulatory solutions. What progress has been made thus far and what solutions are Chinese regulators considering now? These are:

- The attempt from the 2015 Draft Foreign Investment Law: This initiative was the first regulation to clearly state that the VIE structure cannot be used to circumvent foreign investment laws- with the exception of foreign companies ultimately controlled by Chinese citizens. This exception accommodated companies like Alibaba and Baidu that were founded and owned by Chinese citizens. But companies like Tencent were excluded despite their Chinese founding, because Tencent's shares were not controlled by its founders. This draft has been subsequently withdrawn.
- In 2019, an updated Foreign Investment Law (FIL) was enacted: Global investors were disappointed and surprised when the most recent FIL (effective January 1, 2020) did not address the VIE structure. As a result, S&P Global Ratings concluded that China would abandon efforts to restrict VIEs and updated its risk assessment for VIE-structured Chinese companies. The Hong Kong Stock Exchange revised its guidance to continue allowing VIE structures.
- The creation of an annual "Negative List": Since July 2017, the Chinese government has implemented a nationwide negative

list approach with annual updates. The negative list defines prohibited and restricted industries accessible to foreign investors. The list becomes shorter each year, providing more opportunities for foreign investment and eliminating caps of foreign ownership in certain industries. The trend of shortening the negative list will continue to attract additional foreign investment. At the same time, by prohibiting fewer industries, the government will reduce the necessity of VIE structures.
- Anti-Monopoly Guidelines released in November 2020: The "Guidelines for Anti-Monopoly in the Platform Economy" issued by China's State Administration for Market Regulation ("SAMR") made the VIE structure part of an antitrust review and addressed SAMR's additional scrutiny for "mergers control review" involving VIE structure transactions. However, SAMR's focus seems to restrict foreign ownership on certain technology sectors via VIEs, not to eliminate the VIE structure completely.
- It is highly unlikely that China will suddenly ban VIEs without notice or justification. Most well-known Chinese multinational companies today are structured as VIEs. These VIEs are major contributors to China's GDP growth, job opportunities, tax revenues and global expansion. Punishing VIEs would cause financial chaos and disruption to China's economy.

China has been taking a gradualist approach[4] to economic reform and corporate governance development over the past 30 years. The approach has proved to be successful in contrast with the Russian "rush approach[5]", for example. According to *Corporate Governance and Financial Reform in China's Transition Economy* by Leng Jing, countries utilizing a

---

[4] China's "gradualist approach" refers to a constantly experimental and correcting economic reform process. Regulators will issue interim regulations to guide the economic reform through different stages with progressing evolution focus in order to transform from a planned economy to market economy with continuous correction and improvement on the regulatory system, industries' standards and business practice. China's SOE reform through different stages using the "gradualist approach" will be discussed in Chapter 3.

[5] Russia's "rush approach" is a top-down reform package consisting of programs designed to destroy all existing economic structures and replace them with a Western-style market economy. Russia's "rush approach" led to political conflict during firms' privatization, and eventually led to economic reform failure in the 1990s.

gradualist strategy tend to lack well-functioning or updated regulations, which means regulatory development always lingers. It appears obvious that Chinese regulators are concurrently using the same strategy to fix VIEs as they steadily and continuously relax foreign investment restrictions and improve the overall standard of its regulation system.

China's 2019 Foreign Investment Law still needs improvement, but it establishes the principles necessary to create a more equitable environment for foreign investors to simplify the approval process for foreign investments entering and exiting China's market, and to better protect foreign investors' interests. Most reforms of the current FIL still need detailed provisions for practical implementation since these reforms are fundamental to fixing VIEs. It may be too early to conclude if the anti-monopoly guidelines will lead to further regulatory restrictions on the VIE structure. Leaving the VIE structure in an obtuse area as it is at the moment could be a practical decision that indicates the Chinese government is still working to improve its overall regulatory system, which is unlikely to directly prohibit or restrict the VIE structure in the near future.

Chapter 3
An Overview of China's SOE and CG Regulation Reform

Hong Kong, the "Pearl of the Orient", is one of the most beautiful cities in the world. What I love most about Hong Kong is its contrasting beauty of well-mixed Western and Eastern cultures, expensive Michelin restaurants and street gourmet food, worldwide brands and open-air markets.

Historically, Hong Kong has been an important financial center in Asia and the closest connection to China from the west. Despite being warned of the "housing space shock" by two college friends who moved there for bank jobs from the US in the 2000s, I still wanted to live there. I expected opportunities to practice my Cantonese before moving to Hong Kong. However, for the two years I lived there, other than taxi drivers and street shop owners, most Hong Kongers spoke either Mandarin or English. I was impressed indeed by the number of Mandarin speakers who applied for the finance and investment opening positions while we were building the local team, most of whom studied Mandarin in mainland China. Hong Kong's privileged economic position has been fading in the past couple of decades due to China's fast growth. A profound experience I had with our local employees through their words and behavior was their "sense of loss" as native Hong Kongers, and the paradoxical feeling they had working for a company from mainland China. My workaholic lifestyle rapidly earned their respect and trust, and they helped me understand that local professionals were accustomed to Western-style business practices that had been widely adopted over the past few decades in local organizations.

The Hong Kong company was welcomed by local banking and investing communities. With influential support from top leaders of the SOE and several executives from corporate headquarters, we assembled a local team and devised some strategies; supported the SOE parent company to raise a significant amount of US capital at the HKEX by US bond issuances; reviewed a number of investment opportunities including pre-IPO and asset acquisitions; and established a joint venture company in the US. The fast pace of all these activities made my two-year experience in Hong Kong a life-changing journey fulfilled with much excitement that also opened my eyes and mind about Chinese companies' agile growth and regulatory guidance, both of which were evolving simultaneously, in contrast to my years of experience with US companies, where I observed their growth within a well-regulated business environment. I was also forced to acknowledge that certain occasions caused me confusion about decisions made at the top, while comments made by my Hong Kong colleagues detailing their previous experiences with local companies only confirmed my apprehension.

Once I had a chance to study Chinese SOE reform and CG regulatory reform later on, I realized the importance of Chinese SOEs' evolving journey toward China's regulatory reform and CG reform implementation. I also realized the value of my two-year experience at the Hong Kong company, a new but important subsidiary of a fast-growing Chinese SOE. Through these experiences I witnessed China's fast economic growth as the powerful engine that enabled the SOE's access to domestic and international capitals, the SOE's influence in Hong Kong and other Asian regions, and its ability to do business the "Chinese way".

In addition, I had opportunities to engage with certain Chinese authorities (including the State Administration of Foreign Exchange) and experience the application and proven process of China's Renminbi (RMB) internationalization program eg, the RMB Qualified Foreign Institutional Investors (RQFII)[1]. I was introduced to international credit rating agencies and their counterparts in China and now understand the gaps between their rating standards. I also gained first-hand experience

---

[1] The RMB Qualified Foreign Institutional Investors (RQFII) program was established in 2011 to setup quotas for qualified foreign institutional investors to invest in the Chinese bond and stock markets. There are jurisdictional requirements and total asset under management thresholds for different groups of RQFII applicants.

of the perplexing differences between onshore RMB and offshore RMB[2] and the extreme interest rate fluctuation of offshore RMB in Hong Kong's capital market in early 2016 that was caused by the anticipated capital regulation change as a reaction to RMB's weakening pressure at that time (details regarding RMB internationalization and related matters will be discussed in Chapter 10).

In this chapter, I will review China's regulatory reform milestones and examine a few Chinese companies' success stories and notable business activities that resulted from unique experimental policies and regulations conducted during the stages of SOE reform, and the positive aspects of the Chinese governments' commitment to establish a better-regulated investment environment that fosters fair competition.

3.1. Timetable of China's SOE and CG Regulation Reform Milestones

China has taken a gradualist approach on economic reform that has been proved successful when contrasted with the relatively opposite Russian "rush approach". However, countries that employ a gradualist strategy lack well-functioning or have out-of-date regulations, which means the development of comprehensive regulations that support the proper functioning of institutions always lags behind. Consequently, in order to direct and regulate economic reform strategies, regulators have issued many policies (or "stepping-stones") to direct the transfer of China's planned economy to a free-market economy, while simultaneously fine-tuning and refining these transitional regulations over time.

For the purpose of this book, listed in Table 3.1. below are some milestone regulations and guidelines related to Chinese CG development and SOE reform implemented from the beginning of China's modern economy in 1978.

---

[2] Chinese RMB held and used in mainland China is known as onshore RMB (trading symbol: CNY); Chinese RMB held by banks in overseas RMB hubs led by Hong Kong and Singapore is known as offshore RMB (trading symbol: CNH). Although the RMB is considered one currency, the different interest and exchange rates between onshore and offshore RMB often cause confusion as if they are two currencies.

Table 3.1. China's SOE and CG Regulation Reform Timetable

Year	China SOEs regulation and reforms	China's CG regulation reforms	Purpose of the regulation or reform
1981	Introduces a "dual-track" system – an intermediate price system from a State price control system to a free-market price system		To allow some enterprises to sell their surplus products at market prices, while the planned quota product was to be sold at State-set prices
1985	Launches a "responsibility contract system"		To establish accountability mechanisms for SOE managers
1990	Reopening of the SSE & establishment of the SZSE		The first milestone of SOE reform. To build a foundation for CG development by diversifying SOE share structures, allowing SOEs to raise funds in the stock market, and transferring partial SOE shares to investors
1992		Establishment of The China Securities Regulatory Commission (CSRS)	To form the CSRS as a government body to regulate the new stock market
1994	Establishment of the first set of Company Law		The second milestone of SOE reform. To set up a legal foundation for the establishment of a CG structure for Chinese SOEs.
1999	Establishment of the first set of Security Law		The third milestone of SOE reform. The first economic law drafted by State legislatures, not government departments.
2001		The CSRC publishes guidelines for listed companies regarding independent directors	To require at least one-third of the board members be independent directors
2002		The CSRC issues its first CG Code	To establish CG Code
2002		Introduction of Qualified Foreign Institutional Investors	To allow foreign capital entrance to China's stock market via institutional investors
2003	Establishment of the State-Owned Assets Supervision and Administration Commission (SASAC)		SASAC as a government institution to manage and transfer state assets to the market
2005		The CSRC introduces split-share structure reform and begins converting non-tradable shares of the 1000-plus listed SOEs into tradable shares	To diversify the SOEs' shareholder structure

Year			Purpose
2006		Establishment of new Company Law and Security Laws	To increase the liability exposure of directors, improve the management structure of listed companies, and make CSR a requirement for companies
2006		The SZSE issues social responsibility instructions to listed companies	To define CSR as a mandate for listed companies
2007	The issuance of China's first Labor Contract Law		To protect workers' legitimate rights and interests
2007	New Corporate Bankruptcy Laws		To regulate the bankruptcies of SOEs, foreign investment entities and domestic companies
2007		Partial adoption of International Financial Reporting Standards and International Standard on Auditing	To align China's accounting and auditing standards with international standards
2007	SASAC issues a new directive in Enterprise Risk Management		To provide guidance for SOEs regarding risk management
2007	Enterprise Income Tax Laws enacted		To establish a uniform tax rate of 25% for all types of enterprises operating in China (Before this tax reform, income tax for SOEs was 33%, and for foreign-invested companies 17%)
2008	SASAC issues guidelines to SOEs directly managed under the central government to fulfill CSR standards		To make CSR required for all central government controlled SOEs
2008		CSRC requires leading firms to have annual board reviews	To improve CG
2008		SSE releases notice of improving listed companies' assumption of social responsibilities; SZSE releases social responsibility instruction to listed companies	To require CSR for listed companies
2009	The SASAC mandates all SOEs under its supervision to develop CSR mechanisms in their corporate governance		To require CSR for all SOEs
2012	The SASAC mandates all SOEs under its supervision publish their first CSR report by the end of 2012		To require CSR reporting mandates for all SOEs
2012		HKEX releases the first ESG Reporting Guide	To encourage ESG information disclosure
2014		China's State Council issues the Planning Outline for the Construction of a Social Credit System	To initiate China's social credit system including Corporate Social Credit System (CSCS)

Year		Event	Purpose
2015		SASAC issues Guidance on Social Responsibility, Guidance on Social Responsibility Reporting, and Guidance on Classifying Social Responsibility Performance	To emphasize CSR requirements
2015		The HKEX issues a consultation paper increasing the requirement of ESG reports from "suggested disclosure" to "comply or explain"	To encourage ESG information disclosure or require explanation
2017	State Council mandates the majority of external directors be established in wholly owned SOEs		To improve CG for SOEs and emphasize SOE ERM
2018		The CSRC requires companies on the Ministry of Environment and Ecology's list of heavy polluters to disclose details of their pollution and pollution control measures	To mandate ESG information disclosure
2018		Revised code of CG for listed companies (Revised Code)	To improve CG
2018		The SSE & SZSE issue the ESG Disclosure Guide	To encourage ESG information disclosure
2019		The HKEX issues an updated ESG Reporting Guide with mandatory disclosure requirements	To mandate ESG information disclosure
2020		The HKEX issues updated ESG Reporting Guidance and E-training	To better standardize and improve the effectiveness of ESG reporting
2020		The HKEX launches the Sustainable and Green Exchange (STAGE), an online platform that addresses issues such as data availability, accessibility, and transparency	To provide investors with information for investment decisions and provide issuers visibility of sustainable standards and the issuers' compliance status
2021		The CSRC issues new ESG reporting guidelines with a set of risk disclosure rules	To require companies to disclose protecting procedures and measurement systems for environmental factors (eg pollution and waste management), and to encourage disclosures of social factors (eg poverty alleviation and rural revitalization)

As listed in Table 3.1., Chinese regulation reform started with SOE reform. China's CG reform and development started from SOEs and has expanded to all other types of companies, along with SOE ownership diversity and the birth of private companies. This chapter will analyze the trends focused on important milestones in SOE and CG reforms.

3.2. History is Not Repeatable - China's SOE Reform

Before 1978, Chinese SOEs were State-operated enterprises, which exposes the fact that Chinese SOEs were not only owned but also operated by the State. Managers of State-operated enterprises were not entrepreneurs, but government agents and Party officials. Therefore, the most important job of these officials was not to maximize enterprise profit, but to ensure that government quotas instituted by central planning were attained. All strategic decisions involving resource financing, production planning, and all products' selling prices of these enterprises, were controlled by government authorities. This bureaucratic system made Chinese SOEs very inefficient, and the Chinese government has been struggling to improve SOE efficiency for three decades beginning in 1949, when P.R. China was established, until 1978, when comprehensive reforms began.

Therefore, SOE reform has been a priority of China's economic agenda since the beginning. In this section, we will review China's SOE reforms that focus on policies experimented during different stages. To help readers understand the policy priorities of each stage and the opportunities available for companies with these policies and the procedures that some companies took to capitalize on domestic and international growth, we will briefly examine a case study of the Haier Group Corporation, a global Chinese company that implemented certain reforms in their business practice.

3.2.1. Stage One (1978 – 1984): Autonomy and Incentive

The Chinese government realized that a lack of production incentives and employee enthusiasm were the main culprits of SOEs' inadequate performance and inefficiency. In the first stage of Chinese SOE reforms, when regulators were focused on increasing SOEs' decision-making processes in operations, the government started experimenting with ownership structure reforms for local government controlled SOEs. The following are the principal actions during this stage that did not then negatively impact China's planned economy:

- Initially, an "enterprise" was defined as a legal entity with the right to function independently
- The creation of a "dual track system" that allowed SOEs to retain their profit after paying an income tax of 55%, replacing the former policy of forfeiting all profit to the State
- Collectively- owned township and village enterprises were introduced to local SOEs
- No changes to the planned-economy system

The first stage of SOE reforms initiated operational autonomy and ownership diversity, created competitive mechanisms while introducing a "dual track system", and paved the way for additional SOE reforms in later stages.

Case Study 3.1. The Establishment of Haier – Collective Ownership Structure (SOE Reform Stage One)

Haier Group Corporation is a Chinese multinational home appliances and consumer electronics company headquartered in Qingdao. Haier Group's three subsidiaries are listed on the Shanghai Stock Exchange, the China/Europe International Exchange of Frankfurt, and the Hong Kong Stock Exchange (Haier Smart Home was listed in Shanghai in 1993, Frankfurt in 2018, and Haier Electronics Group in Hong Kong in 2016.) Haier's ownership structure has frequently changed and its business growth over the past 40 years reflects different stages of China's SOE reform as discussed here.

Haier's history began in 1984 with Zhang Ruimin appointed as plant director of then nearly bankrupt State-owned refrigerator company. Before his appointment - when the company was known as the Qingdao Refrigerator Plant - Zhang was the deputy manager of the municipal government's household appliance division. Zhang was a young student whose education was disrupted by China's Cultural Revolution, but he was an autodidact and slowly ascended the government's hierarchy.

Haier was initially constructed as a collective ownership enterprise, a structure introduced to local SOEs during SOE Reform Stage One to attain operational efficiency. With the collective ownership structure, local governments granted SOE managers partial or total residual company shares. As a passionate and innovative 35-year-old in 1984, Zhang Ruimin was appointed to the position. In the same year, Haier was introduced to Liebherr, a German technology and equipment company whose product line included refrigerators.

The collective ownership structure provided a strong incentive for Haier's management team led by Zhang Ruimin. The ongoing changes afterwards have facilitated the company's financial comeback.

3.2.2. Stage Two (1985 – 1992): "Neither This Nor That" - Separating SOEs' Ownership and Operating Rights Based on Public Ownership

The most symbolic feature in this stage was the establishment of the Contract Responsibility System (CRS). With CRS, SOEs' managers are assigned operating rights by the government via a three-to-five-year employment contract. In return, the managers rebate predetermined profit to the government and thereafter retention of the excess profit. By the end of the 1980s, over 90% of SOEs were using the CRS system. Although CRS is considered to be successful when the SOEs' operation performance improves, the system experiences systematic shortcomings as mentioned below:

- The three-to-five-year contractual term creates potential conflicts between managers' short-term goals and SOEs' long-term strategies
- The rights to the SOEs' residual profits enable managers to obtain more benefits by extracting resources from SOEs, potentially causing significant State-owned asset erosion

- The fact that the CRS system is not a market mechanism leads to huge resource waste resulting in unsellable products produced by SOEs.
- The term "socialism with Chinese characteristics" was invented in this stage to define the transitional Chinese economic conditions of the early 1990s. Australian economist Geoff Raby describes this as 'The Neither This Nor That Economy', half-plan, half-market; neither-plan, neither-market; pretend-socialism, pretend-capitalism; with ill-defined borders between legality and illegality; socialist moral codes and principles of market efficiency; neither this nor that; in short a condition of 'market socialism', or 'socialism with Chinese characteristics'."

CRS was not considered a successful strategy but is one of many "stepping stones" leading to the ultimate destination to a market economy. According to statistical data, 40% of SOEs were losing money in the early 1990s which created the demand for the third stage of SOE reform in China, an iconic one in SOE reform history, one that established market-supported institutions.

3.2.3. Stage Three (1993 – 2002): SOE Corporatization - the Beginning of China's CG Development

The year 1993 was a pivotal time in Chinese SOE reform, as that year, the government introduced the concept of shareholding companies that initiated shareholding experiments and corporatization programs intended to transform traditional Chinese SOEs into shareholding companies, a new enterprise formality. China's third stage of SOE reform starting that year focused on establishing a modern SOE system based on a free-market economy. Unlike the first two stages of reform that focused on SOE operating rights, the third stage emphasized reforming SOE ownership rights. The acronym "SOE" originated during this stage. Three milestones resulted in successfully bringing China's SOE reform to the next level – the alignment of SOE and CG reforms:

- The reopening of the Shanghai Stock Exchange (SSE) and establishment of the Shenzhen Stock Exchange (SZSE) provided platforms and channels for listed SOEs to raise funds in the capital market
- A company law was enacted in 1994 as a legal foundation for Chinese companies' CG structure
- A securities law instituted in 1999 - the first financial law issued by the supreme legislature of the State, not by a government department - marked the beginning of a separate regulatory system of China's securities market

The third stage of SOE reform made SOEs' inefficiency apparent. According to statistical data, nearly 40% of large and middle size SOEs reported losses in 1997 of RMB 66.6 billion ($10.5 billion). Under the leadership of Prime Minister Zhu Rongji, China's government assembled a three (fiscal)-year (1998-2000) SOE reform goal to rejuvenate unprofitable SOEs, resulting in a noticeable profit achieved by SOEs in the latter period of this stage, although 21 million "over-abundant" workers were laid off throughout China. Nevertheless, regardless of the lack of systematic regulation guidance and enforcement, the third stage of SOE reform created opportunities for some private sector businesses to capture State assets via an internal management buyout system, even though unemployed workers who were laid off encountered re-hiring challenges. The unanticipated wealth distribution imbalance also created social dissatisfaction, which led to future stages of SOE reform.

Case Study 3.2. Haier's Opportunity for IPO and International Growth (SOE Reform Stage Two & Three)

- *China's quota-based IPO system in early 1990s*
  The Shanghai Stock Market that was established in 1990 contained a share-issuing process governed by a quota system. With the quota system, local governments were responsible for the qualification review and nomination of IPO candidate companies to the central government for final administrative approval, while IPO prices were jointly decided by regulators and brokerage firms.

- *Haier's public listing in 1993*
  In 1992, Haier encountered a significant cash shortage prior to pursuing its plan of acquiring land to build the first industrial park of an estimated cost of over RMB 1 billion. With the local government's endorsement, Haier listed its stock on the Shanghai Stock Exchange in 1993, and successfully raised RMB 369 million, which enabled the company to build the industrial park. Haier's timely public listing was one of the profitable outcomes of China's quota IPO system in the early 1990s. The company was then renamed "Qingdao Haier Refrigerator Co. Ltd.". The transaction allowed Haier to survive the cash crisis and furthered its plans for future growth.

- *Haier's Expansion to the Global Market*
  Haier's international journey started in the early 1990s with exports to European countries. In 1994, Haier invested $30 million in a joint venture with Mitsubishi, permitting the company to be one of the first of China's companies to engage in foreign investment. In 1997, Haier formed another joint venture with a Serbian company located in its capital Belgrade.

  Haier entered the US market with low-priced products in 1994 and Haier America was established in 1999. In the early 2000s, the company purchased property for its headquarters in New York, built a factory and industrial park, and began promoting its brand in the US.

- *Organizational Structure and Business Strategy*
  Between 1998 and 2002, Haier reformulated its organizational structure on 40 occasions - exemplifying the Chinese idiom (of) "cross the river by feeling the stones", meaning, "to learn by doing, and keep trying until finding the right route". Throughout those experimental experiences, Haier prepared for the later implementation of the "Rendanheyi Organizational Structure" that was to be instituted throughout the company.

  With Haier's success in the early 1990s, municipal governments persuaded the company to take over poorly performing firms owned by municipal governments in exchange for Haier acquiring all the *employees and debts of these firms. Propelled by governmental pressure between 1995 and 1997, the company procured 15 companies and quickly realized a sizable profit due to its management and quality control strategies. These domestic acquisitions allowed Haier to consolidate its holdings into a group company with diversified household appliance products such as refrigerators, washing machines, and air conditioners, which built a solid foundation for Haier's international growth as a multinational company later on.*

During my conversation with her, Professor Lourdes Casanova - who has devoted decades of research to emerging multinationals - related that one of the primary differences between China's multinationals and other emerging multinationals is Chinese companies' success in its domestic market. That success is attributed to China's fast economic growth that differentiated these companies' global growth motivation and strategies from other emerging multinationals who pursued international growth in order to avoid domestic economic crisis. Haier is one of many successful Chinese companies identified and was provided with growth opportunities through the interim regulation period during China's SOE reform. The company subsequently capitalized on those opportunities to expand the business and achieve domestic success, which became a solid foundation when Haier entered the global market.

The collective ownership structure greatly motivated the management team toward company efficiency. The never-reprised quota-based IPO system enabled Haier to access capital via the stock market, and the success of Haier's joint venture with Mitsubishi benefited from a 17% income tax rate for foreign investment companies in the 1990s, in contrast to 33% for traditional SOEs.

3.2.4. Stage Four (2003 – 2012): State-Owned Asset Management System Reform

The fourth stage of SOE reform targeted large and influential SOEs in order to solve a long-standing undefined property rights issue. If "owned by the people" is such an ambiguous concept, who are the owners of SOEs? The SASAC was established in March 2003 to act on behalf of the central government, who is the shareholder of large and influential SOEs on behalf of the government. At the time of the SASAC's establishment, 189 SOEs were subject to SASAC's authority with total assets of RMB6.9 trillion ($1.1 trillion).

The establishment of the SASAC was a an especially important milestone in Chinese companies' CG development. Company board reforms launched by the SASAC required central SOEs to increase the number of outside directors and oversee boards' monitoring and advisory functions. By the end of 2018, 90% of Chinese SOEs complied with or were in the process of board reform.

Although there is much room for improvement of Chinese SOE board practices, the SASAC's requirement of outside directors to participate in the strategic decision-making process of these companies has established the foundation for future CG development and reform.

3.2.5. Stage Five (2013 – present): Extensive SOE reform

Followed by a nationwide anti-corruption campaign and increasingly comprehensive SOE reform, the Chinese government issued a guidance report, "Guiding Opinions on Deepening the Reform of State-Owned Enterprises" in 2015, in addition to 22 supplementary publications emphasizing that SOE reform should be guided by one core policy (the "one"), plus ancillary policies (the "N"). The "one plus N" policy enables the following elements:

- Classifying SOEs into separate commercial and public service SOEs, which allows government to reduce support to commercial SOEs and provide more resources to public service SOEs.
- Strengthening Party committee leadership in SOEs. SOE boards of directors are mandated to received Party committee's opinions for important decisions.
- Centralized SOE reorganization to promote the competitiveness

of SOEs for China's Belt and Road Initiative (BRI)[3]. During this SOE reform, the number of central SOEs in China decreased from 189 in 2002 to 96 at the end of 2018.

China's SOE reform was in a continuous process under former Chinese president Deng Xiaoping's strategy of the idiomatic "feeling the stones while crossing the river". In well-established Western-style economics, business' "best practices" are admired. However, there was not a "best practice" convention for SOE reform and economic reforms in China. Would China's emerging experience become a "best practice" or guidance for other countries with emerging markets? I hope so, as that will help save the time and resources needed on such a journey and help expedite those countries' contributions to the global economy.

Case Study 3.3. Haier's Rendanheyi Model (SOE Reform Stage Four & Five)

Haier's innovative concept, Rendanheyi, is a win-win management model labeled as "making everyone a CEO". Key elements of Rendanheyi are autonomous micro-enterprises, performance-based compensation structures, and open online user platforms. The ultimate goal of Rendanheyi is to create "zero distance to the user". The Rendanheyi 1.0 concept was introduced and implemented in three phases during a company-wide restructuring plan.

Rendanheyi's phase-one implementation (2005 - 2009). *This model was designed and introduced by CEO Zhang Ruimin and the first group of CEO/owner of micro enterprises (numbers of mini companies under Rendanheyi's model) in 2005 to implement it in the organization in 2010. Supporting infrastructure was built within that period. The actualization of the Rendanheyi management model transformed Haier from a traditional manufacturing company into a service-oriented company.*

---

[3] China Belt and Road Initiative (BRI) is a global infrastructure development strategy launched by the Chinese government in 2013 as an initiative to increase China's economic links to Southeast Asia, Central Asia, Russia, and Central and Eastern Europe for joint projects in infrastructure, energy, and transportation sectors. Some details of BRI will be discussed in Chapter 9.

During Rendanheyi's phase one implementation, Haier established new strategic business units (shared service functions) and implemented new IT solutions and performance measures to connect the organization to customers.

Rendanheyi's phase-two implementation (2009 - 2014). *Haier established 10-20 ZZJYT (a self-operating group that uses the Chinese abbreviation of "Zi Zhu Jing Ying Ti") to operate autonomously to hire team members and set compensation and bonus structures;*

Rendanheyi's phase-three implementation (2014 - 2015). *Haier further restructured the ZZJYT to over 200 6-8 employee xiaowei (micro-entities) permitting them some ownership of the entities and providing authorization for independent decision-making to xiaowei leaders that allowed them to choose external suppliers or obtain external funding, similar to CEO responsibilities in an independent company. A Xiaowei's performance is measured by financial key performance indicators (KPI) and user value added, and Xiaowei members' compensation is entirely tied to their performance. In addition, the innovation of Rendanheyi not only improved Haier's profitability, but also shook the conventional hierarchy of China's manufacturing entities and widely promoted an entrepreneurial spirit in organizations.*

Rendanheyi 1.0 increased Haier's profit margin from 3-4% in 2005 (in contrast to Whirlpool's 6-8% during the same time period) to 5.7% in 2015 (to Whirlpool's 3.9%). However, Haier's workforce declined by 25% (20,000 of 80,000 employees) during Rendanheyi's 1.0 implementation.

Unfortunately, the Rendanheyi model cannot be implemented in Haier's overseas companies due to local regulatory and business practice differences, which has prevented Haier from becoming an industry leader. In addition, it took Haier until 2019 to achieve a top-tier global brand ranking, according to data from Emerging Markets Annual reports published by Cornell University, while other Chinese peers, such as Lenovo and Huawei, have successfully positioned themselves as price leaders across most product categories and have enjoyed higher brand rankings since the mid-2010s. The fact that micro-enterprises focus more on short-term profit using the Rendanheyi model also raises questions regarding a company's long-term sustainability. However, Haier's growth over the past 40 years reflects many positive aspects of policies implemented during China's SOE reforms throughout the different stages of strategic maneuvers.

During China's 40-year SOE reform journey, policy priorities have been gradually shifting over time along with the government's adoption of various strategies. When we look at the percentage of public sector shareholders today, 38% of Chinese companies' public sector shareholders appear to be very high, in contrast to 3% of US companies, 9% of European companies, and a 14% global average. But upon a review of China's SOE diversified ownership process and its "learning by doing" approach, alongside understanding the gradualist strategy of the country's economic reform measures that ensured the smooth transition from a State-planned to market economy, we must recognize that the 38% accomplishment should not be undervalued.

China's SOE reform has generated many encouraging results due to its SOE diversified ownership and financial performance improvements, although problems remain and should not be underestimated. Given China's 14th Five-Year Plan, SOEs will retain important roles in China's future economic growth, and their reform will continue to improve operational and strategic roles to fortify the economy over the next five years and in the decades to come. Details of China's new Five-Year Plan will be discussed in Chapter 8.

3.3. China's CG reform

China's CG reforms started in the early 1990s, when the primary focus was on SOEs. Western-style CG mechanisms of boards of directors, supervisory boards, independent board directors, and general shareholder meetings were introduced to China in the early 1990s, along with the establishment of two stock markets, the SSE and SZSE. The CSR and ESG concepts were also introduced to the Chinese market by Western companies and investors during various stages of China's economic growth, which played fundamental roles in stimulating and facilitating Chinese companies' global expansion.

At this point, it is worth reiterating and summarizing China's CG regulation and ESG reforms that occurred in two phases, according to Table 3.1.:

Phase one (1990 to 2001): In the early 1990s, the reopening of the SSE, the founding of the SZSE, and the establishment of the CSRC as the new stock market regulating authority launched China's modern CG journey. China established various regulations in phase one to build a regulatory foundation for CG development.

Phase two (2002 – present): In 2002, the CSRC issued the first Chinese CG code, followed by a series of regulations and rules to promote and advance the capital markets to global investors, diversify the SOE share structure, initiate CSCS and CSR guidance, and establish a series of guidelines for ESG development to be consistent with global trends. The following are a few points of China's CG reform worth mentioning:

3.3.1. Chinese Companies' CG Improvement Parallels Regulatory Development

Regulations and rules are simply the "hard facts" of CG, like board structures, independent board directors, board committee functions and board report formats. CG is much more complicated, however, subjected as it is to the influence of a country's culture, history, and legal environment. Soft factors like corporate culture, trust between board members, and board directors' knowledge about the company cannot be defined by regulations, but are the result of board members' understanding of the board's functions and fiduciary duties and their commitment to work together to perform these functions. Research shows that these soft factors are actually better indicators of the effectiveness of governance than hard factors. In these soft factors, Chinese companies have the greatest room for growth.

Some companies, such as the Chinese tech giant Lenovo, are ahead of the curve. The company built its high standards of governance using Western CG norms as its benchmark. Lenovo has established systematic checks and balances mechanisms in its CG via a transparent corporate culture, clear governance structure, a professional board of directors, and well-structured board functions with a formal nominating process (See Case Study 3.4.).

Case Study 3.4. Lenovo's CG model

Lenovo was founded in 1984 and became a Hong Kong-listed company in 1994. In 2005, Lenovo's acquisition of IBM's personal computer business not only empowered Lenovo with global market access, technological improvements, a branding strategy, but also exposed it to IBM's CG practice that follows international standards and made the company the pacesetter of other Chinese multinationals on CG practice.

When Hong Kong-listed companies were only required to issue financial reports semiannually, Lenovo followed international accounting standards by issuing quarterly financial reports and conducted semiannual roadshows to meet institutional investors. Lenovo's 12-member board has one executive director, two non-executive directors and nine independent directors. All members of the Audit Committee and Compensation Committee are non-executive directors. Since 2020, the lead independent director chairs the Nomination and Governance Committee. While chairman and CEO are still a combined role, the lead independent director calls and chairs meetings at least once annually with only independent non-executive directors attending.

Lenovo's board emphasizes a transparent corporate culture and maintains formal nomination procedures when appointing new board directors. All directors are subject to retirement by rotation every three years, with nine years as regular tenure for independent directors, and shareholder elections after the first three-year term. The maximum tenure for independent directors is 12 years upon another shareholder's re-election. Lenovo's board provides comprehensive induction and continuing professional development programmes to help directors understand business operations and improve directors' professionalism.

Lenovo's board maintains a structured schedule and an agenda and information dispatch procedure for regular and ad hoc board meetings and an annual board evaluation, a clear matrix for key matters that need board approval and consistent timelines for CG report preparation.

Lenovo demonstrates the best CG among mainland Chinese companies. Since 2012, the company has been consistently honored with Best Corporate Governance Awards and Best Sustainability and Social Responsibility Awards by the Hong Kong Institute of Certified Public Accountants (HKICPA).

Although acquiring IBM accelerated Lenovo's CG improvement, the company and its leadership team also deserve credit for their willingness to learn and follow a higher-standard CG practice since then. As more and more Chinese companies enter the global market, and as some have taken leading roles in particular industries, the global business community has come to regard Chinese companies as global citizens. With this acceptance comes higher expectations of both financial and non-financial performances. This moment presents a unique opportunity for Chinese companies to raise their CG standards to the next level.

3.3.2. China' CG Reform Trends

In order to understand China's future CG reform, I would like to highlight two important movements that have been gradually re-shaping China's economic and social environments.

China's ESG Revolution. Since 2012, China has been taking ESG concerns very seriously since the HKEX ESG reporting guidance standards were issued. The guidelines have provided consistent updates on ESG disclosure requirements to achieve higher standards. The latest HKEX ESG reporting guidance issued in 2020 has placed climate-related disclosure as a high priority for listed companies in Hong Kong in order to align with recommendations from the leading international framework for climate-related disclosure, the Task Force on Climate-Related Financial Disclosures (TCFD). After issuing environmental reporting requirements for heavy polluters in 2018, CSRS's revised guidelines on ESG reporting to including environmental and social factors in June 2021 will broaden ESG reporting requirements from heavy polluters to most listed companies, and will affect Chinese companies' 2021 semi-annual reports and annual reports.

At the time this chapter was written, the ESG revolution has proliferated within the global business community. With China being the world's second-largest economy, and having rapidly recovered economically post-COVID-19, will the ESG revolution further the opportunity for China to advance its CG development and worldwide influence? We will discuss that idea in Chapter 7.

China's Social Credit System (SoCS). The Planning Outline for the Construction of a Social Credit System (2014-2020) launched in 2014 initiated a plan for a nationwide social credit system including the implementation of the China's Social Credit System (SoCS) by the end of 2020. Due to the complexity of establishing such a comprehensive social credit system, the process of standardizing the legal foundations of the SoCS and developing and implementing social credit system policies in various cities and provinces is still in progress at the time of this publication. Although the completion schedule of a nationwide SoCS in China is unknown, according to a 2020 research study by Trivium China, a Chinese politics and economy advisory firm headquartered in Beijing, Chinese social credit regulations in all provinces are expected by 2023. However, SoCS has received increased attention since 2019 due to tension over the trade war between the US and China, especially because of controversial discussions on data security and a lack of transparency in the implementation process. With increasing concerns about data security as digital business continues growing in China, and greater demand for a nationwide credit system, SoCS development will likely speed up via advanced technology and the possibility of consolidating credit data collected by and held on various organizations will continue. China's SoCS will play a significant role in China's future CG development.

For the time being, the most fundamental questions regarding China's SoCS are: How does the system work? What are the impacts to foreign companies' operation and foreigners in China? We will discuss more details about China's SoCS in Chapter 8.

Chapter 4
Key CG Risks of Chinese Companies

Risks and opportunities go "hand in hand." Although we all understand the importance of risk mitigation, eliminating risks is not a good option since "avoiding 'bad' risks at all costs presents a countervailing risk: that we will fail to take 'good risks'", according to Michele Wucker, the American author and policy analyst specializing in world economy and crisis anticipation, and taking the "good risks" often leads us to opportunities. Ms. Wucker also points out in her book, *You Are What You Risk*, that knowledge and awareness in specific endeavors can change an individual's risk appetite and risk attitude and help us make rational risk-taking or risk-avoiding decisions. Ms Wucker contends that active risk-taking is healthy and beneficial when expectations are established, and challenges are not only expected but also conquered.

Business leaders' risk appetites and risk attitudes will be reflected in companies' risk management strategies. Most CEOs I worked with emphasized that businesses should take calculated risks, which means company executives need to be aware of risks for the specific business they are running and be able to measure the maximum damage of these risks and the potential opportunities as a result of taking these risks. Some risks are explicit, some are hidden, and some are more harmful than others. Traditionally, we categorize business risks as economic risk, compliance risk, financial risk (including fraud risks), operational risk, competitive risk, fraud risk, and political risk if operating in other countries. With the fast growth of digital business, increasing the discussion of a corporation's purpose and the coming worldwide ESG movement, reputational risk, data security risk, and CG risk have all become vitally important to business.

Since the topic of this book is CG, what then are CG risks? If CG is how power is deployed and allocated in an organization as explained in Chapter 1, CG risks are risks associated with deploying and allocating systems including the decision-making process, mechanisms for checks and balances, and the nomination functions for board members and executives. With risk management being a basic function of CG, CG risks will not only make the risk management function less effective, but also create systematic risks in the organization and generate fiduciary risks for business leaders who make the decisions. More importantly, most CG risks are not explicit but also difficult to be identified and calculated.

After reviewing Chinese companies CG development, creative CG models, and China's regulatory reforms, what are the key CG risks of Chinese companies that we should be aware of? Let us zoom in on this chapter for answers.

4.1. Insider Share Pledging Risk

Share pledging refers to companies that use a percentage of company stocks as collateral to obtain loans with an agreed stock price at the time of pledging. In practice, the lender will force sales of the pledged shares when the stock price drops to a certain level. The forced selling will cause panic in the Stock market, which leads to a further decline of the stock's price and potential destabilization of the equities market. During the 2008 financial crisis, forced share sales due to margin calls caused further stock price drops for companies with insider share pledging, which exposed serious share pledging risks for investors. Therefore, share pledging has been widely considered as a serious CG risk.

Insider share pledging refers to company insider shareholders who use their shares as collateral with a third party in exchange for cash. Due to the fact that a higher percentage of companies in emerging markets are dominated by family-controlled companies, and most emerging markets countries do not have systematic securities laws, insider share pledging is more prevalent in emerging markets than in advanced countries.

What then are the motivations for CEO share pledging?

4.1.1. CEO Share Pledging Motivations

Studies have summarized motivations for CEO share pledging in three categories:

- **To double the CEO's influence in the company.** A CEO's confidence about the firm's future performance and their desire to increase voting power in the company are the top drivers in this scenario. CEOs normally use cash from share pledging to increase their ownership in their firms despite exposing the company to additional risks.
- **To access additional cash.** Pledging allows CEOs to access additional cash while retaining voting rights without selling their shares. Founder-CEOs are often motivated in this type of monetizing pledge. In addition, the inside pledging disclosure

requirements are not as restrictive as those for stock transactions. Share pledging disclosure is required in a company's quarterly proxy statement, while stock transactions by founder-CEOs are required to be disclosed within two business days.
- **To mitigate risk of personal wealth.** Driven by negative inside information and an uncertainty of a firm's future, CEOs might choose to pledge shares and invest the proceeds in other assets to decrease personal wealth risks. CEO share pledge disclosure is only required for the quarterly proxy statement instead of the two-business day mandate if CEOs enter hedging transactions with their shares.

Regardless of the motivations and reasons for CEOs share pledging, insider share pledging could cause a disaster to company stocks and expose outside shareholders' interests to great risk. Studies also show that CEO share pledging occurs more often in companies with these scenarios:

- those led by founders
- with high levels of CEO ownership
- experiencing considerable stock price appreciation
- led by CEOs with long tenure
- with a history of poor liquidity
- and larger boards of directors

4.1.2. Risk Mitigation of Insider Share Pledging

If share pledging is a CG risk, can CG practice improvements help mitigate the risk? The following are a few CG factors that could reduce share pledging opportunities and the challenges of the effectiveness of these mechanisms.

- **Shareholder engagement.** Many studies today recommend increasing institutional ownership as a path for mitigating share pledging risks, with the assumption that institutional investors are willing to influence companies' decisions using their voting powers, and investors are willing to implement effective monitoring systems to identify early signs of share pledging risks. However, effective monitoring demands have a cost, and investors might have different agendas and strategies that impact their cost expectations. The underlying message is that shareholder engagement mostly occurs with long-term institutional investors. Actively engaging with companies allows investors to understand the business, empowers investors with a sense of share pledging motivation, and enables investors to identify early signs of potential risks.

- **Independent board directors' independent roles.** Share pledging often occurs in controlling structure companies. A well-designed system of checks and balances with independent board directors can help with share pledging risk mitigation. Having a board comprised of a majority of independent board directors has become worldwide CG practice for decades and many countries have made this practice a part of CG regulation. In many countries with emerging markets, the understanding and effectiveness of independent board directors' roles are limited for various reasons (eg, corporate culture and lack of talent) In many cases, most independent directors are still considered "outsiders" who are not involved in critical decisions. Also, a large percentage of independent directors come from academic (approximately 40%) or government backgrounds with little business experience, according to Xin Tang, professor at Tsinghua University School of Law and former member of the China Securities Regulatory Commission. There is room for improvement to ensure that independent voices can be heard in boardrooms, and independent opinions are necessary for important business decisions as part of CG practices. Moreover, an independent director's independence needs to be truly independent, not merely a formality.

- **The corporate repurpose revolution.** Worldwide corporate repurpose discussions were also intensified by the 2020 COVID-19 pandemic. Corporations are under pressure to re-purpose their businesses to consider stakeholders' interests and environmental issues. In the end, a cumulative mindset change is driven by top leaders (board chairs, founders, and CEOs). Since insider share pledging motivations are mostly related to personal interests, would a revised corporate leaders' mindset effectively reduce share pledging transactions? I believe the answer will be revealed in the coming decades.

4.1.3. CEO Share Pledging Landscape in the US

Modern companies often offer various stock packages to motivate CEOs in order to improve their firms' financial performance, which makes company share ownership an attractive element of CEO compensation, particularly for American CEOs. Studies of S&P 1500 companies in 2018 show that 83% of S&P 1500 companies require CEOs to own shares, while 45% of these CEOs' total compensation packages included various stock plans.

Of interest, the infamous 2003 WorldCom debacle revealed that the company's then CEO, Bernard Edders, owned an estimated 11 million company pledged shares valued at $286 million, for which the company's board reluctantly decided (more precisely, the board was "hijacked") to extend a loan because of their fears that the company's stock value would significantly decrease in case of forced sales. When this scheme was discovered, US regulators realized the substantial risk that corporations would encounter with these types of transactions, which led to the Securities Exchange Commission (SEC) 2006 share pledging disclosure requirement for company executives and boards of directors. Notwithstanding the SEC disclosure requirement and the financial crisis, American companies' CEO share pledging became substantial over time. American proxy advisory firms ISS and Glass Lewis issued statements in 2012 and 2015, respectively, to address their concerns regarding insider share pledging risks and related companies' governance weaknesses. In 2015, the SEC amended share pledging disclosure requirements to broaden its scope of shareholder transactions and to include details of the pledging transactions. Due to pressure from the proxy advisory firms and the substantially rising number of American companies adopting anti-pledging policies between 2007 to 2016, the CEO compensation structure between base salary and performance driven incentives has changed significantly over the past few years.

In the US, research studies continue regarding the effect and impact of anti-pledging policies on companies' investment decisions and company value. Although the SEC does not prohibit company share pledging yet, its risks and the impact on companies' stock prices are a vital concern of shareholders and are closely monitored by proxy agencies and regulators.

4.1.4. Chinese Companies' Founders & CEOs' Share Pledge

Although share pledging is a world-wide practice, companies' share pledging risks in China are considerably more dangerous than other countries due to the size of China's economy and the immaturity of the current Chinese securities market. Statistics show that Chinese companies' share pledging amount was $632 billion in October 2018, which represents 11% of the entire Chinese capital market at the time of the analysis. Since China presently has the second-largest Stock Market in the world, such a huge amount of share pledging could place the Chinese market at substantial risk, significantly impacting the worldwide Stock Markets.

The Luckin Coffee scandal discovered in early 2020 is a good example of how a Chinese company was exposed to share pledging risks.

Case Study 4.1. The Luckin Coffee Scandal and Founder Pledge

> Luckin Coffee opened its first store in January 2018, made its IPO debut on Nasdaq in May 2019, quickly grew its business from 2,370 to 6,500 stores, then suddenly crashed in April 2020 after financial fraud was revealed. As a typical insider-controlling founder firm, the founders' group controlled in excess of 50% of company shares, over 60% of the voting power, and 49% of company shares were pledged as loan collateral. As a result, the founders' pledge significantly jeopardized the business and investors' interests.
>
> Additionally, both the chairman and CEO held board committee chair positions that compromised the independence and objectivity of the board

committees. Upon admitting to sales fraud of $310 million USD (42% of 2019 revenue) in April 2020, Luckin's stock price plunged 91%.

In May, the company fired its CEO and COO as part of an internal investigation into the sales fraud. In June 2020, the investigation discovered that the chairman instructed employees via company email to commit sales fraud. The chairman is currently facing criminal charges in China. Consequently, Nasdaq suspended Luckin's stock trading on June 29 and delisting procedures followed. In July 2020, Luckin replaced the entire board of directors with five independent directors with professional backgrounds in management, corporate finance, law, and governance. As of May 2021, Luckin is still trading on Nasdaq with only 14% of its initial stock value at the time the fraud was discovered in April 2020. Although Luckin's business continues, considerable time is needed to repair its reputation.

Since the Luckin founders pledged 49% of their company shares as loan collateral, when the stock price dropped due to the company's financial fraud and the chairman defaulted on the loan, Luckin's lending companies were forced to sell the founder's pledged shares, which amplified the disaster. And the forced sale caused further decline of Luckin's stock price.

Luckin's share pledging criteria were consistent with CEO pledging firms' schemes: companies led by founders; high CEO ownership; and considerable stock price appreciation. Luckin's share pledging is no different from companies from other countries as far as the share pledgers' motivations, the creditors' reactions when stock prices fall, and the harm that caused stock prices to further decline are concerned. However, most Chinese companies' stakeholders, including investors, board directors, and executives, are not as sophisticated as those of US companies, as far as awareness of insider share pledging risks (that probably nourished share pledging abuse opportunities) is concerned, and the potential damage that companies may face.

In addition to share pledging, the Luckin case also revealed the company's significant board oversight weakness – the ex-chairman governed the Nomination & Corporate Governance committee while the ex-CEO chaired the Compensation Committee, both of which jeopardized the independence and objectivity of board functions. Is it possible impartial board oversight could have prevented Luckin's share pledging failure? The answer is not certain. However, an objective, fully functioning board may have prevented this scandal by monitoring and scrutinizing the company's operations policies and procedures, including its share pledging policy.

In my opinion, the question that truly matters to global investors is: will Luckin's share pledging risk and its financially catastrophic results lead to Chinese regulatory improvements that restrict companies' insider share pledging and require information disclosure, just like Worldcom's catastrophic disaster with its ex-CEOs share pledging led to the SEC's regulation reform?

4.2. VIE Structure Risks

In Chapter two, we discussed the history of Chinese companies VIE structure, the regulatory grey area of VIE structure, and how Chinese regulators have handled the VIE structure in recent regulation reforms.

The VIE structure itself has evolved in the past two decades. VIEs have been consolidated into offshore holding companies' (OLOEs) financial reports since the US SEC started requiring off-balance controlling entities to consolidate their balance sheets after the Enron scandal in the early 2000s (see Figure 2.1.). Since VIEs naturally favor founders, and in order to protect investors' interests, some VIE agreements include conditions that include the risks associated with a founder's marital status. However, when companies use a VIE structure to circumvent Chinese regulations of foreign ownership of certain industries or to decrease the approval process for foreign capital access, companies intentionally evade these regulations and enter a "grey area" of Chinese contract law.

VIE structures normally contain a dual natural arrangement: On the control side, the business' VIE is controlled by OLOE through various agreements. The OLOE is listed overseas, which technically has no voting rights with the VIE. On the operational side, the VIE is owned by a Chinese domestic company (WFOE) that has contractual control over the VIE through the OLOE. The VIE structure circumvents the regulator's restrictions on foreign ownership, while the complicated relationship between different entities under the VIE structure exposes VIEs to the following risks:

4.2.1. Legal Uncertainty

The question over whether VIE agreements are legal is their largest vulnerability. According to current Chinese law, a contract written to avoid regulation requirements is void and the courts will not enforce it. The special contracts enabling global investors' controlling interests of VIEs are technically not valid. And Chinese regulators have attempted to address the VIE issues with some regulatory improvements listed below:

In 2006, the former Ministry of Information Technology issued a memo to request all Chinese telecom companies to get its approval before applying for an overseas listing;

In 2009, the Chinese publishing authority issued a direct regulation to attack online gaming companies using VIE structures;

In 2011, some unconfirmed research data implied that the China Security Regulatory Commission intended to attack the overseas IPOs of internet companies that had VIE structures;

In 2015, regulators attempted to amend the Foreign Investor Law to address the VIE issue, but the relevant revision was withdrawn later;

In 2019, the new Foreign Investor Law was enacted but regulators did not address VIE issues as expected by the market, which created many apprehensions regarding Chinese regulators' approaches to close the VIE loophole.

In 2020, the new anti-trust law enforcement guidelines, and the regulators instituted additional scrutiny of mergers and acquisition transactions associated with a VIE structure, focusing on the restriction of foreign ownership in certain technology sectors, whilst not completely eliminating the VIE structure.

Technically, Chinese authorities can choose to close the loophole at any time by banning or restricting VIE structures, which could leave global investors in limbo. The vagueness of the Chinese regulators' attitude to the VIE structure does not appear to imply the government would suddenly prohibit the application of a VIE structure.

However, we should never ignore that, should contracts between a VIE and OLOE fail, these contracts are not governed by Chinese contract law, as they are illegal from the beginning. Perhaps this is the most likely legal risk of VIE structures at the moment.

4.2.2. Investors' Fragile Ownership

Global VIE investors are only shareholders of an offshore holding company (OLOE) that excludes investors from decision-making processes unless agreed upon. The most prominent example is the Alipay spin-off controversy between Alibaba and its partners, Yahoo and Softbank, in 2011, when the Chinese government tightened regulations on online payment businesses. Alibaba decided to transfer ownership of its online payment platform, Alipay, to a private company owned by founder, Jack Ma. Unfortunately for them, Yahoo and Softbank were not part of the decision because of Alibaba's VIE structure and their dispute has become a warning to global investors.

Case Study 4.2.: Alibaba Alipay Ownership Transfer Case - VIE Structure and its Risk to Shareholders

> *E-commerce started in China in early 2000. Foreseeing a fast-growing e-commerce business opportunity in the Chinese market, eBay entered the market in 2002 upon acquiring Eachnet, a Chinese C2C marketplace. However, the limited use of credit cards in China and eBay's dependence on PayPal as the only allowed direct payment method caused a severe lack of trust between buyers and sellers in e-commerce transactions. Because of a better understanding of the Chinese market and consumers, Alibaba launched the mobile payment platform, Alipay, in 2004 with an escrow mechanism to ensure that buyers would make payments upon receiving promised goods. The innovation of Alipay became a powerful engine for the growth of Alibaba's e-commerce business and helped Alibaba successfully conquer its foreign competitor eBay. In 2006, eBay closed its Chinese operations and exited the market. However, during the four years of eBay's operation from 2002 to 2006, Chinese e-commerce*

users more than doubled from 59 million to 138 million. Alipay was later transferred to Ant Finance and became the core business of the latter company.

On March 31, 2011, Yahoo and Softbank were notified that two relevant transactions were pending: Alipay's ownership transfer would take place in August 2011, and the financial statement deconsolidation of Alipay was effective in the first quarter of 2011. The decisions of both transactions were made without the knowledge or approval of Alibaba Group's board of directors, where Yahoo and Softbank both held seats. After the announcement about losing Alipay in May 2011, Yahoo's stock price dropped significantly.

Alipay's ownership was transferred to another domestic company, the majority of stock for which was held by Jack Ma. The reason for Alipay's transfer was a result of China's new regulation that forbade foreign ownership of online payment companies. However, the tricky part of the transaction was Alibaba's VIE structure that excluded Alibaba Group's partners, Yahoo and Softbank, from being involved in the decision of such a significant transaction. As part of Alibaba's VIE structure, Alipay was obligated to distribute its revenue to Alibaba Group while Alipay was valued at RMB 330 million at the time of the ownership transaction. Forfeiting Alipay's revenue caused a substantial drop in Yahoo's stock price.

Jack Ma claimed that the Alipay ownership transfer transaction demonstrated his intention to follow Chinese regulations by terminating the VIE operation. However, the exclusion of its business partners to take part in the decision-making process significantly impacted the magnitude of losses in Yahoo's stock value which provides strong evidence of the risk that the VIE structure may create for investors.

4.2.3. How do Chinese Companies Handle VIE Structure Risks?

The VIE structure is a regulatory as well as a contract enforcement risk, both being beyond Chinese companies' purview. How then do Chinese companies manage VIE structure risks? Sophisticated companies like Alibaba choose to be transparent with investors regarding VIE structure risk factors by providing proper disclosure and adequate communication. Alibaba began disclosing VIE risks in its 2018 SEC filing by highlighting its VIE structure's significant uncertainties and potential tax liabilities that may impact the company's future revenue. In addition, to comfort investors' concerns over the VIE structure, Jack Ma, the primary and controlling shareholder of Alibaba's VIEs in China, committed to forego all financial benefit from his ownership of these VIEs to benefit Alibaba, and expressed his willingness to enter into agreements to transfer proceeds to Alibaba whenever permitted by law.

4.3. The Founder Controlling Company's Key Person Risk

Many large Chinese companies are controlled by the founders. Although some of these companies have successfully grown within the global market and become industry leaders, their governance models and decision-making processes still function as if they are early-stage companies. That means, the most important company decisions are made by the founders without a systematic decision-making process. The advantage of this centralized control and decision-making system is efficiency, which allows companies to grow rapidly. In addition to the functional disadvantages including the lack of a checks-and-balances mechanism and a lack of independent objectivity, there are two factors that cannot be overlooked: the significant impact to companies caused by a key person's absence, and a key person's poor reputation that damages a company due to malfeasance.

The following case study of JD.com, the second largest e-commerce business in China, reveals the impact on company value and stock price due to the founder's poor personal behavior.

Case Study 4.3.: JD.com Founder's Poor Reputation Impacts Company's Stock Price

> JD.com was founded by Liu Qiangdong in 1998 and is the second- largest Chinese e-commerce company. The company has been listed on Nasdaq since May 2014, and secondarily listed on HKEX since July 2020. The significant difference between JD.com and Alibaba is that JD sources

various products and process to fill its own orders with a much lower operating margin, while Alibaba is an e-commerce paid listing platform for third-party sellers. JD's operation model allows the company to better control its product quality and delivery schedule.

In September 2018, Liu Qiangdong was arrested in the US after being accused of raping a Chinese student at the University of Minnesota, where Liu was taking a doctoral business administration course. Although Liu denied any misconduct and was released with no charges three months after the arrest, JD's stock price hit an 18-month low during the week of Liu's arrest, resulting in a $7.2 billion loss (16% of its market share) caused by investors' fears that JD.com would significantly lose consumers due to Liu's arrest. A November 2018 report showed that the company's customer base declined dramatically, as projected.

As the controlling founder, Liu Qiangdong has heavily-weighted voting rights, tight control of the company, and is the major decision-maker on the company's board of directors. Jiu's case raised many questions about JD's CG risks regarding:

- Succession planning - who is the company's immediate successor?
- The decision-making process - who has the authority to provide major decisions if/when Liu is unable to lead the company?
- Minority shareholders' interest protection - what options are available for minority shareholders who have limited voting rights?

JD.com founder's case may be an egregious example, but the CG risks exposed by companies like JD.com should serve as a warning for investors and companies. While many might believe tightening regulatory compliance requirements can help eliminate CG risks, for Chinese companies, such as JD.com, the best approach to avoid CG risk and business risks due to a key person's wrongdoing or inability to perform leadership roles caused by a founder's personal behavior is not to enhance compliance, but to improve board oversight including optimizing board committee functions and decision-making processes. At the moment, institutional investors' influence in Chinese companies are still limited due to their small share percentage, and many obstacles (eg.the language barrier) remain for investors to raise their voice. Over time, though, investors' active engagement and their outspokenness via voting rights should have an impact.

4.4. Party Committee in Chinese Companies – Risk or Support?

Party involvement in Chinese companies has been one of the top historical concerns of the Western business community. Although China's fast-growing economy and Chinese companies' close collaboration with the West appears to have eased fears over the past few decades, the 2018 CG code provisions requiring Party Committee involvement have brought this legitimate concern to prominence. The focus of recent discussions is the opaqueness of the actual roles of the Party Committee in Chinese companies. However, I suggest we consider another vantage point:

First, the Party Committee as an additional layer in organizations involved in a company's decision-making proceedings admittedly may slow down the process and make an organization less efficient. However, while the Party Committee plays a supervisory role in an organization, it actually enhances a checks and balances mechanism that reduces an opportunity for management malfeasance. Therefore, the Party Committee's involvement has a positive influence on an organization's internal control system and CG function.

Second, it is important to evaluate the Party Committee's involvement based on its impact on companies' CG functions, instead of focusing on the "formality" of the Committee in an organization. If the Committee's involvement minimizes a boards' ability to establish independent and objective board functions, promote information and decision-making transparency, or protect investors' interests, it is certainly a CG risk to the company. If the Party Committee's involvement does not jeopardize board oversight but instead helps build stakeholder relationships with government and the community, we might need to reconsider the concerns of the Party Committee's role in Chinese companies.

Third, since the PR of China's establishment in 1949, the Party has been performing leading roles in establishing economic and social development strategies, launching economic reforms, and guarding the success of Chinese economic development. Party Committee involvement represents the Chinese government's support. According to Professor Lourdes Casanova, Director of Emerging Markets Institution at Cornell University, the Chinese government's support is an essential key to Chinese multinationals' success, for both SOEs and private companies. From this perspective, Party Committees humanize the relationship with government authorities who are important stakeholders that help sustain a business.

Have you, the reader, reconsidered any doubt (presuming some existed) of the government's benevolence toward Chinese companies? Which is greater: risk or support?

4.5. Other Risks

In addition to the key risks discussed above, below are other CG risks that often occur in Chinese companies. Interestingly, all these risks appeared with the Luckin Coffee matter.

Audit quality and audit information transparency: All foreign companies listed in US Stock Markets are required to have their financial statements audited by an independent firm. Most of these multinational companies are audited by firms in their own country. This practice is not just for Chinese multinationals, but for companies from around the world. Under the Sarbanes-Oxley Act, the Public Company Accounting Oversight Board (PCAOB) has established formal co-operative arrangements with foreign audit regulators, which allows the PCAOB to conduct an inspection of audit firms in these countries. However, an equivalent arrangement has not yet been established between the PCAOB and the Chinese regulators. Therefore, although many Chinese companies listed on the US exchanges are audited by the "Big Four" accounting firms, without Chinese regulators' authorization, these firms conducting business in China cannot yet relinquish their audits to the PCAOB. At the time this book is written, the Big Four auditors have been compressed between the US and China after spending nearly three decades building their operations in the Chinese markets.

In the Luckin Coffee case, Ernst & Young Hua Ming LLC, a member firm of Ernst & Young LLP (EY) in the US, has been Luckin's auditor. Although EY did not audit Luckin's 2019 financial statements at the time the scandal was revealed, EY issued a "comfort letter" to investment banks in early 2020 to underwrite Luckin's stock and bond sales, which damaged the accounting firm's reputation - despite EY's denial of irresponsibility.

Board function independency and objectivity: Most Chinese companies have established a Western-style board structure with independent board directors. I want to emphasize that two traditional characteristics exist in Chinese companies' governance models and business practices that are invisible, inherited, and unlikely to evaporate from Chinese culture: a patriarchal culture and a nominal board. A patriarchal culture implies valuing a considerable depth of familial-like relationships, and nominal boards allow controlling shareholders to manipulate company board decisions. Because of these two features, most important decisions are still made by one individual without a transparent decision-making process including any checks-and-balances mechanism, regardless of the company size. Most Chinese companies choose to breed home-grown talent for critical positions instead of hiring professional executives selected from the marketplace. In recent years, increasing numbers of Western executives are taking positions in Chinese companies, and more overseas-listed Chinese companies hire local independent directors to make company boards appear more professional and independent. But most Western executives are not in the "core cycle" (people who have been following the founder since the early stage of the company), and most independent board directors are treated as outsiders or consultants without access to core information or are prohibited from participating in important decisions. The dual existence of the patriarchal culture and nominal board feature are obstacles for Chinese companies' board functions' independence and objectivity.

Luckin Coffee is a typical patriarchal company, where former chairman Charles Lu and former CEO Jenny Qian held 30.53% and 19.68% of company shares and voting rights of 36.86% and 23.7%, respectively in each category. In addition, before jointly founding Luckin, Qian was COO of another public company founded by Lu. The patriarchal culture, combined with Lu's and Qian's control of the board committees, eliminated any possibility that Luckin's company board could perform proper functions as prescribed in Luckin's CG documents.

Related transactions: At the time of writing, details of Luckin's fabricated sales in 2019 have not been revealed. It is likely, however, that Luckin's complicated supply chain linked to both its founder and then chairman Charles Lu, almost certainly explains the reason. Although investors will not be able to access the company's internal information, Luckin's 558% third quarter and 400% fourth quarter sales revenue increases in 2019 should be treated as early warning signs and should be questioned by investors whose interests may be jeopardized, as well as by independent board directors, who tied their personal reputations to the company and could be held liable for the company's misconduct.

Some of the key CG risks to Chinese companies will diminish while improvements of CG practice and government regulations continue. However, some remnants may remain as Chinese companies' unique identities. Has my exploration of Chinese companies' key CG risks helped you adopt a different risk appetite when considering an investment or a career opportunity? I hope the discussion in this chapter brings awareness and stirs some consideration about these key CG risks.

Chapter 5
What is Driving China's CG Development?

Is it necessary we "navigate in the dark" while working with Chinese companies?

After two years of research, I believe the answer to this question lies in the understanding of three fundamental features of China's CG development: the difference between Chinese companies' governance models from those in more developed economies due to Chinese culture, China's special economic growth strategy, and the country's regulation reform progress; the immaturity of Chinese companies' CG practice and their potential for future development; and most essential, the rise of the "China model", that signifies that China's CG development will continue to evolve following its own path instead of duplicating those of more developed economies.

Perhaps the first two are much easier to grasp and accept than the last. The emergence of the "China model" indicates the necessity and demands of building different economic growth models for emerging market countries. The Western business world often expects that their models should be the path and destination of emerging market countries' economic growth and CG development. Therefore, when China took a different path and proved its success, there was much resistance to accepting the "China model". Moreover, China's success testified that given the differences of many economic growth elements such as culture, demographic characteristics and the regulatory environment, the Western models might not be suitable for emerging market countries. The rise of the "China model" suggests the emerging trend of diverse CG models, business practice models, and collaboration models between emerging markets and more developed markets, and among emerging market countries.

However, if China's CG development will follow its own path in contrast to those in the West with whom we are familiar, what are the drivers of China's CG development? Let us start with reviewing the key characteristics of Chinese companies' CG practices.

5.1. Pros and Cons of Chinese Companies' CG Practices

The case studies we discussed in the first four chapters represent the prevailing CG models employed by different categories of Chinese companies: Haier (an SOE); Huawei (a privately-owned company); and Alibaba, sina.com, Pinduoduo, Lenovo, Luckin Coffee and JD.com (all are overseas-listed companies). Regardless of the different CG models, these companies' CG practices share common characteristics as summarized below.

5.1.1. Government Influence

Chinese SOEs and listed companies are required to establish Party Committees, and many established private companies have voluntarily established their Party Committees to remain "politically correct and connected" with the government. In Chinese SOEs, the chairperson, most members of the boards of supervisors, and most executives are assigned by the SASAC. Members of the Party Committee are from different business positions within the organization. A Party Committee is not a functional department, but a communication channel between government and a business, which enables government's understanding of the business and provides support to help a business grow whilst ensuring that it is also involved in important business decisions to ensure that a company's growth aligns with government's strategy.

During an interview with Professor Lourdes Casanova, the professor shared her opinion regarding the key reasons for Chinese multinationals' success compared to other emerging multinationals. Given her years of research experience in emerging markets multinationals from Latin American countries to China, Professor Casanova concluded that the Chinese government's support enables companies (including SOEs and private companies) to be innovative, allowing them to be more resilient in the global marketplace. In the book *Innovation from Emerging Markets: From Copycats to Leaders* co-authored by Casanova and her emerging markets research group, various case studies were analyzed and ultimately arrived at the same conclusions. Haier's case studies from Chapter 3 are good examples of how the Chinese government supports an SOE's business growth over time. I was convinced from my experience working with the company in Ningbo that private companies' successes cannot be separated from the government's support. In addition, recent news regarding the fast growth of Xpeng Motors, a leading Chinese electric car manufacturer provided with favorable terms on land acquisition, a low interest loan, and tax breaks by local government, is another testimony in this regard.

Government support leads to easy access of capital, other resources, tax breaks (eg, Haier's IPO 3.2.), and a sophisticated mechanism of checks-and-balance that enhances internal control. The alignment with government strategy reduces regulation compliance risks and promotes good relationships with stakeholders including authorities, banks and local communities who are also of vital importance.

However, government intervention is the biggest concern for global investors, especially because of a lack of transparency regarding the government's role in the business decision-making process. Instead of clamoring over whether government intervention in companies is necessary, perhaps it is more important for investors to consider and evaluate whether government intervention impacts the integrity of business decisions or disturbs compliance with international standards.

The government's assignment of executives to SOEs also cause concerns regarding the executives' professionalism and their motivation for business success, especially in Chinese multinationals who require they have "international vision" and global business experience to lead a company in the global marketplace. Moreover, in Chinese SOEs, the CEO's compensation amount must align with government-mandated salary limits, while company boards do not have the power to decide Chinese SOEs' executives' compensation (as discussed in Chapter 1), which could also affect the efficacy of a board's oversight.

5.1.2. Creativity and Quick Reaction Capacity

Growing alongside China's regulation reforms that have been constantly subjected to trial and correction, and taking this adventurous journey without practical guidance, most Chinese companies became creative with their governance models and business practices and developed their capacity for quick reaction to regulation changes. Most notably are

Alibaba's partnership controlling structure (case study 1.1.) and Huawei's rotating CEO system and "superfluid" organizational structure (case study 1.3 & 1.4). Both companies' CG models have contributed to their companies' success, but areas for debate and potential future improvement exist for Alibaba, due to its extraordinary control of keeping investors' involvement at a minimum, and Huawei's "superfluid" organizational structure that unfortunately offers negligible job security to its employees.

Investors should keep their collective eyes on the creative governance models to verify that basic board functions are sufficiently outlined, a mechanism to protect investors' interests is invoked, and business practices comply with both Chinese regulations and international standards. While language barriers and other inconveniences may be present, investors should be highly encouraged to participate in AGMs and other shareholder meetings to familiarize themselves with a business and not be reluctant to raise their voices with respect to any concerns.

Chinese companies' quick reactions to global business uncertainties seem suitable for today's ever changing business environment due to the COVID-19 pandemic and worldwide disaster interruptions. However, the impact of these "knee-jerk reactions" to a company's long-term sustainability will need to be further examined, given the complexities of today's global business environment.

5.1.3. The Vernal Years

Most Chinese companies are young (merely thirty to forty years old) since corporation formation and the concept of shareholding companies were introduced only as recent as 1993 (as discussed in Chapter 3). Therefore, most Chinese companies are still operated or highly influenced by the founders' generation. These founders are dedicated and have substantial personal and financial investments in their companies, having secured the success of their business by including an efficient decision-making process and less bureaucracy, while also enhancing investors' confidence despite regulatory uncertainties. This notably contrasts with some CG concerns from more developed countries' CG practices today since their boards can suffer from a "disconnect" with their business, making board oversight less effective and less efficient. For example, Alibaba's Jack Ma's personal engagement with that business helped the company establish and retain investors' confidence despite the company's VIE structure (see case study 2.3).

However, because of Chinese companies' young age, even if some of them are growing quickly domestically and internationally, their CG practices are still in the early stages of development, similar to Western startups that lack comprehensive board procedures, well-monitored board functions, sound decision-making and succession planning processes. The Luckin coffee and JD.com case studies in Chapter 4 are good examples: in both cases, the founder/chairman made most of the decisions, and a well-functioning monitoring and enforcement mechanism was missing to ensure that policies and procedures were followed and executed.

In addition, the absence of a sophisticated internationalization strategy that includes a global talent component reveals another weakness of young Chinese companies. This tendency is typically reflected by a lack of understanding of host countries' business practices and regulations, while they also overemphasize the "China model". The main reason for this scenario is a lack of business leaders with professional knowledge and international business experience. Although some Chinese multinationals started to hire Western board members and executives, the absence of a talent recruiting strategy, together with these companies' governance models and leadership styles often lead to challenges of qualified acquisition and retention. With dual cultural background and bilingual skills, it's quite challenging for me to navigate the decision-making process and understand many business behaviors. I can only imagine the challenges for Western executives working for Chinese companies, which lead to the difficulties for Chinese companies seeking to hire and retain business leaders who have international experience.

According to Christine Raynaud, a former director of the European Chamber of Commerce in Hong Kong and business owner in China, Western companies have historically internationalized by deploying their home country's model to overseas subsidiaries. Those models are no longer applicable due to an increasingly complicated global business environment underpinned by proliferating regulations and competition from domestic market players. These challenges equally apply to Chinese companies seeking to become multinationals; they will need to understand, respect and legitimize a host country's culture and business practices and empower local management in order to succeed. Highly-centralized management styles and the lack of international business experience among senior executive teams are challenges both for Chinese companies and for seasoned international Western executives. In addition to facing difficulties with these leadership styles and governance models when working for Chinese companies, Western executives are not entirely trusted and are often treated as external consultants despite their executive titles or board directorship roles. Relying on her experience advising Western and Asian companies' global talent strategies since the 1980s, Ms. Raynaud suggests that China's education system and Chinese multinationals should establish comprehensive international talent development strategies as part of their global business growth plans.

Establishing a sophisticated board process and global internationalization strategy to overcome related CG challenges both take time, and the learning process may be painful and costly for Chinese multinationals until their higher-standard CG practices are established and implemented. At the same time, I hope pointing out these key characteristics and their strengths and weaknesses will help build understanding in Western business leaders and companies so they do not have to be "navigating in the dark" while working with Chinese companies.

At the same time, Chinese companies' CG practices have been evolving with domestic and international drivers. The following are the key factors driving China's CG development:

5.2. Key Domestic Drivers

Paralleling Chinese companies' perpetual growth domestically and internationally are some concomitant challenges that may occur during that growth, possibly revealing these companies' CG weaknesses which must be quelled in order to capture future CG improvement. The process of searching for solutions to these challenges will identify CG improvement opportunities allowing these companies to realize that improving their CG practice and conquering obstacles simultaneously will improve competitiveness in the global marketplace. A "helping hand" from Chinese regulators may minimize or prevent problems due to regulation lagging, possibly resulting in improving Chinese companies' development of digitally-based businesses.

5.2.1. Global Branding Challenges

Despite many success stories, some Chinese companies have overlooked the key elements of CG while chasing growth and expansion. These CG weaknesses eventually became obstacles to their global growth. Specifically, one of the primary challenges for Chinese companies is global branding.

Although there is no research yet establishing a direct relationship between a company's CG practice and brand value, it is understood that high-standard CG practices significantly increases a brand's valuation. Since BrandZ and Brandirectory began ranking the top 100 and 500 most valuable brands in the early 2000s, many international brand valuation firms have been testing brand valuation models and identifying factors that influence brand value. According to Cornell University's annual Emerging Markets report, some Chinese brands have shown steady rank improvements on both BrandZ's and Brandirectory's lists from 2009 to 2018, while other Chinese companies have struggled with brand recognition because they have failed to view CG practice improvements as a part of their global branding efforts. Consider Haier as an example: As the largest home appliances and consumer electronics manufacturer in the world and one of the first Chinese multinational companies, Haier planned to build their brand upon entering the global market in the 1990s and made sizable investments in a branding strategy. However, the price of Haier's white goods was at the lower end compared to its counterparts in North America, Japan, and South Korea. Haier struggled to achieve top-tier global brand rankings until the late 2010s, unlike their Chinese peers, Lenovo and Huawei, who have successfully positioned themselves as price leaders across most product categories and have enjoyed higher brand rankings since the mid-2010s.

Case Study 5.1.: Corporate Governance Weaknesses of Haier's Rendanheyi Model

Haier spent ten years designing, experimenting, and implementing the Rendanheyi model, known by the slogan "making everyone a CEO" by dividing the entire organization into semi-autonomous micro-enterprises to encourage superior service-oriented employee performance while promoting the idea of "zero distance" to the customer. The model provides authorization for business, recruiting, and compensation decision-making responsibilities to micro-enterprise leaders, connects the largest part of an employee's compensation to performance, and creates an entrepreneurial corporate culture, significantly improving the company's net profit of Haier's China operations.

However, Haier was not able to implement the Rendanheyi model in its acquired subsidiaries due to the following weaknesses of the model:

1. **The model's lack of consideration for other societies' cultures and its inherent inability to appreciate host countries' regulation systems and business practices.** *Haier's implementation of the Rendanheyi model led to a 25% domestic workforce reduction in 2016. The company acquired its subsidiaries, GE Appliances, from the US in 2016 and Sanyo White Goods from Japan in 2011. In the former case, the model failed due to stringent labor laws prohibiting massive layoffs; in the latter, a disavowal of Japanese social history and understanding of the country's shareholders.*

2. **Lack of a long-term sustainable strategy.** *The compensation structure under the Rendanheyi model created conflicts between the micro-enterprises' desire for short-term profit and Haier's long-term corporate strategy.*

Haier designed and refined their Rendanheyi organizational model in approximately the same amount of time as Toyota took to create their "Lean Manufacturing" model, but so far, Haier has failed to enjoy the same kind of global success. Toyota's Lean Manufacturing model has been widely replicated by global manufacturers and has successfully helped worldwide companies enhance their operational efficiency and save costs, establishing Toyota as a global industry leader for decades while contributing to its consecutive No. 1 Global Auto Brands position. Haier's Rendanheyi model has successfully improved the company's corporate culture and increased its domestic operations profit, but its limited application slowed its global scaling strategy and prevented the company from maximizing the business value they expected from the model. Also, the company's failure to consider the model's legal and social implications restrained it from being recognized as a good corporate citizen and industry leader in the global marketplace. Although its brand's value has increased since 2018, enabling the company to become a top-tier global brand in 2019, Haier decided to establish the Rendanheyi-Silicon Valley Center in Menlo Park, California in 2020 to improve and promote the model and inspire ongoing innovation. The Rendanheyi model will continually improve over time and eventually align with international standards.

5.2.2. Leadership Transfer Challenges - Founder Generation Retirement

In Western countries, it is not difficult to recognize those companies that have nearly or over one-hundred-year histories. Some of those companies have become industry leaders or famous multinationals, such as JP Morgan Chase (founded in 1799), DuPont (founded 1802), and Macy's (founded in 1858), all of which are lucrative businesses managed by professionals. Some are still controlled by small-size founder-families, whose members have transferred their businesses in perpetuity, which has enabled their success despite various (and sometimes detrimental) problems.

With PR China's establishment in 1949 and the tumultuous political and economic reforms afterward, Chinese private companies became officially "legal" no earlier than the early 1980s. Most successful Chinese companies are still managed or overseen by the founders' generations, although many of these founders are close to or already at their retirement age. Leadership transfer upon a founder's retirement has become one of the top challenges for many companies and that challenge makes CG weaknesses apparent. These companies have been searching for solutions by experimenting with different approaches over the past two decades. The case study below demonstrates the CG weaknesses and challenges due to the founder's retirement from Wahaha Group, the largest beverage producer in China. The lessons learned will hopefully present opportunities to improve their CG practices and develop useful strategies to overcome these challenges.

Case Study 5.2.: Wahaha's Corporate Governance Weakness Revealed Through its Leadership Transfer

Hangzhou Wahaha Group (WHH) was founded in 1987 as a local SOE owned by the Hangzhou Shangcheng District. The company has been led by Zong Qinghou since its establishment. In 1996, WHH signed a joint-venture agreement with Singapore-based Jinjia Investments Co., a joint holding company formed by Groupe Danone, a French multinational food products company and Peregrine Investment Holdings, a Hong Kong-based investment company. In a WHH joint venture holding structure, foreign partners hold 51% of the stock, and Chinese partners hold 49% (39% by WHH and 10% by employees). With the formation of the joint venture, Zong Qinghou became an important minority shareholder, board chairman, and CEO of the holding company, as well as five additional joint venture companies. The WHH joint venture holding company's board was then comprised of four members: Zong Qinghou as chairman, two members from Danone, and one from Peregrine. During the 1998 Asian financial crisis, Peregrine collapsed. Groupe Danone confiscated Peregrine's shares in Jinjia Investments Co. and replaced Peregrine's board seat on the WHH board and as a result, became WHH's majority owner with 51% of the shares.

While Danone owned the majority of WHH's shares, they were interested in remaining a shareholder only, without being involved in WHH's operations. Nevertheless, its embedded board presence and financial interest led to frequent clashes between them and Zong Qinghou, the most significant of which occurred in 2007 when both parties warred over a trademark dispute. The following are a few CG weaknesses revealed during the trademark battle as described in a Forbes article at that time:

- With the WHH JV agreements, Danone agreed not be involved in JVs' operations as majority owner (of 51% ownership);
- Zong Qinghou operated the WHH joint ventures and made important decisions without consent from the board
- Zong Qinghou was able to create many non-JV companies selling WHH JV products
- Zong Qinghou's family members held critical positions in the WHH Group

These elements accepted WHH JV's CG weaknesses regarding board structure and process, decision-making, compliance, and transactions involving family members, all of which were revealed at the time of the trademark ownership battle. Chinese companies' CG development over the past two decades has brought improvements to these weaknesses, but the primary challenge presently facing WHH Group and Zong Qinghou is the company's succession plan regarding Zong Qinghou's retirement.

In 2007, Zong Qinghou's only child, Zong Fuli, became president of one of the company's subsidiaries. Contrasted to her father, who was not interested in attracting additional capital to WHH, Zong Fuli was more open- minded so Qinghou began delegating authority to allow his daughter's ascension to CEO. However, an acquisition failure with a Chinese candy company in 2017 has stalled the leadership transfer. In recent interviews with the media, the 76-year-old founder mentioned that preparing for a management succession includes establishing a decision-making structure and the creation of more executive positions in the decision-making process. Zong Qinghou has also commented that the challenges facing the 30-year-old company are a "sickness". In mid-2020, WHH announced its plan for a Hong Kong IPO.

The WHH's founder's retirement case study represents the challenges many Chinese companies are currently - or will soon - encounter via generational inheritance or selection. The most important points to ponder from WHH's case are that its founder, Zong Qinghou, after nearly a decade of promoting his daughter to take over the company's leadership, has recognized the importance of building an organizational structure and a feasible decision-making process, as well as a professional management team as salient parts of succession planning. Since Zong Fuli is anticipated to take over the helm of WHH, the newly established structure and succession process will enhance her and WHH's long-term success. Therefore, WHH's journey while seeking a comprehensive succession plan solution has become the impetus of its CG development.

Becoming a listed company requires more compliance and board oversight, including optimizing a board's structure and process. WHH's IPO plan indicates Zong Qinghou's desire for new governance models to cure the company's "sickness", another driver that is needed for its CG development.

WHH was not the only company going through succession planning challenges due to a founder's retirement. Founders' mindset changes during that process, together with the trend for these Chinese companies to converge with the CG practices of their contemporaries in more developed countries, will better prepare CG practices to sustain these companies' competitiveness in the international marketplace. At the same time, some young entrepreneurs' retirements in China that transferred the leadership position to partners - such as Huang Zheng's retirement from Pinduoduo (see Case Study 2.3) and ByteDance's Zhang Yiming's resignation from the CEO role (see Case Study 8.2)- not only provided pertinent examples of the different succession plans of traditional Chinese entrepreneurs, but also indicated the modern mindset of the younger generation of Chinese entrepreneurs regarding "social responsibility" and companies' long-term sustainability, which will accelerate the momentum for Chinese companies' corporate governance development in the future.

5.2.3 China's Continuous Regulation Reform and Enhancement of Regulation Enforcement

With the fast growth of Chinese e-commerce companies and digital businesses over the past few decades, regulators have been trying to correspond with a similar pace of new and various business models. The ultimate goals of these new regulations are to prevent systemic failures, establish an effective monitoring system, prevent fraud and other crimes, and eventually provide continuous improvement guidelines for companies' corporate governance practices.

Like most emerging market countries, the Chinese regulatory system was unfortunately well-known for its lack of enforcement mechanisms. Therefore, some companies did not take the new regulations seriously and subsequently paid huge costs for their neglect. The best example of this was Ant Group's IPO incident that occurred at the end of 2020 (see Case Study 5.3. below).

Case Study 5.3.: Ant Group IPO Incident

In the summer of 2020, Ant Group (Ant) was on the verge of releasing its highly-anticipated IPO—the world's largest with a $312 billion valuation—and was seeking to raise $34.4 billion for dual listings in Shanghai and Hong Kong. Despite the tension between the US. and China, many American tier-one investment banks and institutional investors had taken part in this iconic transaction with other global players. Fewer than two days before Ant's shares were to begin trading, China's regulators suspended Ant's IPO. The news shocked the financial world and left many people speculating about what really happened and what the future held.

Ant (originally "Ant Financial" until June 2020) was launched by Alibaba in 2012 as a microloan solution provider for Chinese small businesses (hence the applicable name "Ant"). Back in 2012, the thresholds for small and middle enterprise (SMEs) receiving loans from Chinese banks were about $1 million, which disqualified financing possibilities for most Chinese SMEs. Ant filled this need to extend an average loan size of RMB8,000 (about $1,200), with the lowest financed amount available of RMB324 ($50). Ant extended its lending business to individual consumers in 2014. In 2019, the smallest credit limit offered by Ant was RMB45 ($7).

Because of the vast amount of consumer data generated by small businesses on Alibaba's platform, and Alibaba's advanced algorithms, Ant was able to analyze borrowers' profit margins, transaction histories, and affordability, then simultaneously determine a borrower's finance terms, such as loan amounts, interest rates, and payback periods. The prompt process enabled Ant's microloan business to operate with a default rate of only 1% (much lower than the worldwide average of 3.9% in 2018 according to S&P Global Ratings). In contrast to the complicated application process and documentation required for receiving traditional bank loans, Ant offered a user-friendly financing process by offering customers the ability to apply via a smartphone and receive cash if their applications were approved. The entire process took roughly three minutes and no personal bankers were involved. (Of interest, Ant also sold insurance, investment products, and financial technology to enterprises.)

To pave the way for its IPO, Ant significantly expanded its international business in 2019 by acquiring the London-based payment company, WorldFirst, to establish a European foothold, invested aggressively in Asian and South American countries, and established payment channels with 35,000 merchants in the US. The large transaction volume from Alibaba's e-commerce platforms (Taobao and Tmall), combined with the growth of overseas consumer activities driven by Chinese tourists and students, and the wide acceptance of Alipay by overseas merchants, made Ant the largest fintech in the world and precipitated its Asian IPO in January 2020.

In early November 2020, Chinese regulators halted Ant's IPO. In late December, regulators ordered Ant to return to its roots as a payment service provider and revamp its insurance and money management businesses which were both in need of regulatory compliance. Moreover, regulators mandated that Ant improve its CG procedures due to Ant's proclivities to "cut corners" that allowed the company to "skirt" regulation compliance that culminated in a weakened company board that impaired its functions and responsibilities. Regulators also launched an antitrust investigation into Alibaba, who owned one-third of Ant Group.

Ant purposely positioned itself as a technology company for a higher IPO valuation due to technology companies' having higher PE ratios than finance companies. According to PE ratios of Chinese main banks' stock indexes, Ant's valuation would only be $33 billion as a finance company vs. $312 billion if valued as a technology company before its 2020 IPO application, based on the same reported net assets.

In February 2021, Ant agreed to restructure as a financial holding company directly under the auspices of China's central bank. At the time of this writing, Ant was ordered by Chinese regulators to take the first step of the restructuring plan by setting up a consumer finance company to take over its consumer credit business. The consumer finance company is a joint venture with six other shareholders that includes two State-owned financial institutions and one of China's largest distressed assets management firms. Setting up the new company is deliberately designed to cease Ant's current consumer lending models, and establish a new consumer-finance business under regulatory supervision.

The timing of the suspension was dramatic, but regulatory reforms that led to the decision have been decades in the making. Let us take a brief look at the reforms that played particular roles.

Online payment and mobile payment. While Ant has been the largest fintech in the world since early 2019, the company has tried to position itself as a technology company in order to obtain higher valuation status, as well as to minimize the regulatory pressure from China's new online and mobile payments regulations from the following:

- The Measures for the Administration of Online Payment Business of Non-Bank Payment Institutions, issued by the People's Bank of China (PBOC) in 2016, requires non-bank payment platforms to standardize the processes for client registration, credit worthiness evaluation, risk management implementation, client data usage notifications, and data privacy protection.
- In 2018, the PBOC established the Online Settlement Platform for Non-Bank Payment Institutions as a centralized clearinghouse. All mobile payment transactions must be settled at the centralized clearinghouse.
- China's new rules for financial holding companies issued in September 2019 and effective Nov. 1, 2019, require large companies possessing two or more financial businesses with 85% or higher debt-to-asset ratios to register with authorities and secure at least RMB5 billion ($731 million) for their financial businesses (eg online payment and lending).

After suspending Ant's IPO, China's regulators determined that Ant was not a technology company.

Antitrust Laws. Immediately after rescinding Ant's IPO, the State

Administration for Market Regulation drafted a series of new antitrust laws in November to stop anti-competition practices of internet-based businesses while also protecting consumers. The new anti-monopoly rules applied to China's internet giants Alibaba, Tencent, Pinduoduo, JD.com and Meituan. Although these large companies have been praised during the COVID-19 pandemic for minimizing the disruption to Chinese society, the use of an exclusivity agreement between one of Alibaba's e-commerce platforms and the food delivery service company Meituan transgressed these new antitrust laws, prompting regulators to forcefully respond. The Chinese government started its investigation of Alibaba because of the company's suspected monopolistic conduct in December 2020 and issued a record fine of $2.8 billion for violating antitrust laws in April 2021. By enforcing these laws, the Chinese government intervened in a timely way and prevented other Chinese multinationals from operating outside the law.

These were some of the reforms that were front and center resulting in Ant's suspended IPO. Perhaps more important than the story behind the suspension is how it will impact China's business development, particularly in the area of CG.

Narrowing the antitrust enforcement gap between China and the US. Due to a huge consumer market and a burgeoning middle class over the past few decades, Chinese multinationals have learned to grow their domestic companies before expanding into the international marketplace, leveraging the domestic market for further global growth. China's regulators have incurred suspicion from the global business community for allowing unfettered growth of Chinese companies at home due to the country's flexible regulation system. With this suspension, China has shown it is willing to enforce its antitrust laws. This mirrors what we are seeing in the US, as big tech companies such as Google, Facebook, and Amazon face greater scrutiny and antitrust investigations.

Improving the quality of China's economic environment. China's antitrust enforcement is sure to impact other Chinese internet giants such as Tencent, Meituan, and JD.com and may possibly damage China's economy and investors' interest and faith in Chinese companies for the time being. However, over the long-term, a well-regulated economic environment is essential, especially as China's economy—the oft-repeated second largest in the world—transitions to the digital era and plays a greater role in the global economy. Since China suspended Ant's IPO and penalized Alibaba's monopolistic behaviors to demonstrate its commitment to higher regulatory standards, it may have come just in time - not only to prevent systemic and credit risks, but also to sustain and strengthen Chinese companies and the country's entire economy.

5.3. Major International Drivers

The globalization process over the past few decades has significantly improved worldwide economic exchanges but created complicated commercial relationships between some countries and the rest of the world. With Chinese companies increasingly participating in global business activities, the demands for these companies' CG practices from the rest of the world are rising too. The following are two prominent external drivers that will likely have a quick and significant influence due to their persuasive impact on Chinese companies.

5.3.1. US scrutiny of US-listed Chinese Companies

Perhaps April 2020 was the darkest month for US-listed Chinese companies. Less than one week after Luckin Coffee admitted to its $30 million financial scandal (see Case Study 4.1.), two additional Chinese companies were reported for inflating sales revenue figures – the online education company, Tomorrow Advancing Life (TAL) Education Group that admitted to employee misconduct, and the video streaming company, iQiyi, who denied accusations of two activists short-sellers after an internal review was performed. Regardless of the investigative outcomes of these incidents, the coincidence of all three having occurred in such a short time period troubled global investors who already had serious doubts regarding Chinese companies' CG practices. The April incidents exceeded the US stock market's tolerance limit that led to consequential scrutiny of US-listed Chinese companies in the following months. US Stock Exchange regulators then initiated a series of legal and regulatory changes targeting China-based, US-listed companies. The following are a few highlights:

- On April 21, 2020, in a joint statement by the US SEC and the US PCAOB, directors of both organizations addressed their concerns regarding the reporting and disclosure quality of US-listed companies operating in emerging markets, particularly in China, due to the SEC and the PCAOB's inability to enforce US disclosure standards for listed companies. The directors also urged that the risks of these US-listed emerging market companies should be carefully evaluated and disclosed to investors.
- On May 18, 2020, Nasdaq offered three proposals to the SEC suggesting additional listing criteria for companies whose operations are in countries with regulations restricting US regulators' access to company information. China is one of these countries. Upon approval of these three proposals, Nasdaq will evaluate new listing applications based on additional criteria or greater measurements of applicant companies' financial numbers, due-diligence efforts, and organizational structures.
- On May 20, 2020, the US Senate passed the Holding Foreign Companies Accountable Act as an amendment to the SOX Act. According to the amendment, certain US-listed companies are either required to certify that these companies are not owned or controlled by a foreign government, or permit the PCAOB to inspect these companies' audit firms for three consecutive years. The failure to meet either one of these two requirements disqualifies a company from trading its securities at any securities exchanges within the SEC's jurisdiction, and will result in delisting from US stock markets.

On June 4, 2020, the US White House issued a presidential memorandum that recommended US financial markets participants to react accordingly should Chinese companies fail to meet transparency and accountability requirements of US regulations.

Regulatory changes in the US are obviously targeting the stalemate that US and Chinese regulators are encountering regarding the PCAOB's lack of access to Chinese companies' information. As many of the US-listed Chinese companies are SOEs in energy, transportation, communication and pharmaceutical industries, Chinese securities law has been prohibiting any documents and materials of Chinese companies from being disclosed overseas, which has stymied China-based US public accounting firms from obtaining audits of overseas securities, as these audits may involve sensitive information.

This increasing pressure from the US caused Chinese companies' "homecoming wave" in 2020. Game developer NetEase and online retailer JD.com entered secondary listings in Hong Kong in 2020 with more companies to follow. In 2000, the Sina Corporation, one of the first Chinese internet IPO companies in the US, led fellow companies to delist their companies' stocks from the US stock market and "go private". As this chapter is being written, three additional Chinese State-owned telecommunications companies, China Mobile Ltd., China Unicom, and China Telecom Corp, are expecting to be de-listed from the NYSE.

Conversely, led by Tencent-backed Chinese popular podcast app Ximalaya, Ant-backed, bike-sharing platform Hello, Taobao-backed media and data cloud service platform Qiniu, and many additional Chinese companies are still seeking IPOs in the US stock market for various reasons. These newcomers will be compelled to improve their reporting and disclosure standards to follow US regulations.

Although the US regulatory scrutinization of Chinese companies seems political at the regulatory level, the increasing compliance requirements of US regulators and Exchanges are one of many powerful drivers for Chinese companies to improve their CG development in the decades to come.

5.3.2. The Increase of Foreign Investments in Chinese Companies

Pressures for CG improvements apply not only to overseas-listed Chinese companies, but also for Chinese-listed companies, due to the increasing amounts of foreign investments and increasing numbers of foreign investors in these companies.

In addition to China's forecasted 4% annual average economic growth in the coming decades and the country's economic boom led by growth themes such as high-tech innovation, digital infrastructure, urbanization, and renewable energy, China has been continuously making the country's A-Share market more accessible to foreign investors by removing restrictions and including the availability of SSE and SZSE-listed companies to global equity indices such as MSCI indexes.

At the same time, China's strategy to strengthen domestic growth and to shift the economic model from investment-driven to consumption and service-driven models has led to a dramatic rise of new economy sectors in the total A-share market over the past decade (in 2008 new economy sectors were less than 20% of Chinese A-Share market capitalization, and the percentage has risen to over 50% in 2021), which paves the way for investors easy access to the new themes opportunities.

Although institutional investors' shares of the A-Share market are still limited at the moment (with 4% of market capitalization), Chinese-listed companies will be increasingly attractive to more global investors. The global trend toward board- shareholder engagement to sustain stable economies will not only allow global investors to demand higher standards of CG practices, but also facilitate corporate repurposing, long-term value creation, and systematic CG improvements using the "voice of capital".

Should the domestic and international drivers perform well, Chinese companies' CG practices will evolve in the coming years, and hopefully become more transparent and compliant with international standards. However, due to the unique features of Chinese companies' CG practices as we discussed in early chapters, we should also expect and honor China's CG development to have its own path instead of following any of the models from more developed economies. With the rise of emerging markets and the different economic environments within emerging market countries, the trend of developing suitable economic growth models and CG practice models for emerging markets is rising too.

How can we step out from the feeling of "navigating in the dark" while working with Chinese companies? I hope the discussion in this chapter helps you find your own path.

Chapter 6

Chinese CSR and ESG Evaluation Systems

The terms "Corporate Social Responsibility (CSR)" and "Environmental and Social Governance (ESG)" have appeared more frequently in various media outlets over the past several years. An increasing number of discussions have taken place regarding employee well-being concerns about health and work-life balance issues, social equality and inclusivity due to worldwide demographic changes and diversity demands, the increased frequency of natural disasters such as wildfires, floods, and the fatal environmental problems of air pollution and plastic waste. Globalization is not only an economic term, but an important part of all global citizens' lives. CSR and ESG were accelerated by the unpredicted worldwide COVID-19 pandemic that provided a clear understanding that surviving a global crisis such as COVID-19 requires global collaboration. Fighting the COVID-19 pandemic highlighted the world's awareness of the interdependency among countries, and that no individual country can survive if others are suffering, which is comparable to fighting other environmental and social battles. Not being responsible for others is not an option any longer.

Although I had learned throughout my career that modern business operations must care about environmental protection, social responsibility, and regulation compliance, especially when operating a business in the global marketplace, I was not familiar with the relevant international standards, requirements, and practices before researching them. Since studiously watching serious social and environmental issues (such as workforce safety protection, food safety concerns, and severe air and water pollution) that China and the Chinese people have been experiencing – all the while observing improvements in certain areas over the past few years - I was curious to learn what the Chinese government has done to address these international business movements and how they may impact China's future growth.

Considering air and water pollution as examples, I remember an incident regarding the 2008 Beijing Olympic Games when the Chinese government, in preparation for the Games, ordered many manufacturers in the surrounding Beijing area to cease their operations months before the Olympics in order to sanitize the air quality. They complied and most returned to full operating capacity after the Olympic Games, ironically creating the term "Olympic Blue" that has described a blue sky in Beijing since then. "Olympic Blue" ironically indicates the trade-off between healthy air quality and economic development that creates job opportunities resulting in improvements to household incomes. After all, *who objects to economic development?* The Chinese people have reluctantly accepted air pollution as "normal" and have found ways to deal with it as part of daily life. In areas with serious air pollution, Chinese families install air purifying home appliances to help improve the air quality in their homes. Runners in China rely on air quality index mobile apps to decide if it's a good day or not for an outdoor run. What can the Chinese government do to improve the air quality in its capital city, and to further control the historical sandstorms that northern China has been suffering for generations?

I also remember a horrible pollution incident on the beautiful, elevated Dianchi Lake (6,189 ft above sea level covering 115 square miles) located in my hometown, a second-tier city in China, that provided so many pleasant childhood memories. With its nickname "Sparkling Pearl Embedded in a Highland", Dianchi is one of Asia's biggest freshwater lakes. Before the first wastewater treatment plant was built in the 1990s, 90% of untreated wastewater from the city (including industrial wastewater) was pumped into the lake, and the lake became seriously polluted as a "consequence" of local economic growth. Dianchi's water quality recovery has been on the local government's agenda for decades, but the process has been awfully slow. Is the reason for the slow progress because the city has to balance the trade-off between economic development and better water quality? I don't have a simple answer.

While considerable research and analysis has been performed to establish whether a positive relationship exists between ESG performance and a company's financial return, ESG is still widely considered to be a non-financial factor at the time being. CSR is not a financial concept either; notwithstanding, CSR has been widely implemented by many Chinese companies and the concept has been implemented primarily as companies' philanthropic efforts such as donations and free service offerings. Although China contributed approximately 18% to global GDP in 2020, let's not forget that the average household income of rural households in 2020 was RMB 17,131 ($2,675), and nearly 40% of the Chinese population lived in rural area in 2020.

How do China and Chinese companies embrace non-financial factors and measurements that have been promoted by the international business movement over the past decades?

Let us start by understanding how CSR was introduced to China . . .

6.1. Corporate Social Responsibility in China

Corporate Social Responsibility (CSR) is defined as "business' contribution to sustainable development" according to the OECD. Milton Friedman, the Nobel Prize-winning American economist, first connected CSR to CG in 1970. Bob Tricker, widely known as the father of Corporate Governance, attests in his latest publication *The Evolution of Corporate Governance* to Friedman's contributions of the integration of CSR thinking with future CG research. Mr. Tricker also pointed out that CSR was not a part of Western CG development consideration until the late 1990s and early 2000s because of increasing societal concerns over environmental and social issues, although for decades, CSR has been used as a powerful tool by developed countries' multinational enterprises when they selected suppliers from developing countries.

6.1.1. CSR History and Development in China

As in many other developing countries, CSR was introduced to Chinese companies by their Western partners as a requirement to meet Western CSR standards when China started its economic reform in 1978.

Compliance with CSR standards was the precondition for conducting business with Western multinational companies. From the late 1990s to the early 2000s, when China's economy grew quickly (driven by exports with mostly labor-intensive manufacturing goods), rapidly embracing CSR became a necessity for both China's government and Chinese companies. China's first Code of CG in 2002 encouraged listed companies to integrate CSR into their business operations.

Many Chinese companies started to incorporate CSR as part of company philanthropy that focused on donations to charitable programs and company participation in poverty-relief and disaster-relief efforts. CSR concerns grew and extended to corporate environmental protection efforts due to the sense of urgency caused by increasing amounts of serious air and water pollution issues worldwide.

At the same time, Chinese companies' increasing global expansion and their growing influence in international markets impacted on the rest of the world, especially the host countries of Chinese companies' overseas subsidiaries, where the expectation was for these companies to contribute to local sustainable development, particularly for those involving resource-extraction projects in African countries and other developing countries.

The involvement of conscientious consumers and investors domestically and internationally and the need to meet their growing expectations drove CSR into Chinese companies' consideration of their strategy. When establishing overseas operations, an increasing number of Chinese companies realized the importance of building trust and long-term relationships with local communities and started to promulgate effective communication channels with multi-stakeholders. A growing plethora of Chinese multinational companies adopted a new strategy of human capital growth, a trendy business model of increasing the number of positions by hiring "locals" and offering them training opportunities instead of importing staff directly from China.

CSR in Chinese companies has transcended mere compliance and philanthropy over the past ten years. With the positive conclusions drawn from studies about the relationship between investors' confidence and good corporate reputation, corporate image and brand value, an increasing number of companies have been using CSR as a tool to respond to stakeholders' expectations in order to build their reputations, while also to improving their business practices by becoming increasingly proactive in two-way communication opportunities with stakeholders. Some companies have even established official communication channels for stakeholders to raise concerns and/or provide recommendations pertaining to company operations.

Similarly to companies from other countries, embracing CSR as a corporate strategy or corporate culture involves a mindset-changing process for Chinese companies that takes time and requires behavioral changes. Due to the wide income gap between the rich and the poor in China, the emerging middle class, and the divergence of corporate practices between companies from different geographic regions, the challenge should not be underestimated. The rising number of conscientious citizens, entrepreneurs, and support from the Chinese government will stimulate Chinese companies' CSR performance, which has improved their potential competitive advantage.

6.1.2. Chinese Government's Influence in CSR development

The Chinese government has played an important role in driving CSR development. China's new company law, issued in 2006, is widely recognized as the turning point in CSR regulation reform. The law provides guidelines for a CSR standards framework and requires companies to implement these standards. In the same year, the SSE released its "Notice of Improving Listed Companies' Assumption of Social Responsibilities," and the SZSE issued "Social Responsibility Instruction to Listed Companies" and made CSR a requirement for listed companies. In 2008, 2009 and 2012, the SASAC issued a series of policies requiring CSR mechanisms be established in companies while mandating CSR reporting for all SOEs (see Table 3.1.). Between 2006 and 2012, 1,600 CSR reports were published in China in contrast with only 22 such reports between 1999 and 2005. The Chinese government, therefore, has showcased its powerful influence toward implementing significant changes with regulatory requirements.

Not only have these CSR regulations and standards enacted in the 2000s helped Chinese companies remain competitive within the global marketplace, but they have also shifted China's attitude from a defensive adoption of CSR standards engagement because it was a requirement to a proactive position of propelling forwards standards development.

Despite these improvements, there were no CG reporting or measuring standards, including the 2002 CG code, that were established or required by Chinese regulators at that time. In 2005, when the China Securities Index Co., Ltd. established the first CSI 300 Index to reflect the performances of the top 300 stocks traded on both the SSE and the SZSE, the measurements used by the index companies were based mainly on stocks' performances according to their daily average trading and market values. No CG factors were incorporated into Stock Market performance measurements.

However, before China had the chance or motivation to explore and develop CG rating systems comparable to those used in the US - CGQ, GRID, QuickScore ISS, and AGR by Governance Metrics International (GMI) - the establishment of its Socially Responsible Investing (SRI) strategy in the late 2000s drove the demand for a CSR evaluation system in the country.

6.2. Chinese CSR Evaluation Systems and ESG Rating Systems

As an investment strategy that considers financial returns as well as social and environmental factors, SRI's origins can be traced to the 18th century in the US but has accelerated in the West since the 1960s. Today, SRI and ESG investing are both considered as sustainable investments that align with both financial and social returns, with ESG investing covering a broader range of E, S and G factors, while SRI focuses on societal impact.

China's SRI started in 2008 with AEGON-Industrial Social Responsibility Hybrid Securities Investment Fund. Following the first socially responsible fund, the Chinese Federation for Corporate Social Responsibility and the Chinese Corporate Development Academy of Shanghai Jiao Tong University launched the first SRI index in 2009. This marked the official beginning of the demand for CSR reporting and measurement in China. Chinese authorities also introduced subsequent policies and guidance for CSR reports and information disclosures. In accordance with the growth of socially responsible investment, Chinese rating firms have developed various CSR rating systems since then.

6.2.1. Chinese CSR Evaluation Systems

Runlin (http://www.rksratings.cn) and Hexun (https://m.hexun.com) were the two main ratings firms to provide CSR quantitative research scores for Chinese companies in the early 2010s. Runlin's RSK scoring system focused on the quality of CSR information analysis with no horizontal comparison and only covered companies with published CSR reports. Hexun's HX scoring system covered a broader base of public companies and focused on CSR performance analysis with data collected from companies' CSR and annual financial reports. RSK and HX scoring systems established the foundation for future designs of quantitative research. However, RSK's and HX's scoring methodologies did not incorporate governance as a factor, and the results from these two systems were hardly synchronized.

Driven by the Chinese government's series of regulations, sustainable investment has grown rapidly in China and made the country the world's largest green bond market in 2016. The growth of sustainable investment created demand for a rating system with environmental and governance factors. At the same time, with China's ESG reform in the 2010s, research on a comprehensive ESG rating system began in China in the late 2010s alongside a global trend of ESG ratings, replacing CG rating systems. This development led to a transition from CSR ratings to ESG ratings systems in China.

6.2.2. Chinese ESG Rating Systems

Chinese ESG evaluation research started in the middle 2010s following the development of global ESG ratings. The most elemental ESG evaluation system in China is "Beautiful China ESG 100 Index," which was launched jointly in August 2019 by the International Institute of Green Finance at the Central University of Finance and Economics (IIGF), a key Chinese research university under direct administration of China's central government authority, and Sina Finance, a media platform providing global financial market coverage and commentary in Chinese. This index comprises the top 100 ESG performers from China's stock markets (35 companies from the SSE, 42 companies from the SZSE and 23 companies from the HKEX). Beautiful China ESG 100 Index's ESG rating system was developed solely by IIGF and considers Chinese characteristics including China's economic development status and industrial distribution, economic and environmental regulation development stages, while incorporating an in-depth understanding of China's markets (since IIGF is directly administrated by China's Central Government authority). In addition to basic ESG factors, Beautiful China ESG 100 Index's ESG rating system added negative and risk elements that consider violations and lawsuits in regard to E, S and G measurements respectively, and uses A (excellent), B (good), C (qualified) and D (needs improvement) to categorize ESG evaluation results. Beautiful China ESG 100 Index's December 23, 2020 report reveals the top 10 companies of the Index without publicly disclosing each company's ESG rating scores (see Table 6.1.).

Table 6.1. Top 10 portfolio weighted constituents of Beautiful China ESG 100 Index

Rank	Code	Issuer	2021 Portfolio Weight	Sector
1	0941.HK	China Mobile Ltd.	15.64%	Telecommunication
2	601318.SH	Ping An Insurance (Group) Co.	11.54%	Finance
3	000858.SZ	Wuliangye Yibin Co.	9.18%	Consumer Discretionary
4	2388.HK	BOC Hong Kong Holdings Ltd.	5.11%	Finance
5	601012.SH	Longi Green Energy Technology Co. Ltd.	4.58%	Information Technology
6	0960.HK	Longfor Properties	4.40%	Real Estate
7	1109.HK	China Resources Land Ltd.	4.19%	Real Estate
8	2007.HK	Country Garden Holdings Co. Ltd.	4.06%	Real Estate
9	00294.SZ	BYD Company Ltd.	3.25%	Consumer Discretionary
10	0981.HK	Semiconductor Manufacturing International Corporation	4.52%	Information Technology

Source: Author's based on data from Sina Finance, June 21, 2021, retrieved on June 30, 2021.

Another leading Chinese ESG rating firm is SynTao Green Finance (STGF), an independent consulting firm promoting sustainable finance in China. In December 2017, STGF and Caixin Media, a privately-owned Chinese media group providing financial and economic news, jointly launched the China ESG50 Index (SGCX ESG50 Index), the first equity index incorporating the ESG performance of listed companies in the mainland Chinese stock market. STGF has been publishing its monthly "Landsea China ESG Development Index Report" since then with regular updates. STGF and Moody started a strategic partnership in October of 2019 with the expectation of developing effective ESG methodologies that consider both global ESG standards and Chinese characteristics. After China's COVID-19 pandemic outbreak in early 2020, STGF published "ESG Evaluation for SSE 50 Index Constituent Stocks on Epidemic Control" on February 24, 2020. In this report, STGF developed an ESG Epidemic Control Valuation model (ESG-ECV) with indicators of "S" to assess how companies handle corporate social responsibilities and "G" to measure the timeliness of corporate actions against the pandemic and quality of relevant information disclosure in response to the coronavirus outbreak in China. The ESG-ECV system graded all SSE 50 companies using five performance levels and nine companies received the highest-level score.

XinHua CN-ESG System which launched in December 2020 closely aligns China's ESG evaluation with global ESG evaluation standards. XinHua CN-ESG System was jointly launched by Ping An Insurance (Group) Company, one of the largest financial service companies in the world, and Xinhua News Agency's China Economic Information Service, one of the largest economic information service organizations in China, under guidelines from MSCI ESG Ratings and the Dow Jones Sustainability World Index. Built with cutting-edge technology and comprehensive indicators designed for Chinese companies, XinHua CN-ESG System provides real-time analysis and ESG scores for companies. With Ping An's leading role in ESG engagement, its leading position in Beautiful China ESG 100 Index, and China Economic Information Service's State backing and broad range of services, XinHua CN-ESG System rose quickly and contributed to China's ESG evaluation and reporting standards improvement.

In April 2021, Chinese Securities Index Co., LTD. (CSI), launched a series of ESG-themed indexes, including the CSI 500 ESG Index and CSI 800 ESG Index. CSI, a joint venture between the Shanghai Stock Exchange and the Shenzhen Stock Exchange, was established in 2005 as the leading index provider in China and has approximately 4000 indices under its management. The CSI 500 ESG Index is designed to cover only the top 80% of performers, which will help establish ESG performance benchmarks and promote ESG performance improvement.

China's self-developing ESG rating systems are still in their infancy. However, Chinese ESG firms' continuous efforts to explore different ESG models to align with global ESG standards are auspicious signs. As the disruption caused by the COVID-19 pandemic opened opportunities for ingenuity and creativity, these same disruptions may uncover unseen possibilities with ESG evaluation development as well.

6.3. MSCI ESG Rating Systems and MSCI China ESG Index

Owned by MSCI Inc., a leading American finance company and global provider of equity, fixed income, hedge fund and Stock Market indexes, MSCI ESG Indexes' broad international coverage makes it the most popular tool for global institutional investors with international portfolios.

6.3.1. MSCI Global Sustainability Indexes

MSCI's Global Sustainability Indexes, launched in January 2009, are free-float-adjusted, market capitalization weighted, indexes with high ESG performing companies from two sectors—MSCI World ESG Index and MSCI EM ESG Index. MSCI World Leader ESG Index, launched in October 2007, covers 23 developed markets (DM) countries. MSCI EM ESG Leader Index, launched in June 2013, covers 27 emerging markets (EM) countries. The US and China weigh heavily in these two sector indexes at 65.71% and 39.02% respectively as of May 31, 2021.

MSCI Global Sustainability Indexes' constituent structure with its sequential selection criteria and quarterly review system is aimed at encouraging companies in both sectors to succeed according to financial and ESG standards. According to MSCI World ESG Index data as of May

31, 2021, US companies' ESG ratings dominate the top 10 list (See Table 6.2.), and Chinese companies continue to make steady progress in ESG ratings as reported by the MSCI EM Leader Index (See Table 6.3.). While the ESG ratings of top 10 companies in the MSCI World ESG Leader Index have been up and down during the past five years, the top 10 companies in the MSCI EM ESG Leader Index have steadily improved their ESG ratings within the same time frame.

Table 6.2. ESG performance trends of top 10 weighted constituents of MSCI World ESG Leader Index

Rank	Issue	Sector	Country	2021 Index Weight	2016	2017	2018	2019	2020	2021
1	Microsoft Corp	Information Technology	US	6.26%		AAA	AAA	AAA	AAA	AAA
2	Alphabet C	Communication Services	US	2.49%			A	AA	BBB	BBB
3	Alphabet A	Communication Services	US	2.48%			A	AA	BBB	BBB
4	Tesla	Consumer Discretionary	US	1.68%			AA	A	A	A
5	Johnson & Johnson	Health Care	US	1.56%	BBB	BBB	BBB	BBB	BBB	
6	NVIDIA	Information Technology	US	1.41%		AA	AAA	AAA	AAA	AAA
7	Visa A	Information Technology	US	1.35%		A	A	A	A	A
8	Home Depot	Consumer Discretionary	US	1.20%		A	A	A	A	A
9	Procter & Gamble Co.	Consumer Staples	US	1.16%		A	A	A	A	A
10	Disney (Walt)	Communication Services	US	1.14%		BBB	BBB	BBB	BBB	A

Source: Author's based on data from MSCI date on May 31, 2021, retrieved on June 30, 2021.
Note: MSCI World ESG Leader Index had 726 constituents as of May 31, 2021.

Table 6.3. ESG performance trends of top 10 weighted constituents of MSCI EM ESG Leader Index

Rank	Issue	Sector	Country	2021 Index Weight	2016	2017	2018	2019	2020	2021
1	Taiwan Semiconductor MFG	Information Technology	TW	11.17		AA	AA	AA	AA	AAA
2	Tencent Holdings LI (CN)	Communication Services	CN	9.63%		BBB	BBB	BBB	BBB	BBB
3	Alibaba GRP HLDG (HK)	Consumer Discretionary	CN	8.64		B	B	BB	BBB	BB
4	Meituan B	Consumer Discretionary	CN	2.86%				AA	A	
5	Naspers N	Consumer Discretionary	ZA	2.03%	BB	BBB	BBB	A	A	
6	Reliance Industries	Energy	IN	1.78%	A	A	A	A	A	
7	China Construction BK H	Financials	CN	1.66%	BB	BB	BB	BBB	A	
8	Ping An Insurance H	Financials	CN	1.44%	BB	BB	BB	BBB	A	
9	Infosys	Information Technology	IN	1.37%		AA	AA	AA	AA	A
10	Housing Dev Finance Corp	Financials	IN	1.26%	A	A	A	A	A	

Source: Author's based on data from MSCI date on May 31, 2021, retrieved on June 30, 2021.
Note: MSCI EM ESG Leader Index had 494 constituents as of May 31, 2021.

However, there's no comparing the two indexes. The deviation of industries represented by selected constituents in each sector, especially considering the avoidance of certain sectors in EM due to ESG quality considerations, and the differences of the overall quality of regulation development and economic environment between developed countries and countries with EM, make MSCI World ESG Index and MSCI EM ESG Index impossible to compare at the index level or individual company level. Data shows that in the first three years of the MSCI EM ESG Index (2013 – 2016), that index significantly outperformed MSCI World ESG Index, which amplified the impact of selected sector avoidance in EM. As EM countries increasingly contribute to the global economy, demand for one comprehensive ESG index system will likewise grow as companies from EM countries seek an assessment on a unified platform that recognizes their leading position. Establishing a unified global ESG standard will take time, require more research and reform, and require leading companies in EM countries to continuously improve their ESG performance and influence other companies in the EM world to bridge the gap between EM and Western countries. As Table 6.3. demonstrates, leading companies in the EM have started to do just that, with consistent improvement over the past five years and one company making it to the top tier (AAA rating) in 2021. The fact that companies are competing with higher ESG rating scores leads us to ask: What is the relationship between ESG scores and a company's financial performance?

6.3.2. MSCI China ESG Leader Index

MSCI's "Corporate Governance in China" report issued in September 2017 summarizes Chinese CG practices through a global investor's lens. The report highlights three fundamental realities of Chinese CG—VIE structure[1], State involvement, and controlling ownership. This report points out the legal uncertainty and unequal voting power risk of the VIE structure and reveals the extremely low CG scores that MSCI gave leading Chinese companies that have VIE structures, like Alibaba and JD.com. The report then reviews a large percentage of Chinese SOEs, lists the CG weaknesses of SOEs, and details China's incremental SOE reforms. The report also documents the various controlling ownership structures of Chinese companies and corresponding CG risks and concludes that Chinese companies' CG scores cluster around the median of EM peers and VIEs while SOEs have obvious governance risks. In essence, the report laid out a framework for future Chinese ESG evaluation research.

The MSCI China ESG Index was launched in March 2018. Around

---

[1] Variable Interest Entity (VIE) structure is a unique business structure in which investors do not have direct ownership but have controlling interest of the entity through special contracts (Greguras, 2020).

200 A-share listed companies have been evaluated by MSCI since China A-share officially became part of MSCI EM Index and MSCI Global Index in June 2018. Many overseas-listed Chinese companies have been evaluated by MSCI since 2015. The number of Chinese companies participating in MSCI's evaluation slightly more than tripled from 152 companies in 2017 to 459 companies in 2018, and the response rate of these companies doubled from 13% in 2017 to 26% in 2018. The overall performance of the MSCI China ESG Index in 2019 improved from 2018 with fewer bottom-rated companies (20% CCC-rated companies in 2019 vs. 22% in 2018; 36% B-rated companies in 2019 vs. 37% in 2018), an increase in BB-rated companies (26% in 2019 vs. 21% in 2018), with minimal changes in the other rating categories.

The MSCI ESG rating system builds and maintains companies' positions and reputations. Chinese companies participating in MSCI ESG evaluation are working on improving ESG scores because they understand that global investors welcome higher scores. The ESG rating improvement of the top 10 companies in MSCI's China Index demonstrate this trend (see Table 6.4.).

By exposing Chinese companies' ESG performance to the global capital market, MSCI China ESG Index is motivating companies to enhance their ESG and building a foundation for further Chinese ESG rating system development. Although Chinese companies' ESG ratings are not in the top tier yet, the fact that ESG ratings of most MSCI China Index Top 10 companies have been moving from BB to A and AA classes since 2015 indicates steady improvement of their ESG performance (see Table 6.4.). This improvement also reflects the fact that Chinese lawmakers, financial institutions, and Chinese-listed companies understand the importance of an ESG rating and are committed to standardizing and encouraging ESG information disclosure, enhancing regulatory guidance, and advocating ESG investment. With China's commitment to become carbon neutral by 2060, China's government has already established plans in its newly created 14th Five Year Plan (starting in 2021) for environmental protection and industrial green transformation. This will facilitate regulatory requirements for Chinese companies' ESG performance and information disclosure.

Table 6.4. ESG performance trends of top 10 weighted constituents of MSCI China ESG Leader Index

Rank	Issuer	Sector	2021 Portfolio Weight	2016	2017	2018	2019	2020	2021
1	Tencent Holdings LI (CN)	Communication Services	24.67%		BBB	BBB	BBB	BBB	BBB
2	Alibaba GRP HLDG (HK)	Consumer Discretionary	22.14%		B	B	BB	BBB	BB
3	Meituan B	Consumer Discretionary	7.34%				AA	A	
4	China Construction BK H	Financials	4.25%	BB	BB	BB	BBB	A	
5	Ping An Insurance H	Financials	3.70%	BB	BB	BB	BBB	A	
6	Wuxi Bilogics	Health Care	2.83%			A	A	AA	A
7	Nio A ADR	Consumer Discretionary	2.68%				A	A	BBB
8	China Merchants Bank H	Financials	1.94%	BBB	BBB	BBB	BBB	BBB	
9	Yum China Holdings	Consumer Discretionary	1.53%		B	B	BB	BB	BBB
10	Shenzhen International	Consumer Discretionary	1.15%			BB	BB	BBB	A

Source: Author's based on data from MSCI date on May 31, 2021, retrieved on June 30, 2021.
Note. MSCI China ESG Leader Index had 174 constituents as of May 31, 2021.

6.4. China's ESG Evaluation System's Future Development

6.4.1. Non-Government Advocate Organizations

In addition to the Chinese government's ESG regulations and reporting guidance (see Table 3.1.), industrial organizations have been pushing China's ESG reform by leading ESG research, recognition, and corporate engagement.

The Asset Management Association of China (AMAC) was established in July 2012 with 147 members from the fund management and distribution industry. As a self-regulatory organization formed to enhance and supervise compliance, fiduciary duties, social responsibilities, sustainability, and healthy growth of the fund management industry, AMAC published a "Research Report on ESG Evaluation System of China's Listed Companies" in November 2018 and opened a new chapter in China's ESG investment practice. In May 2020, AMAC published a "2019 Research Report on ESG Evaluation System of China's Listed Companies" with updates regarding China's ESG evaluation development and challenges.

The China Alliance of Social Value Investment (CASVI) was founded in May 2016 with a mission to develop a quantitative assessment system of social value. Initiated by YouChange China Entrepreneur Foundation, with 60 institutional members and a broad network across many sectors, CASVI is the first licensed international non-profit organization promoting social value investment in China. CASVI published "Discovering 'SV 99' in China" reports in 2017 and 2018 to compare SV 99 (social value of the top 99 companies) and CSI 300 (top 300 stocks on the SSE and the SZSE) on various social and environmental indicators and economic contribution indicators.

The China ESG Leaders Association (CESGLA) was founded in August 2019 with 30 founding organizations led by Sina. CESGLA's founding firms are publicly traded companies like Ping An, Haier, COSCO Shipping, Bank of Communication and Fosun Pharma. One of the association's goals is to standardize ESG report frameworks, ESG education, ESG information disclosure, and ESG evaluation.

ESG has slowly obtained recognition from different industries in China, as evidenced by the timeline of these organizations' founding and the nature of their different missions. The fact that publicly traded companies have realized the value of ESG and started to engage in ESG improvements in order to stay competitive in the global market indicates that an ESG revolution in China is coming.

6.4.2. The Necessity to Develop a Chinese ESG Evaluation System

Although global ESG rating firms and credit rating firms have developed various ESG evaluation systems, due to the application of different data resources, data analysis methodologies and ESG rating modeling, ESG ratings from different rating firms are not at all comparable. Lack of universal ESG ratings significantly limit the reliability and utilization of existing ESG scores. Moreover, investors prefer more qualitative ESG analysis rather than quantitative rating scores. As a result, major institutional investors establish internal ESG teams for their own analysis.

Since ESG ratings are determined by each country's standards, a bias exists, as discussed in section 6.3.1, which negatively impacts the ESG scores of companies from emerging markets due to the nature of these countries' economies. In particular, industrial sectors have the lowest ESG scores, as most of them operate in developing countries. Emerging markets countries also face challenges with underdeveloped regulatory frameworks, a shortage of expertise on ESG reporting and integration, and a lack of systematic readiness for ESG adoption.

As China's economy continues to grow rapidly, Chinese companies are trying to catch up with their competitors from more economically advanced countries regarding ESG performance and ESG rating scores. Increasing numbers of Chinese companies are committed to improve their ESG performance to attract investors, reduce capital costs, and stay competitive. Developing a Chinese ESG evaluation system based on China's local market situation will become essential for companies to receive fair ESG scores compared to their competitors in more developed economies.

6.4.3. The Context for China's ESG Evaluation System Development

Chinese rating firms and leading ESG firms worldwide continue to optimize mechanical processes like data collection, information disclosure, and integration of global ESG and CG standards as they seek a comprehensive ESG evaluation system. At the same time, it is necessary to consider four unique Chinese factors—legal environment, culture, shareholder structure, and government relationship during this process, as these four factors have had a profound impact on Chinese companies' CG practice. These factors will also play a part in how ESG implementation is integrated into Chinese companies. Though measuring the four factors could be challenging, doing so will make the ESG evaluation system much stronger.

China's Legal Environment. A country's legal environment has a major influence on its CG practice. This is an important factor to consider when evaluating the overall governance level of companies in a particular country. In a country with a weak legal system, companies have to apply extra efforts to maintain sound CG to offset the negative impact of the legal system. Along these lines, the S&P 360 Degree scoring methodology developed in 2004 suggested a "Country Governance Review" as part of the CG scoring framework.

In China, the lack of enforcement of laws and regulations is a weakness which stems in part from the ongoing development of China's legal system and also from a lack of practical details regarding existing regulations. Misinterpretation of regulations and numerous grey areas of enforcement are all too common. Factoring China's legal environment in ESG evaluation can also help identify the weaknesses of the existing legal system and facilitate future regulation development.

China's Cultural Influence. Chinese culture inevitably and profoundly influences Chinese companies' CG. Many of these cultural elements contribute to Chinese companies' success to some degree, but some of these elements cause blind spots in their corporate culture and operation.

China's Confucian philosophy, inherent paternalism, and relationship-based nominal board culture are good examples of elements that exert dual influences on CG. Ancient Confucian philosophy advocates etiquette and justice, which is helpful when establishing CG rules for an organization, but it also emphasizes compromise and tolerance, which makes it harder to establish checks and balances in an organization, as many employees will refuse to tell the truth simply to stay out of trouble. Paternalism values and maintains long-term relationships with customers and suppliers and rewards and looks after loyal employees, but paternalistic companies are normally controlled by an insider group with opaque decision-making processes. A relationship-based board can be very supportive at a company's early stage by unifying board directors and executive teams, but a nominal board (as opposed to one composed of experts) tends to perform few CG functions and meetings and decisions are simply formalities, which nourishes opportunities for mismanagement or fraud and becomes an obstacle when trying to attract investors. Integrating these cultural elements into ESG evaluation systems requires further research and study on cultural roots and potential solutions. But ESG evaluation systems without these cultural factors will fail to accurately measure Chinese companies' CG.

Chinese Companies' Controlling Shareholder Structure. According to MSCI's Chinese CG report in 2017, 81.9% of Chinese companies have a controlling shareholder structure, including SOEs and founder firms. The percentage was reduced to 79% in MSCI's 2019 research, which shows a trend of Chinese companies' shares opening to global investors at a slow pace. A controlling shareholder structure is not necessarily indicative of poor CG, but from an ESG evaluation standpoint, it is essential to examine whether the board acts in the interests of all shareholders. Alibaba serves as a good example for how a founder-controlling firm engages investors with transparent succession planning as part of its CG practice. On the other hand, Luckin Coffee founders' abuse of the controlling power led to the company's crash and unnerved the market.

Founder-controlled firms also face succession plan obstacles as founders reach retirement age, and it is natural in Chinese culture for one generation to pass the business to the next. However, some founders' children lack the interest or ability to take over the business from their parents. Those willing to take over normally carry on the founder's core values, although younger generations are exposed to Western education and are less emotionally attached to the business. Therefore, whether a company's succession plan is to prioritize long-term business sustainability with the possibility of cultivating outside talent, or to remain a founder-controlled structure by bequeathing the business to the next generation, companies are sure to inherit a very particular set of challenges and opportunities.

More research is necessary to understand the impact of founder firms with a controlling shareholder structure on CG and ESG.

Chinese Companies' Relationship with the Chinese Government. One of the most common questions regarding Chinese companies is: "Are Chinese companies (non-SOEs) controlled by the Party?" The relationship between the two has been an enduring mystery to many Westerners. Alibaba's Jack Ma used to characterize the relationship between his company and the government as being in love with the Party, but not marrying them. Having strong ties with the government is obviously risky, especially to the extent it allows external influence on board decisions, but a good relationship can also mean companies have access to domestic resources and government support for long-term growth, which ultimately benefits all shareholders. When we emphasize stakeholder interest and CSR from a corporate purpose standpoint, the relationship between Chinese companies and the government might be viewed differently.

Ultimately, it is more fruitful to examine areas where board decisions could be influenced by government, and whether those decisions will help businesses maximize value creation and optimize all stakeholders' interests, than to object to the relationship entirely. Further research on measurement factors and methodologies is needed.

Chapter 7
China's ESG Revolution in the Post COVID-19 Era

2020 was destined to be an extraordinary year for many people, for the world, and for China. As the ESG movement gained more traction, the concept became the predominant focus of the "movers and shakers" of the global business community, and China, which began the ESG revolution journey as the world's second-largest economy and one of the most dynamic ones, decided to "take up the mantle" toward becoming the world's ESG leader. The country's leaders pledged to no longer be a "follower". Taking the lead role in ESG regulation reform, ESG integration within companies' operations, and ESG reporting improvements both domestically and internationally, has become the primary mission of the Chinese government and Chinese companies. However, becoming the world's pre-eminent economic engine will not only result in a global expectation of a commitment to higher standards, but more importantly, also invite increasing scrutiny of its compliance with these standards. Will China be able to capitalize on this opportunity, and if so, how?

In *The Era of Chinese Multinationals – Competing for Global Dominance*, co-authored by Professor Lourdes Casanova and Professor Anne Miroux, the authors connect the 2008 global financial crisis to a successful turning point for Chinese multinationals. When companies' asset values from more developed economies significantly depreciated after the crisis, Chinese multinationals' active overseas acquisitions enabled many Chinese companies to become global industry leaders. Will Chinese companies be able to exploit the worldwide COVID-19 pandemic as another growth opportunity? During my interview with Professor Casanova, she cautioned that the COVID-19 pandemic is a different economic situation than the 2008 financial crisis. The worldwide business landscape changed dramatically between the two crises: hosting countries' regulatory scrutiny of foreign acquisitions increased dramatically; and overseas acquisitions will no longer be Chinese companies' primary growth strategy in the coming decades. While most developed economies are still contending with the coronavirus and the reopening of their domestic economies, China's effective control of the coronavirus and nimble economic recovery will enable the country to switch its development strategy from a high-speed to a high-quality model.

Professor Casanova also opined that while global ESG adoption has intensified during the COVID-19 crisis, a "one size-fits-all" strategy is not practical or feasible. Although ESG momentum has been driven by more developed economies over the past few decades, emerging market countries' ESG adoption models will not replicate those models.

After decades of high-speed growth, China now needs time to review, refine, and retune its legal, cultural, financial, and economic institutions. How will the country align its new economic development strategy with the international ESG movement? More importantly, how will China's ESG adoption model contribute to the establishment and implementation of a suitable model(s) for emerging market countries?

2021 became the "year of action" for everyone, in every country, and in China, especially with regards to China's ESG revolution. After kicking off the year with several integrated regulation reforms, the momentum of the ESG revolution has seen non-stop growth with various financial instruments being issued, the launching of a national carbon trading market and collaboration among international organizations. The Chinese government's new regulation reform strategy and international consideration strongly indicate that China is on the verge of adopting ESG according to internationally-recognized standards, which might also become the impetus and opportunity for China to shift from "a laggard and handbrake to a pioneer and accelerator" in the worldwide ESG revolution, as well as economic growth leader in the post COVID-19 era.

Let us take a look at China's exciting ESG movements in the first half of 2021 and enhance our knowledge of its accomplishments in the post COVID-19 era, while also examining new overseas growth strategies created by Chinese companies to overcome ESG challenges and take ESG integration as opportunities to reshape their international operations strategies and corporate images.

7.1. ESG Movements in China

China's highly ambitious plan to reduce the country's carbon dioxide emissions by at least 65% by 2030 and achieve carbon neutrality by 2060 will require a rapid transformation of the economy. In September 2020, President Xi Jinping announced the government's intention to attain a zero-carbon emissions goal by 2060 as part of China's 14th Five-year Plan. By 2025, an expectation of a decrease in fossil fuel energy consumption of 13.5% and a carbon emissions reduction of 18% is anticipated. Thereafter, the government intends to increase the amount of renewable energy sources into its energy supply mix from 15% in 2018 to 85% by 2050 to achieve the 2060 carbon neutral goal. Kicking off 2021, China has made some progress in numerous areas to demonstrate its commitment to the UN's Sustainability Development Goals (SDG) initiative.

7.1.1. Regulation Reforms

Issuing new green bond regulations to align with international standards. In March 2021, a Notice on Clarifying Relevant Mechanisms of Carbon Neutrality Bond was issued by the National Association of Financial Market Institutional Investors to guide and ensure that the usage of carbon neutrality bonds' proceeds are only for green projects. In April 2021, *Green Bond Endorsed Projects Catalogue (2021 Edition)* was jointly issued by the PBOC, the National Development and Reform Commission, and the CSRC, with three advancements: to clarify eligible projects (excluding coal and other fossil fuels projects), to unify a set of consistent standards in China; and to integrate an international Do No Significant Harm (DNSH) principle. At the time of writing, China and the EU agreed to reach common classification standards of "green projects" by the end of 2021. The common standards will enable European investors to have easy access to Chinese green bonds.

Issuing new ESG reporting rules. On June 28, 2021, the CSRS released new ESG reporting rules that mandate environmental factors (eg pollution and waste management) disclosure, and encourages social factors (eg poverty alleviation and rural revitalization) and carbon emission reduction related information disclosure for China-listing listed companies. The new ESG report rules stipulate ESG reporting as a requirement for most listed companies effective from 2021 half-year and annual reports, while the previous CSRS ESG reporting guidelines issued in 2018 only required disclosure of environmental factors for heavy polluters.

As discussed in previous chapters, most Chinese regulation reforms were lagging, and lacked practical guidance or lacked alignment with international standards, so regulators took a different approach on the green bond and ESG reporting regulation reform in 2021. The new Notice and Catalogue were issued at the beginning of the year before significant amounts of Green Bonds were issued. Both provided timely guidance and practical clarification for funds usage to avoid misunderstandings, and were integrated with international principles while unifying domestic standards to ensure the alignment between China's regulations and international standards. The new ESG reporting guidelines were issued before companies filed their half-yearly reports to ensure the reporting requirements would be reflected in the 2021 reports. In addition, issuing ESG reporting guidelines in June 2021 allowed China to maintain the same pace as more developed economies.

The improvements of both regulation reforms in the first half of 2021 are proof of the Chinese government's new strategy for future regulation reforms.

7.1.2. Transforming to Green Finance

Promoting "green" finance movements. In March 2021, the China Development Bank (CDB), China's top policy bank[1] issued its first "carbon neutrality" bonds supported by the Shanghai Clearing House, one of several securities depositories in the country. (The CDB was established in 1994 with the initial purpose of financing government's infrastructure projects in China. The CDB is under the direct administration of the Central Government, and is the world's largest development financial institute[2].) The three-year bonds with a total value of RMB20 billion

---

[1] There are three policy banks in China - the China Development Bank (CDB), the Agricultural Development Bank of China, and the China Export and Import Bank.

($310 million) were offered to global investors. The funds raised by the sales of CDB's green bonds will be utilized for green projects that are designed to reduce carbon emissions. Given the largesse of China's financial market, the bond sales are expected to have a significant impact on carbon emission reduction goals. The China International Capital Corporation (CICC), the underwriter of this green bond, is a leading player in the country's green financial market. This year, the CICC underwrote China's first transition bond[3] with the Bank of China's Hong Kong branch; in 2017, the first real estate green bond with Longfor Chongqing Enterprise Development; and in 2016, the first financial green bond with Shanghai Pudong Development Bank.

Also in March 2021, the State Grid International Leasing Company Ltd. issued asset-backed commercial paper, China's first innovative asset securities product designed to facilitate carbon neutrality. The RMB1.75 billion ($270 million) raised by the ABCP supports clean energy leasing projects in wind power, hydropower, and photovoltaic power. The fact that this asset-backed commercial paper was issued and managed by various Chinese trust companies, including the State Grid-backed Yingda International Trust Co. Ltd and the Bank of China, indicates the leading roles that lenders are taking to encourage a nationwide green finance movement and to hopefully compel additional Chinese financial institutions to participate and support climate change initiatives.

Collaborating with international climate bonds organizations. In March 2021, the Shanghai Office of the Climate Bonds Initiative (CBI)[4] was launched in Shanghai Lujiazui Financial City that confirmed Lujiazui's green financial center role to promote green bonds, green standards, and green transition finance. In June 2021, CBI issued *Green Infrastructure Investment Opportunities,*

---

[2] Development Financial Institutions are national or regional financial institutions designed to provide medium- and long-term capital for infrastructure projects or other large-scale projects in poor countries (eg Asian Development Bank).

[3] A transition bond is a new financial tool to fund the climate change initiatives and energy transition.

[4] The CBI is a not-for-profit international organization launched in 2012. By providing annual studies on the evolution of the green bonds market and standards and guidance on green bonds, the CBI advocates climate change considerations through financial institutions' investing and lending activities.

The Guangdong-Hong Kong-Macao Greater Bay Area 2021 report to promote the green infrastructure investment opportunities in the Greater Bay Area (GBA) and help raise funds for these infrastructure projects.

Taking a new strategy on green bond regulation reform, actively promoting diversified green finance programs, collaborating with international organizations, setting up common standards with the EU, (which has been leading the green finance initiative over the past few decades), strongly indicates China's commitment to higher standards to provide green financing, as well as the country's intention to become an active player in the global green finance initiative.

7.1.3. Carbon Emission Control

Establishing focuses for carbon dioxide emissions. In March 2021, the chairman of the Global Energy Interconnection Development and Co-operation Organization published an article to discuss and propose solutions to achieve China's 2030 carbon dioxide emissions and 2060 carbon neutrality goals. The solutions include four focus points for emissions reduction and the means to accelerate the increase of non-fossil energy consumption. More importantly, the article calls for collaborative efforts between government, corporations, and non-profits to facilitate and advance the transition to a green economy.

Launching a national carbon trading market. China has established eight regional pilot exchanges for carbon trading since 2013, and launched a national carbon trading market in Shanghai in July 2021 with the first 10 companies signing deals on the first trading date of July 16, 2021. The national carbon trading market with 2,225 companies joining as the first group will be overseen by the Shanghai United Asset and Equity Exchange (SUAEE) and the Shanghai Environment and Energy Exchange (SEEE). According to an article in the South China Morning Post news on June 23, 2021, the SEEE's national carbon emissions trading platform will operate like the SSE and SZSE, with the same trading hours, daily trading limits, and a ten percentage point trading price cap. All transactions conducted in the eight regional pilot exchanges will eventually be taken over by the SEEE. The main purposes of the carbon emission trading platform are to enable carbon credit trading and establish similar financial instruments such as those in the US and European Union to help China achieve its carbon neutrality goal by 2060. China's national carbon trading market will expand to cover eight industries, a few of which are cement, electrolytic aluminum, steel, and chemicals, within the next five years.

Kicking off renewable energy spot trading in Guangdong. In June 2021, Guangdong province launched renewable energy trading with four renewable energy generators and seven retailers who signed contracts during the first day of the trading. The fact that these four generators were making higher profits from the contracts than traditional power generators will motivate energy generators' conversion to renewable energy and facilitate the country's energy transformation in the long-term.

The active progress and the continuing momentum of China's ESG initiatives will help China catch up with ESG leading countries. What are the drivers of China's ESG movements which have been accelerating these initiatives then?

7.2. Major Drivers of China's ESG Revolution

The ESG revolution is a long-term journey for the world as well as China. The COVID-19 pandemic, social and political protests, and environmental disasters have highlighted the roles that businesses can and should play in society, pushed ESG discussions to a "boiling point" and launched the beginning of this endeavor. Since China is the second-largest economy in the world, what are the major drivers of its ESG revolution?

7.2.1. Policy Makers and Regulators

Chinese lawmakers and regulators have been the biggest drivers for the ESG movement over the past several decades and will continue their important roles of prodding China's ESG revolution. Since the end of 2020, market participants have been expecting new ESG reporting regulations for mainland China's listed companies (A-Shares[5]) that will

---

[5] A-Shares are RMB-denominated stocks of China-based companies listed on the and Shenzhen Stock Exchanges.

be issued by Chinese lawmakers in late 2021. When that occurs, the new requirements will become the biggest driver of ESG reporting in mainland China, and the requirements will significantly increase public availability of ESG information for listed companies. In addition to the upcoming and new ESG regulations, Chinese companies will be required to provide ESG compliance reports by the Stock Markets in Hong Kong, Shanghai, and Shenzhen, all of which are, incidentally, members of the UN Sustainable Stock Exchanges Initiative.

HKEX has been actively driving the ESG reporting initiative since 2012 (see Table 3.1.) and released its first ESG reporting guidance that year. The HKEX has updated their guidance a few times since then, with the most recently updated guidance in July 2020. ESG reporting became mandatory for listed companies on the HKEX beginning in 2015 and mandates the disclosure of detailed investment-relevant information on climate-related risks and the board of directors' involvement in ESG adoption as part of a company's business strategy. In addition, the HKEX provides educational tools (ESG reporting E-training was launched in 2020) and materials such as "How to Prepare an ESG Report, a Step-by-Step Guide to ESG Reporting", "Leadership Roles and Accountability in ESG: Guide for Board and Directors", and "Making Inroads into Good Corporate Governance and ESG Management" to help companies improve their ESG reporting quality. In addition, the HKEX recently launched STAGE. STAGE is an online platform addressing ESG reporting data availability, accessibility, and transparency issues. STAGE provides visibility for companies regarding how their financial products meet sustainable standards; provides investors information for their decisions; and provides all stakeholders with related information regarding green finance.

In mainland China, the Shenzhen and Shanghai Exchanges issued ESG reporting guidance data in 2006 and 2008 respectively, and since 2018, the CSRS has required companies that are industrial polluters to be listed with the government's Ministry of Environment and Ecology to disclose details of their pollution amounts and pollution control measures. Furthermore, the Shanghai Stock Exchange's Science and Technology Innovation Board (STAR) requires companies to report their efforts to fulfill their corporate social responsibilities. According to data from SynTao Green Finance, as of June 2020, 86% of CSI300 A-Share companies have issued ESG reports compared with a 90% reporting rate among S&P 500 companies. Although neither the SSE nor SZSE have yet to issue new ESG reporting requirements at the time of writing, the anticipated growth of green finance and green bonds in China indicates the undoubtedly important roles of the SSE and SZSE in China's ESG movement.

7.2.2. Domestic Asset Owners, Asset Management Firms and Investors

Since the UN launched its "Principles for Responsible Investment" (PRI) in 2006, being a PRI signatory has been widely recognized as a requirement for obtaining the public status of a responsible investment company. Confirmation of this is shown by the dramatic increase in the number of PRI signatories – from 63 firms in 2006 to 3,100 firms in 2020, with the total amount of assets under management increasing from $6.5 trillion to $110 trillion in the same period of time. The top 10 asset management firms worldwide are PRI signatories with a combined AUM of over $30 trillion.

Most large international asset management firms have their own ESG teams that analyze portfolio companies' disclosure and collect information on industry-specific ESG issues and companies ESG risk management via questionnaires, in addition to 3rd party ESG rating score and ESG data. However, these international asset management firms' current ownership of A-share companies remains relatively low. China's relatively quick recovery from the COVID-19 crisis and anticipated positive GDP growth in the coming decades statistically indicate that these international asset management firms will steadily increase their standing in Chinese A-Share companies over time. However, their influence on China's A-Share companies' ESG reporting compliance and performance may be limited in the short-term.

Conversely, China-based asset owners and asset management firms have been rapidly adopting ESG themes in recent years. At the time of writing, five asset owners and 89 asset management firms in Hong Kong and mainland China have become PRI signatories, which represents 3%

of total asset owners and investment managers globally who have signed the PRI. Chinese domestic asset owners and asset management firms will play important roles in China's ESG revolution in the coming decades.

The following case study of Ping An will help us understand how the China-based asset management firm integrated ESG as part of its business strategy.

Case Study 7.1. Ping An Insurance Group ESG Adoption in the Post COVID-19 Era

Ping An Group (with over 30 subsidiary companies) is China's leading asset management firm listed on the Shanghai and Hong Kong Stock Markets. At the end of 2020, Ping An launched the XinHua CN-ESG System, which currently provides quarterly ESG scores for 3,900 A-Share companies.

Ping An's ESG efforts started two decades ago. The company has already completed the first two stages of building its CG and management system according to international standards, and has fulfilled its corporate social responsibilities with projects such as non-profit education, public donations, poverty assistance, disaster relief, etc. Ping An considers itself within the third stage of ESG adoption with clearer ESG requirements from domestic and international regulators. In order to integrate ESG as part of their business strategy, Ping An has taken the following steps:

Phase One: Identify three main drivers of Ping An's ESG effort

1. *To align and balance different stakeholders' interests*
2. *To maintain long-term sustainable goals and long-term value creation of the business*
3. *To remain within high-standards of CG*
4. *To comply with regulatory requirements and meet the growing demand from asset owners regarding ESG integration*

Phase Two: Establish ESG Strategy Execution Plans

- **Externally**:
Committed to support the Chinese government's strategy to achieve carbon neutrality and to fulfill China's commitment under the Paris Agreement

    1. Launched the XinHua CN-ESG System to establish technology-enabled ESG evaluation tools to help other Chinese companies with their ESG performance analysis and improvement
    2. Launched a group-wide "Green Finance" project to become a pioneer in the field, and to lead the nationwide Green Finance movement

- **Internally:**
To modify its organizational structure to enable regular communication between the board and different levels of ESG committees and senior management teams regarding its ESG strategy integration status

    1. To establish an operational policy and procedure system to support ESG reporting and ESG practice reviews in different levels of the group
    2. To utilize cutting-edge technologies to simplify its ESG-related procedures and improve ESG reporting efficiency.

Phase Three: Integrating ESG into an Investment Decision Process

1. Establish Ping An's Responsible Investment Policy around key principles: ESG integration; active ownership; theme-oriented investment; risk management and information transparency
2. Set-up requirements for subsidiary companies' investment procedures and asset class attributions
3. Establish ESG-oriented risk management and asset allocation
4. Establish AI-empowered tools to apply key principles criteria into an ESG evaluation system

While many companies still view ESG integration as regulatory compliance, Ping An took steps ahead of the field to embrace ESG as part of its business strategy. In addition, Ping An's AI-empowered ESG system focuses on helping other Chinese companies improve their ESG enhancements and ESG reporting, which enabled Ping An to become a pioneer and leader in global ESG digitalization. ESG adoption helped strengthen Ping An's overall competitiveness and enhanced its global brand reputation. Moreover, ESG integration will further assist Ping An with better risk management and investment performance. By supporting the government's ESG strategy and helping other Chinese companies improve their ESG performance, Ping An will continue to create and promote a sustainable business and investment environment not only in China but also globally.

In addition to domestic asset owners and asset management firms, Chinese public pensions and sovereign wealth funds are likely to stimulate domestic ESG assets due to the significant amount of AUM and the top-down decision-making structures managing these funds. The Hong Kong Monetary Authority signed the PRI as the first public sector asset owner in China. In mainland China, the government-backed pension programme, together with the National Council of Social Security Fund (NSSF), represents about 80% of mainland China's pension assets. NSSF issued its first ever responsible investing mandate in September 2020, which may be a tell-tale sign of the ESG trend in Chinese public pension and sovereign wealth funds, but this trend may need to be further monitored for confirmation.

Moreover, the growing number of China's middle class and their increasing wealth will drive the growth of professionally managed funds with ESG-themed investments. With younger generations worldwide increasing their focuses on corporate purpose and environmental and social issues, similarly Chinese younger generations' purchasing power will promote ESG products and eventually push ESG-themed investments also.

7.2.3. Chinese Corporations

As we discussed in Chapter 2, SOEs have been dominating the Chinese economy and playing important roles in the country's economic reform and growth. According to statistical data in 2020, a total of 1,150 SOEs were listed on the SSE and SZSE, representing 30% of 3,800 listed companies in these two exchanges, and 300 SOEs were listed on the HKEX exchange accounting for 15% of 2,000 companies. Most SOEs are in energy, minerals, infrastructure, utilities, and financial services sectors resulting in a considerably large amount of capital, so they consequently have been the most significant allies of China's environmental, social welfare, and long-term strategies and will continue to fervently advocate for other Chinese companies to strive to improve their own ESG reporting and performance standards.

In addition to SOEs, some leading private Chinese companies have also initiated ESG integration into their business strategy process. Let us consider the Xiaomi Corporation, for example.

Case Study 7.2. Xiaomi ESG integration in the Post COVID-19 Era

Xiaomi Corporation, headquartered in Beijing, China, was founded in April 2010 by Lei Jun and six co-founders, and has been listed on the HKEX since 2018. The company employs 18,000 workers and has successfully expanded its business throughout China, Southern Asia, Southeast Asia, and Europe.

As one of China's leading multinational electronics companies, Xiaomi's main products are smartphones and home appliances. Since the first quarter of 2018, Xiaomi has been ranked the fourth-largest smartphone manufacturer in the world, following prominent global brands Samsung, Apple, and Huawai. According to a global smartphone quarterly market data report, Xiaomi exceeded Huawai to become the third-largest manufacturer in the fourth quarter of 2020. Xiaomi has also produced a large variety of home appliances in recent years.

In 2014, the company was ranked the most successful technology start-up with a valuation over $46 billion, and by 2019, Xiaomi was ranked 468th as the youngest company on Fortune's Global 500 list. In 2021, they announced its investment in a new electric vehicle project for the near future.

Considering Xiaomi's success as one of the fastest-growing technology companies of the previous decade, what is its position on today's worldwide ESG movement? Let us glance at the company's perspective, current strategy, and future plans:

Phase One: Establish the company's ESG approach in three stages:

1. Foundation – ensure the business entity has operational compliance at all levels
2. Fulfill social responsibility as a good corporate citizen
3. Create social value and brand value via ESG integration

Phase Two: Identify the most significant ESG-related risks facing major stakeholders:

1. Large number of stakeholders including network suppliers and users
2. ESG engagement with suppliers to mitigate supply-chain risks and protect brand reputation
3. Focus on data security and user information privacy and commit to meet privacy requirements

Phase Three: Establish procedures to address ESG-related issues in manufacturing and the online environment:

1. Ensure regulatory compliance as a minimum requirement
2. Set-up supplier social responsibility agreements to specify ESG requirements (including business ethics, environmental and labor rights) and establish an annual audit system
3. Establish an ESG risk management procedure including monitoring and an online education mechanism
4. Establish an information security control system throughout the entire supply chain and conduct strict privacy compliance assessments with an internal professional team
5. Establish "whistle-blowing" channels with a 24/7 reporting platform open to all stakeholders
6. Build an ESG-themed environment by providing supply-chain financing, and drive ESG adoption for small and middle-sized companies.

Since companies around the world are searching for and exploring ESG integration solutions, a KPMG 2018 ESG research report advised that businesses need to identify ESG factors that most significantly impact risks and opportunities, build roadmaps to determine productive strategies, and communicate key ESG risks that stakeholders may consider to be important elements for corporate ESG integration. Xiaomi's ESG approach demonstrates how that thriving company embraces ESG as part of its business strategy, as the KPMG report suggested.

Xiaomi's phase one approach simply repeated the founder's value creation approach: begin with the little things (a practical foundation) then focus on building the social and brand values instead of starting by aiming for perfection (an erudite maxim), a two-pronged philosophy that has driven Xiaomi's success from the beginning.

Xiaomi's phases two and three were the highlights of the technology company's ESG adoption as significant parts of its growth strategy and execution plan. Given the broad range of ESG factors, all industries and companies are exposed to assorted ESG risks, and individuals' ESG interpretations may also differ. The company emphasized the identification of the most important ESG factors and risks to stakeholders for it and built an ESG-themed environment to protect and influence them which focused on applying these factors in its daily operations. While bringing innovation into new areas, Xiaomi's ESG approach might not be perfect yet, but may inspire other companies while continuing to improve Xiaomi's over time.

Moreover, Xiaomi's approach to drive ESG integration in its supply chain demonstrated the company's ability to exert influence with its purchasing power, similar to the Western companies who introduced CSR compliance to Chinese companies in the 1990s. Xiaomi's approach exemplified Chinese companies' initiative at enhancing their lead roles within the international business community to promote the evolution of ESG.

According to Professor Andrew Kakabadse, global business communities need to think about how to determine meaningful engagement on ESG with critical stakeholders as an important part of their ESG agenda. Xiaomi's two-step approach echoes the professor's perspective, and demonstrates to the world how a company identifies its most important stakeholders and establishes operating procedures in its day-to-day business to address ESG-related risks and protect these stakeholders. In addition, Xiaomi included in its agenda influencing the under-addressed small and medium-sized companies, which represent a significant percentage of every economy. By doing so, Xiaomi not only setup good examples for other companies in China and other countries, but also explored innovative approaches to facilitate ESG adoption for the entire society.

7.3. Challenges and Opportunities in China's ESG Revolution

Lack of talent and funding resources are the biggest challenges for Chinese companies' ESG adoption, the same as for companies from every country across the world today. ESG experts are short in various functions, sectors and throughout each organization. On the other hand, ESG implementation is costly in both the short-term and the long-term: short-term costs occur when hiring ESG professionals, setting up ESG KPIs and establishing ESG reporting systems; long-term costs include infrastructure investments across energy, industrial, transport, building sectors, and new emission technology development. According to Tsinghua University's Institute of Climate Change and Sustainable Development data, China will need an estimated RMb170 trillion ($26 trillion) to achieve its 2060 carbon neutral goal.

7.3.1. Moving up the Value Chain

It took China over thirty years to become "The Factory of The World" with over 50% of total global manufacturing output. Apple's global supply chain system in China that allowed iPhone's worldwide success is the best testimonial for China's comprehensive supply chain system, its sophisticated and skilled workers, and affordable and scalable engineering resources. However, let us not forgot that China's export-oriented manufacturing started two decades before the era of iPhones, and the manufacturers have been rapidly moving up the value chain, and shifting from mass production of cheap, low-skilled required, labor-intensive products (eg textiles), to high-value, more sophisticated goods.

China's industrial shift has created a skilled and higher-paid workforce, which significantly enhanced Chinese workers' household income and average education level. The process has also triggered global supply chain relocation with lower-skilled and low-paid jobs moving from China to other Asian countries (such as Vietnam, Indonesia and India) starting from the mid-2010s, and the relocation was accelerated by COVID-19, while the region's supply chain system will continuously rely on China's support network in the coming decades.

Global supply chain relocation from China to other countries will generate positive social impact for everyone. The receiving countries will gain more job opportunities, manufacturers and exports; China will be able to achieve its new development goals of a high-quality economy and greater consumption market; the global consumers will be able to enjoy less expensive products; and the global business community will have less supply-chain disruption risks due to over-dependence on one country.

In addition to social impacts, moving up the value chain will stir technology innovation, productivity improvement, and cost reduction. The momentum will then lead to regulation reform, business model optimization, and less energy consumption which will drive China's ESG movements. The "Made in China 2025" strategy introduced in 2015 highlights the Chinese governments' plan to address the country's manufacturing cost pressure from the increase in labor costs, and the social pressure with the upcoming shrinking workforce and growing ageing population.

Moreover, according to research regarding currency internationalization, staying in the downstream of the global value chain was one of the top reasons that prevented Japanese currency's global usage despite the fact that Japan had led the Asian economy for four decades. Taking the lessons learned from Japan, Chinese manufacturers moving up the global value chain will accelerate China's RMB internationalization too.

However, China and Chinese companies have to deal with challenges during the transformation of its industry, such as potential unemployment issues due to labor-intensive production being relocation to other countries; workforce skillset transformation; and the technology advancement needed to support the transformation. The trend of shifting some labor-intensive manufacturers from the coastal regions to inland regions over the past few years helped to absorb a certain number of extra labor resources, and the necessary technology upgrade occurred in most industry sectors. China's rural re-vitalization strategy which was proposed in 2017 with detailed plans promoted in China's 14th Five-Year-Plan is critical for China's continued industry transformation.

7.3.2. Trend of Business Mindset Change

While different resources are concurrently progressing China's domestic ESG revolution, warning calls came from the global market via a 2020 US technology ban on Chinese companies such as Huawei and TikTok that reminded Chinese companies to proactively integrate an ESG mindset with positive impacts on other societies, which will become a survival strategy in the global market.

Learning from Huawei and Tiktok and other Chinese companies who have paid high costs by not establishing trust with their host countries or spending very little effort on stakeholders' interests, the current generation of Chinese companies is taking different approaches in the international market to create social impacts and become good corporate citizens financially and otherwise. Perhaps the primary purpose at the moment is to mitigate potential political and policy risks while "riding the worldwide ESG revolution wave", but this strategy will help Chinese companies promote an inarguably positive image globally and pave their way toward becoming industry leaders in the future. The business mindset changes needed to overcome global survival challenges may lead to greater success for these companies.

Let us review the VIPKid case study below regarding this new initiative.

Case Study 7.3. VIPKid's Social Impact Strategy

> VIPKid is a privately-owned education technology company founded in 2013 and headquartered in Beijing, China. The VIPKid platform connects

800,000 paying students from over 60 countries with approximately 100,000 North American English teachers. The VIPKid online classroom allows students to receive English language lessons via a video chat platform. The company's five US offices focus on curriculum development, teacher recruitment and management, global business development, public relations, legal matters, and compliance issues.

The company's teachers are independent contractors and VipKid does not provide any benefits, including health insurance. It also has been exposed to various political challenges and policy risks, including worker classification issues, US-China diplomatic tension, personal data privacy, children's online safety, and racism allegations, all heightened during the 2020 COVID-19 crisis.

After realizing the importance of not only complying with local administrative policies and regulations but also the investment of social impact, VIPKid initiated the following measures:

- **Proactively sought regulatory protection to mitigate legislative risk.** With nearly 4,000 teachers in California alone and in order to protect its "gig-economy" business model, VIPKid hired a lobbying firm from Sacramento, the State's capitol, which pursued regulatory protection of the company's business model that included the exemption of their tutors/teachers' employment status as contractors, the ability for tutors/teachers to provide testimony to the legislature, and provided extensive outreach services to the California governor's office, labor groups, and teachers' unions, etc.
- **Public relationship management.** To avoid a deleterious impact on its business, the company proactively removed potential politically related topics from its online curriculum and adopted a restrained approach in its public and media profiles.
- **Data security and personal information privacy protection.** VIPKid took a proactive approach in providing transparency of its data collection and storage to the public on its website, and attests to its adherence with the most recent compliance requirements of the EU's General Data Protection Regulation and the California Consumer Privacy Act. In addition, to avoid potential personal data security conflicts due to its data storage location, VIPKid updated its practice

to store all American-related data on a US-based server.
- **Proactively protect children's online safety**. To avoid any online safety controversy, VIPKid not only remains cognizant of its compliance with relevant regulations, but also joined local children's online safety organizations to participate in best practices discussions.
- **Properly address potential discrimination conflicts due to cultural differences**. Bridging culture differences through sensitivity awareness training, open communication, and thoughtful review of all curriculum and training materials to ensure diversity and inclusion practices.

VIPKid's approach regarding public relations, regulatory protection, and active involvement in online education standards and best practices, demonstrates a new generation of Chinese companies that are determined to expend considerable energy to succeed in the global market, unlike traditional Chinese multinational companies who, by avoidance, focused on growing their business and generating profit while eschewing communication with the local community and stakeholders.

In contrast to companies with well-functioning boards that oversee their business strategies that include ESG adoption, VIPKid is still in its early stage of having a social impact toward furthering its international growth. Regardless, the company's modern and innovative approach may inspire other Chinese companies' advancement toward CG development and ESG adoption.

Following Deng Xiaoping's "feeling the stones while crossing the river" axiom, Chinese companies have demonstrated considerable creativity in their CG development as we previously mentioned in this book. Will more innovative initiatives, ideas, or business models result from Chinese companies' ESG revolution? We will see. At the moment, companies such as VIPKid have been exploring various paths to establish not only their business but also a corporate image in the global market. Today's worldwide ESG revolution will likely be engraved along their journey and will hopefully empower them toward greater competitiveness and better brand reputation.

Chapter 8
Trends to Watch

China's social credit system (SoCS) was first brought to my attention in the fall of 2019, when I was told that a college friend, Jason, (not his real name) was placed on the Chinese government's "travel restrictions blacklist". Jason owned a microloan business in China in the early 2010s, and filed for bankruptcy a few years ago due to a loan default. Upon closing the business, he has been working for a small consulting firm. However, being on the "blacklist" has restricted him from traveling by air or high-speed train and staying in expensive hotel rooms (relegating him to "regular trains" or bus use and staying in "cheap" hotel rooms only). These travel restrictions have made it difficult for Jason to travel long distances for business trips or conferences.

The new SoCS reminds me of the differences between China's prior credit check process and the process in the US. While the personal credit score system in the US and other more developed economies has been widely used for mortgages, job applications and other important social and business references, in China, a stamped recommendation letter containing an applicant's salary amount provided by an employer was required to attest to an individual's credit worthiness for a mortgage application approval. I then became curious about the pending updates to the new credit system in China, as well as any possible alterations of the existing travel restrictions.

Having now learned about the new credit system, sympathy is extended to my friend Jason. However, my research of China's new SoCS has enlightened and now convinced me that the new system will serve an important role in changing individual and businesses' behaviors, in order to accelerate the establishment of a trustworthy society and help improve the regulatory standards of China's business landscape and

Chinese companies' CG development and ESG adoption.

China has changed so rapidly since I initially left. As I write this book, changes are occurring so quickly that companies are designing initiatives to improve their CG practice, become and remain in compliance with newly released regulations, and be in alignment with international standards. Two case studies in this chapter perfectly demonstrate the trend of China's resolute evolution of CG development in the new era.

Before we consider the sensitive SoCS topics and case studies, please allow me to begin this chapter with a brief review of China's upcoming Five-Year Plan that will guide its economic development over the next five years.

8.1. China's 14th Five-Year Plan (FYP)

China's Five-Year Plans (FYP) are a series of social and economic frameworks that have been issued by the Chinese government since 1953, focusing on tasks and goals to be accomplished within each five-year timeframe. The objectives and policies covered by the FYPs include economic, population, environment, public service, and the quality of each citizen's life. Since the establishment of the PR China in 1949, the Party, which has developed and directed all the plans, has taken part in important functions by establishing economic strategies, growth targets, and various reform initiatives.

In the early period of China's social and economic development, an FYP was the "planning" established by the central government to provide detailed development guidelines for all provinces. The initial concept of a "planned" economy subsequently evolved into a "socialist market" economy, then in 2006, when the 11th FYP was enacted, the government labeled forthcoming plans as "guidelines" that describe the means for local governments to establish their own individualized development strategies and policies without the encumbrance of complying with a "centralized" plan. As time progressed, FYPs also became the "thermometer" for the rest of the world to observe the Chinese government's social and economic development process and progress during each successive FYP.

China's 14th FYP (2021 – 2025) was released at the end of 2020 with a set of economic targets including energy intensity, low-carbon intensity and increased self-reliance on technology. The 14th FYP will also mark the beginning of China's economic transformation from a moderately prosperous society into a modern socialist country. While the 14th FYP contains an ambitious and broad range of activities in various social and economic areas, in this section, I will focus on the three key features, also referred to as "new development dimensions", that define goals and objectives proposed in the new FYP. These features will, with purpose, inevitably foster China's ESG movement.

8.1.1. The Three Development Features of the 14th FYP

Unlike previous FYPs, the 14th FYP is the first that does not set a specific GDP growth target. Instead, the new plan addresses other economic indicators such as the unemployment rate, energy consumption, and carbon dioxide emissions - all aimed at improving peoples' lives and environmental protection with a shifting focus towards the *quality* of economic development.

Also, for the first time, the new FYP comprises clear proposals for national security development and capability, food production, energy and financial security, an assessment of current global conditions, and evident challenges facing China's domestic economic recovery and international growth, all of which indicate the improvement and maturity of China's economic and social development.

The following new dimensions have been recommended in the 14th FYP to guide the nation:

The development stage – transition from a high-speed development model to a high-quality model. China's consistently formidable GDP growth rate over the past 20 years (averaging 9.29 percent per year) has enabled the country to become the second-largest economy in the world. Given global economic and political uncertainties, not setting a specific GDP growth target allows the Chinese government and companies to focus on economic recovery from the COVID-19 pandemic as well as to review and refine its strategic response to domestic and international challenges and risks.

The development philosophy – innovation, co-ordination, environmental protection, openness and sharing. The new philosophy is consistent with targets established in the new FYP, such as accelerating technology independence, digital transformation, intelligent manufacturing, promoting a green economy and renewable energy methods, and strengthening comprehensive supply chain networks.

The development strategy - "dual circulation" led by "internal circulation" (aka, the domestic market) with "external circulation" (aka, the global market), each reinforcing the other. China's large domestic market has been the impetus of the Chinese economy's rapid growth over the past several decades so the "dual circulation" strategy will help expedite its domestic economic recovery and growth, which will ultimately boost the global economy by the purchasing power acquired from the ever-expanding consumer goods market in China. In addition, a strengthened domestic market will enhance Chinese companies' competitive advantage globally.

According to Professor Lourdes Casanova, the two elements that most applicably warrant the success of Chinese multinationals are: *China's fast-growing economy and domestic market,* both of which allow multinationals to cultivate the domestic market first before "going global", thus making their domestic markets as "base camps" for their continuous international growth; and the *Chinese government's support and guidance* which advocates nationalism when needed, allowing Chinese companies to be more resilient during a crisis.

8.1.2. How will the 14th FYP Reshape China's ESG Landscape?

Since ESG has been at the top of the global business communities' priority list and China's ESG evolution has made significant progress during the past few years, how will the three key features of China's 14th FYP facilitate the country's ESG progress?

E - Environmental. Improving performance on "E" factors is an especially important feature of the high-quality development model that runs concurrently with China's 2060 carbon neutral goal. The 14th FYP integrates indicators related to energy consumption and carbon dioxide emissions and makes environmental protection one the of the main themes and an integral part of its new development philosophy. In addition, the plan's recommended new development philosophy is characterized by innovative environmental protection to encourage and support green finance, renewable energy vehicles, and investments in renewable energy projects. Making environmental protection a part of the development philosophy, combined with the "dual circulation" strategy, will prompt the discovery and refinement of alternative domestic resources to help improve "E" factors and further China's energy transformation, attract direct foreign capital in related business sectors, and eventually help to raise environmental protection standards and influence good business practices to benefit the global ecosystem.

S – *Social*. Shifting from high-speed to high-quality models will allow the Chinese government and companies to increase their focus on improving peoples' livelihoods and social well-being. The 14th FYP's philosophy and "dual circulation" strategy will encourage technology development in healthcare and life sciences, and also promote social responsibility considerations while companies pursue value branding and the advancement of their supply chain networks. Eventually, the Chinese business community will experience a collective mindset change toward "S" factor improvements.

G – *Governance*. A high-quality economic model indicates a higher standard regulatory system and CG practice. Shifting from high-speed to high-quality models will allow Chinese regulators to focus on improving the regulatory system standards and close the gap between Chinese regulations and those of more developed economies and allow opportunities for Chinese companies to refine and sharpen CG models and improve their CG practices. With regulatory challenges due to the surge of digital and sustainable economy transformations, the new development philosophy and "dual circulation" strategy will help encourage and improve collaboration with different sources domestically and internationally.

The three key features of China's 14th FYP indicate the country's economic growth is moving into a mature stage. After chasing rapid growth over the past few decades, the Chinese government realizes social and economic priorities have dramatically shifted; what is now needed are improvements in the quality of institutional guidance for the economic environment, citizens' living standards, and strategic relationships with other countries to enhance a healthy and sustainable global economy. The new dimensions and objectives initiated in the 14th FYP supports China's commitments of carbon emissions peaking by 2030 and carbon neutrality by 2060 to align with the global ESG movement.

8.2. China's Social Credit System (SoCS)

The China's SoCS was launched in 2014 and originally planned for nationwide implementation by the end of 2020. The system's structure is built to comprise a credit score ranking system for all Chinese citizens and businesses, looking to eventually establish a high-trust society whose compliance with regulations provides rewards. Ideally, China's SoCS will function as well as the system of credit scores in most developed economies. Although full implementation of the system was delayed for various reasons including the impact of COVID-19 in 2020, significant progress has been made in the pilot cities that have taken part in a trial period.

In 2020, the COVID-19 pandemic tested the efficiency of SoCS that proved SoCS's role as a highly flexible platform that enables new policy priorities, although the initiatives and different stages of the SoCS infrastructure across regions and administrative levels in China were still being set in place. Chinese government agencies were issuing a series of COVID-19 pandemic-related regulations that were enacted concurrently without delay thanks to the SoCS infrastructure. SoCS' resiliency and efficiency made 2020 a cornerstone year to prepare for the next step in China's SoCS development. Pivoting from an IT construction phase to the installation of key data-supported frameworks and mechanisms will fulfill SoCS' digitization process to perfectly align with the 14th FYP's new development goal of technology independence.

Therefore, it is important to understand that China's SoCS, as a national credit system, is a mechanism to encourage and enforce organizations and individuals' behavioral changes for the good of the society, and a platform to support the enhancement of China's regulation reform will evolve quickly in the coming years and become mandatory soon.

8.2.1. The Traditional Version of China's SoCS

A social credit system is not new in China. Being born and raised there, I am familiar with two terms, "Huko" and "Dangan", that have existed since the 1950s, and in my opinion, have been serving as China's social credit system in traditional hard copy versions.

"Huko" is the official government registration of household members. Every Chinese household must have one "Huko" booklet that lists all the household members who have historically lived at a residence. "Huko" is required to be updated by local government authorities with stamps and all citizens must register their "Huko" with the local government authorities when moving to another city due to education or a job opportunity. "Huko" was used as a citizen's official identification before China began issuing citizen ID cards in 1984. Today, a citizen's ID card is used for travel and hotel registration, for example, similar to Americans who use their US driver's license. However, "Huko" can also serve as the substitute for the citizen ID card when needed.

"Dangan" is the official government record of a Chinese citizen's education and employment history and is noted if/when a Chinese citizen changes jobs or schools. Any rewards or penalties incurred during an education and/or employment, as well as any legal consequences from criminal or civil law cases, will be recorded on an individual's "Dangan".

China's SoCS is an advanced modern system with the combined functions of "Huko" and "Dangan". Today's technology with the broad range of information obtained from "big data" systems enable SoCS to dynamically monitor and record an individual's social activities and behaviors. In addition, the SoCS has already been extended to include businesses, which is the China's Corporate Social Credit System (CSCS) often referred to in recent reports from some policy consulting firms.

8.2.2. Punishments and Rewards of China's SoCS

Gathered from a research report *China's Corporate Social Credit System* published in November 2020 by the strategy and Chinese policy consulting firm Trivium China, I sensed a "scary" feeling in addition to "a lack of privacy" concern regarding CSCS from Westerners who are accustomed to their well-established legal system containing social contract codes, but more importantly, the serious respect and demand they have for privacy. The CSCS mandate covers all companies registered in China, which has inadvertently led to the widely held concern of critics who regard the impact on foreign companies' operations in China - including the confidentiality of these companies' personnel information such as compensation data - as a violation of their privacy.

Perhaps the following violation consequences incurred by poor social credit performers are the main reasons why China's SoCS and CSCS are facing such strong resistance from the West:

- Travel bans: Individuals on a "blacklist" are prohibited from traveling by airplane or high-speed train and may not reserve rooms at expensive hotels. A citizen in violation remains on a "blacklist" for two to five years.
- School bans: Children whose parents have poor social credit scores are restricted from attending certain universities or schools.
- Public shaming: The government maintains a publicized list of individuals and businesses who have poor social credit scores.
- Privacy: The government monitors as much of a citizen's daily actions as possible. Individuals can lose credit points due to walking a dog without putting it on a leash, smoking in a non-smoking area, or cheating in online videogames.
- Joint liability: Engaging with companies with poor social credit scores can reduce the score of an individual or business.

While restricted punishment was established for poor performers, the purpose of China's SoCS is to reward good performers. In 2021, social credit rewards for businesses contributed to COVID-19 containment, while penalties were imposed on companies that took advantage or violated restrictions during the pandemic. Due to the availability of social credit data, Chinese citizens and businesses are able to access a simplified loan-granting process and expedited access to funding, both geared to help high-score individuals and businesses who have been seriously affected by the COVID-19 pandemic.

In addition, individuals who help take care of disabled people or non-relative elderly people, or who donate to college funds to support poor students will receive positive credits and be rewarded with special discounts to better hotel rooms, or other benefits.

Considering Western standards, the violation consequences of SoCS may sound "extreme" as far as a citizen's freedom and privacy are concerned, and the joint liability for companies may also appear to be unfair. However, for a country with nearly 19% of the world's population and 18% of global GDP, what can be more effective than these punitive and rewarding measures to quickly draw peoples' attention and force behavioral changes?

8.2.3. China's SoCS Impact on ESG Revolution

Although "G" is the last factor in the concept of ESG, I believe it is the precursor. "G" ("Governance") defines an organization's culture, standards of behavior, and attitudes toward innovation and failure. When considering SoCS's impact on business' performance and the results of that relationship to society, "Governance" is the primary element of the three. For this reason, I will address how SoCS accelerates China's ESG movement in reverse order ..

Facilitate regulatory enforcement. In the same year that the Chinese government launched the SoCS, in 2014, President Xi Jinping declared its top priority was to establish a "comprehensive law-based governance" system. Enhancing the enforcement mechanism of existing laws and regulations has been on SoCS' agenda since its beginning. The new roadmap for the "construction of a 'rule of law society until 2025'" issued by the Party's Central Committee in January 2021 further highlights SoCS's role in supporting China's regulatory system development over the next five years. Regulatory enforcement will surely help improve China's CG standards, Chinese companies' CG development, and also facilitate the country's ESG evolution.

Establish a trustworthy economic society. As silly as the negative comments of poor SoCS score performers could sound about consequences they've experienced, China's SoCS scoring system will help foreign businesses find faithful business partners in China by publishing a poor performers list. "Public shaming" (a borrower) and joint liability will also stimulate internal and supply chain audits to eliminate bad partners, force individuals and business to avoid adverse behaviors, and eventually establish a more trustworthy society for people's livelihood and for business.

Enhance environmental protection. Businesses' environmental protection compliance is a significant criterion to evaluate a company's SoCS scores, which will definitely promote "E" responses from the business community. However, let us not forget that compliance is just a *basic* requirement of a high-quality economy. The business behavior changes and business purpose changes led by other initiatives of the SoCS will help in upgrading environmental protection standards to a higher level along with China regulators' effort to establish a higher standard regulation system.

From a business' operational viewpoint, the implementation of SoCS is in line with China's ESG evolution, which will accelerate the company's ESG improvement in many aspects. With its mechanism to reinforce behavior changes, China's SoCS will stimulate the development of China's ESG landscape and help to establish a fair and competitive market with information transparency, which will benefit both Chinese and foreign businesses and investors.

China's SoCS implementation is facing many domestic challenges at the moment, such as a unified definition of "credit", an accumulation of thousands of documents from regional sources, and lack of a standardized evaluation system. The central government is taking steps to tackle these challenges with an upcoming social credit law and many other approaches, with a clear determination and commitment to building a streamlined and digitally integrated SoCS.

Although my Chinese background helps me better understand the "extreme" approach of China's social credit system, I personally do not feel comfortable having to scan my face upon entering the neighborhood of my in-law's residence in China. However, if considering most political and economic systems in Western society that I am familiar with, am I satisfied should they continue with the functioning status quo? Probably not. I am simply just either used to them, or never had an opportunity to voice my opinion when those systems were implemented. Since China's social credit system is new and contains peculiar mechanisms of which they and most countries are not familiar, we may rush to judgement based on habit, similar to a preconceived notion of a new Enterprise Resource Planning (EPR) system criticized by many who may be forced to change their behavior to allow that protocol to work properly. Understandably, each and every one of us values a good EPR system that performs a magnificent job on behalf of a company's internal control and financial reporting operations.

In another words, while we from the West expect Chinese multinationals to respect our well-established regulations when they conduct business in the West, Westerners should reciprocally do the same when doing business in China, especially when matters of trust and compliance are concerned. The purpose of SoCS is to enforce behavior change and to establish a faithful society, which will ultimately benefit both foreign and Chinese domestic businesses and individuals. In the end, it is about understanding and respect.

8.3. China's Commitment to a Higher Standard Regulation System

Like many other emerging market countries, China has a very restrictive legal system, but the problems have always been an absence of practical guidance and a lack of enforcement mechanisms. Since China is now the second-largest economy with many pundits predicting that it will surpass the US and become the largest in the coming years, many have questioned if China is still considered an emerging markets country. What are the lines between developed and emerging markets? How can China become a real leader in the global economy? According to Professor Andrew Kakabadse, who has been researching leadership and government policies and has provided consultation advice to the British government, a strong and high-quality institutional system is one of the top criteria for a country to be considered a global economy leader. The Chinese government has been on a mission to accomplish this goal.

China has realized that the traditionally lagging regulatory system does not fit its ambition in the global economy, and establishing a high-standard regulation system and closing the standards gap between itself and other developed countries must become a priority. Therefore, the improvement of regulation standards is a vital part of China's 14th FYP's new development strategy of transitioning from a high-speed development model to high-quality model, and also on the SoCS agenda of enhancing the enforcement mechanism of existing laws and regulations. The sense of urgency led by the government will be reflected by more guidance, monitoring, and measurements.

Various regulatory reforms and improvements initiated by Chinese lawmakers were addressed in Chapter 3. In this section, I will highlight three topics that occurred recently which are closely related to Chinese companies' ESG improvement and are likely to have an energizing influence on regulatory reform.

8.3.1. Intellectual Property Protection

Intellectual property (IP) rights protection is an especially important topic in CG development, and one of the top concerns of Western companies - primarily the US - about doing business in China. IP protection is a common problem in all emerging market countries due to lack of innovation ability and IP protection regulations, and China's enlarging economy and growth pace have exaggerated this problem. IP protection should be initiated from corporate boards as part of the businesses ethical and moral standpoint and executed as a basic business practice of regulatory compliance. Otherwise, violations of IP rights will continue to cause tragic consequences for Chinese companies, as we have witnessed with the notable banning of Huawei from the US market.

At the same time, Chinese tech companies' fast growth has catapulted the country from a technology importer to an innovator over the past decade. China's proliferating economic global value and its plan to transfer the country's economic development strategy from a high-speed to a high-quality style, have introduced innovative improvements which have created a powerful engine for the country's industrial and economic transformation. A mindset change has been occurring in the country that is reflected by an increasing number of IP applications granted to Chinese companies as a result of regulation reforms.

The following points highlight remarkable changes in the Chinese IP landscape since the landmark year of 2019:

China became the top IP filer in 2019. China bypassed the US in 2019 with a total of 58,990 IP applications filed with the World Intellectual Property Organization (WIPO)[1], versus a total of 57,840 IP applications from the US. In addition to China, the number of other participating Asian countries also soared over the past few years which resulted in total Asia-based IP applications to be over half of the total worldwide number of applications, according to WIPO information. The 2019 surge

---

[1] The World Intellectual Property Organization (WIPO) is a specialized United Nations agency consisting of 193 member countries. The WIPO was founded in 1967 and is headquartered in Switzerland. WIPO's main functions are to promote worldwide IP protection and offer IP administration services according to treaties signed by member countries.

of IP filers from China and other Asian countries indicates a trend toward an innovation shift in Asian emerging markets in the coming years. The number of IP applicants from China (68,720) topped the WIPO list again in 2020 (the number of US applications was 59,230). Of particular interest worth mentioning is 2005, when China first entered the WIPO IP application top ten list with 3,020 IP applications verses the US, which was number one with 48,482 filings. The contrast between China's fast growth and the US's stable but slow growth in numbers over the past fifteen years echoes the trend of China's technology growth and industry transformation from low-value, high-labor intensive industries to high-value, mid-range products manufacturing.

Establishment of a new IP Court of Appeals at the national level. In January 2019, the new IP Court of Appeals was formally introduced, subservient only to the Supreme People's Court (SPC), (China's equivalent to the US Supreme Court), with highly experienced IP judges. Since the establishment of the IP Court of Appeals, several cases have been adjudicated by the SPC, including Michael Jordan's trademark case against the Chinese company Qiaodan Sports who has used the "Qiaodan" company name to identify its products brand and other commercial applications, in addition to approximately 200 trademarks closely related to Jordan's name, image, and likeness. Jordan's trademark case was filed in 2012 and finally resolved in 2020 in Jordan's favor after the establishment of the IP Court of Appeals.

China's Patent Law Amendment enacted in 2021. On June 1, 2021, the fourth amendment to China's Patent Law became effective, many years after the previous amendment that took effect in 2008. The amended patent law has made adjustments on enhancing an enforcement mechanism with a significant increase in the maximum amount of statutory damage inflicted on a petitioner; extending the patent protection term from ten years to fifteen years; joining the Hague Agreement[2] on industrial design patent practice and allowing partial design patents; and granting pharmaceutical patent holders extended terms with additional

---

[2] The Hague Agreement is an international industrial design protection system administered by the WIPO and covers 92 countries. The Hague system protects the lifecycles of industrial design via a mechanism of protection for renewal applications.

tools for protection. Although there is still room for further improvement in China's new patent law, the new amendment made significant improvements on patent rights protection, in alignment with international patent practices, and the spurring of pharmaceutical and biotech development in China. The fourth amendment also includes a broad anti-monopoly provision to align with Chinese regulators' anti-monopoly law movement, which will be discussed below.

8.3.2. Anti-Trust Law Enforcement

Immediately after the Chinese government suspended Ant Group's IPO, the State Administration for Market Regulation issued a draft of *Guidelines for Anti-Monopoly in the Platform Economy* on November 10, 2020 and placed Chinese tech giants "under a microscope". The following April, Alibaba was fined a record RMB 18.2 billion ($2.8 billion) by Chinese regulators, and more than 20 Chinese tech giants made public pledges to comply with China's anti-trust laws. Other than preventing monopolistic activity, protecting a fair and competitive market and promoting equality and inclusion in the business environment, China's anti-trust law enforcement will likely lead to regulatory reform in the following areas:

Consumer data collaboration and protection. Chinese tech companies have collected a large volume of consumers' data containing a wealth of information and individual behavior. Alibaba has established its own credit system that has been used to collaborate with the SoCS to establish a unified credit scoring system. Obviously, the government's access to a tech company's database has become a security consideration of other countries where local consumers' information has been collected by these companies. The lamentable Huawei and Tiktok scenarios have demonstrated the legitimate concerns regarding the challenges for these companies' international growth. On the other hand, enhancing anti-trust law enforcement to prevent these tech giants growing uncontrollably will also protect consumers' data collected by these companies. With the "dual circulation" new development strategy initiated by China's 14th FYP, future regulation reform should support Chinese companies' growth strategy in both domestic and international markets and protect consumers' interests in both markets as well.

M&A transactions involving VIE structures under anti-trust review. After the regulator's most recent attempt to fix VIE structure loopholes in the 2015 FIL draft, regulators have been staying silent regarding VIE structure issues until the new anti-trust law guidelines clearly address the fact that those M&A transactions involving a VIE structure are subjected to anti-trust review. Although the anti-trust review of M&A transactions is not directly targeting the legal status of a VIE structure, the government's review will tighten VIE structure utilization. This approach could be duplicated in other regulatory reforms to indirectly eliminate a VIE structure as a side effect of improving regulations in other areas.

New legal framework with severe penalties for violations. Enforcement of the new anti-trust law primarily targets Chinese tech giants and sends a strong warning signal of the government's intention to exert State power over companies who violate the law. The message is in accord with the 14th FYP to transform the economy from high-speed to high-quality models, particularly for companies that were accustomed to maneuvering in legal "grey" areas and which will now face severe consequences and punishment for any violation.

This law will awaken all tech giants and may possibly damage China's economy and investors' interest and faith for the time being. However, in the long-term, a well-regulated economic environment is essential, especially as China's economy transitions to the digital era and plays a greater role in the global economy. Enforcement of the new anti-trust law clearly indicates Chinese regulators are committed to a higher standard of regulations that will sustain and strengthen Chinese companies and the country's entire economy.

8.3.3. Minority Shareholders' Interest Protection

Compared to investors from countries such as the US and UK, Chinese investors are much less sophisticated. Given the short history of China's Stock Market, limited ownership of institutional investments in Chinese companies, and China's nascent CG code, "shareholder engagement" and "minority shareholders' interest protection" concepts are new to Chinese investors. However, at the time of writing, the new law's validity was tested when the first minority shareholder interest protection lawsuit was litigated in favor of 315 minority shareholders, becoming an important milestone in Chinese Stock Market history. Adding drama with symbolism, the defendant in this case was the first publicly traded company in modern China's history. Below is the case study:

Case study 8.1. Feilo Acoustics Co Ltd Minority Shareholders Interest Protection

> Feilo Acoustics Co Ltd. (FEILO) is the PR China's first joint-stock listed company. The company was approved by the People's Bank of China to issue shares to the public in 1984. The company's shares were listed and traded from the Trust Business Department of the China Industrial and Commercial Bank of China in 1986, and transferred to the SSE in 1990 after its re-opening.
>
> FEILO is one of the oldest Chinese brands of sound reinforcement equipment, electro-acoustic components (speakers), ballroom lighting, and other related products. Over its nearly 40-year history, FEILO has extended its product offerings to include software, multimedia communications, intelligence systems, etc. The company has restructured many times due to the rapid change of the Chinese consumer market.
>
> In July 2019, the China Securities Regulatory Commission (CSRC) issued an "Investigation Notice" to FEILO due to suspected violations of information disclosure requirements and in November, the Shanghai Regulatory Bureau of the CSRC issued an administrative penalty decision based on two findings: FEILO's failure to meet projected revenue recognition requirements; and, incorrect 2017 half-year and third quarter financial reports that indicated a false revenue forecast and inflated profit.
>
> In August 2020, several FEILO investors filed a lawsuit claiming that the information from FEILO's financial reports caused significant investment losses and demanded compensation from the company of RMB146 million ($23 million). The Shanghai financial/civil court determined the scope of the shareholders' rights, issued a "notice of rights

registration", and, according to "Guidance on Represented Litigation" rules, of the 315 plaintiffs (most of whom were retail investors) only five of them could act as class-action representatives.

On May 11, 2021, the court ordered FEILO to compensate the plaintiffs a total amount of RMB123 million ($19 million), averaging RMB390,000 ($61K) per plaintiff. This case was the first judicial practice of ordinary represented litigation since the Chinese Supreme Court issued its "Guidance on Several Issues of Represented Litigation in Securities Disputes" manual on March 24, 2020.

The outcome of the FEILO case provides a precedent for the further promotion of China's Class Action Lawsuit system, and has become a symbolic milestone of the country's regulatory reform – the establishment of a fair, efficient, and effective legal protection system for small and medium investors. As a result of the FEILO case, Chinese society will benefit from:

- An increased understanding of retail and minority shareholder rights
- Investors deepening trust in the Chinese legal system
- The establishment of a representative litigation mechanism in Chinese regulation reform
- Chinese regulators' commitment to establish a higher-standard legal system

The FEILO case was not only the first but also a momentous event in China's representative litigation trend that shows minority shareholders are able to protect their interests within the legal system. However, shareholder engagement, which is a significant part of today's ESG movement, has broader scope than shareholders' interest protection. To establish shareholder engagement mechanisms in the Chinese market demands a more comprehensive regulatory system and CG code; trusted and experienced proxy agency firms; and significant share structure changes in Chinese companies to allow a higher percentage of institutional investors, who are considered the most significant influencer of shareholder engagement in more developed countries. These elements will take time but change will happen quickly with the government's participation. For now, it is prudent to be patient.

8.4. The Rise of Social Entrepreneurship in China

2020 was globally significant due to an increase in discussions about business' purpose and social responsibility, a shift from shareholder-focus to stakeholders' interests, the worldwide ESG revolution, the unpredictable COVID-19 pandemic, and the Chinese government's anti-trust scrutiny of its tech giants. Despite domestic and international turmoil and the global business agenda, two Chinese tech companies' leadership transitions are worth mentioning. In Case Study 2.3., Pinduoduo founder Huang Zheng's retirement revealed an emerging trend in Chinese companies' succession planning and social entrepreneurship. Upon his March 2021 retirement, at 41, Huang Zheng resigned as board chairman and relinquished his majority voting power status to devote his time exploring food science.

In addition to Huang Zheng's retirement, the founder and CEO of Tiktok's parent company, ByteDance, Zhang Yiming, also announced his retirement approximately one year earlier. The following is his and the company's case study.

Case study 8.2. ByteDance Founder CEO Zhang Yiming's Resignation

> ByteDance Ltd., a Chinese multinational internet technology company, was founded by Zhang Yiming in 2012. The company is registered in the Cayman Islands and headquartered in Beijing.
>
> Zhang Yiming, who was named one of Time magazine's 100 Most Influential People of 2019, received his education from Nankai University in China, majoring in microelectronics and software engineering. Before starting his first company in 2009, he worked for Microsoft and Kuxun, a Chinese travel website.
>
> Unlike other Chinese tech giants who are focused on domestic market growth, ByteDance - which is 40% owned by US venture capital firms -

has concentrated on expanding into the global market. Interestingly, Zhang's management style of ByteDance is modeled on Google's management style.

As a result of Zhang Yiming's vision and leadership, ByteDance had several successful products in addition to "TikTok" including: a news app "Toutiao" that attracted tens of millions of followers daily (Toutiao's platform contained a missing person alert that helped find 13,116 missing persons as of 2020); an AI research lab led by a former executive from Microsoft Research Asia; an online education app "Gogokid "that connected children with native English-speaking tutors, and a ride-hailing application "Didi Chuxing".

Over the past few years, ByteDance has faced serious scrutiny on three occasions from the Chinese government: in 2018 by Chinese regulators for improper content of its news app "Neihan Duanzi"; in 2019 by US regulators due to TikTok's violation of children's online privacy protection; and in 2020 by Chinese regulators due to its collaborative tool "Feishu"'s potential circumventing of internet censorship attempts.

Tiktok and "Douyin" (the latter is the former's Chinese version) have been popular since 2017 while the former was caught in diplomatic tussling between the US and China in 2020. ByteDance announced its new division "BytePlus" in April 2021 with the intention of selling Tiktok.

ByteDance's platform supports 800 million daily active users and over 1 billion accumulated users across all content platforms. In 2018, ByteDance became the world's most valuable startup with a valuation of $75 billion, surpassing Uber, and in April 2021 announced its IPO plan was valued at $185 billion.

On May 20, 2021, 38-year-old Zhang Yiming, an AI coding genius, announced his resignation as CEO will occur by the end of the year to better focus on the company's long-term strategy as well as to provide a public service to the country. Zhang named his college roommate, current HR head of ByteDance, Liang Rubo, to be his successor.

There are different opinions regarding Zhang's resignation. Some think his resignation is a strategic move to allow Liang to navigate the rising tide of Chinese regulations targeting tech giants, while others believe ByteDance's planned IPO will significantly increase Zhang's wealth and draw considerable media attention; therefore, Zhang's resignation is to avoid potential adverse publicity with being a wealthy entrepreneur within the current social climate.

Zhang Yiming's resignation letter became public knowledge while I was writing this chapter. In contrast to companies that I have studied, Zhang Yiming's leadership style centered on "social entrepreneurship" with recognition that retreating from leadership and installing a competent executive would soon benefit the company. Zhang Yiming represents the new generation of Chinese entrepreneurs, who grew up in an advanced technology era, sharing the same senses of purpose and "social mission" as those from more developed economies.

This generation will re-shape Chinese companies that differ entirely from older generation Chinese companies which either established controlled structures that heavily relied on their founders' charisma and personal commitment, or which were deeply influenced by traditional family business mindsets that have struggled with a leadership transition process from founders to their children or other family member successors. We may find that these young entrepreneurs and companies under their leadership will bring positive influences on Chinese companies' business purposes, corporate cultures, CG development and ESG adoption.

Upon conclusion of this chapter, I believe it is appropriate to quote from Zhang Yiming's resignation letter:

"With our business growing well, it is time to think about how we cannot simply scale, but make innovative, meaningful, long-term progress towards our mission to 'Inspire Creativity, Enrich life'." – Zhang Yiming (A Letter from Yiming on May 19, 2020, from ByteDance's website)

Chapter 9

Future Trends of Regional Agreements and Partnerships

China's quick recovery from the COVID-19 pandemic enabled the country to prepare for the next stage of its economic growth and global position. However, perpetually complicated globalization has created an intricate interdependence among many countries across the globe, so no country can consistently grow if the remaining countries of the world are struggling. Helping those countries who suffered deeply during the crisis and contributing to rebuilding the regional and international ecosystem, while seeking its own opportunities has inevitably become China's task and mission for the coming years.

On the other hand, the increasing tension between China and the US due to their relationship turning from strategic partners to strategic competitors is concurrently impacted by the accelerating pace of the ESG movement that has expanded to the rest of the world. As a result, a multitude of divergent reactions including concerns from Western and emerging countries regarding Chinese companies' business practice and ESG performance have been voiced. There are vociferous demands for improvement! The tension has also forced China and other major countries to reconsider their global strategies and roles in the current international business climate.

Although the global business landscape in the post COVID-19 era offers more opportunities and challenges for China and Chinese companies, for the purposes of this book, I will focus on reviewing three regional agreements and partnerships, in which China is the dominant country, so addressing these opportunities and challenges and their resulting effects on the country's CG development and ESG movements are of the utmost relevance.

Forming productive partnerships with other emerging market

countries and neighboring countries has been China's long-term strategy, most notably the recent Regional Comprehensive Economic Partnership (RCEP), China's BRI launched in 2013, and the Forum on China-Africa Cooperation (FOCAC) that was initiated 20 years ago.

Signing RCEP agreements that had been negotiated and ratified since 2012 seems like a natural move for China and other member countries of the region, due to the assistance needed for some member countries to recover from the pandemic, and China's desire to strengthen its influence in the region as well as to advance its internationalization strategies.

However, China and Chinese companies have struggled with the rising criticisms regarding project quality and other ESG problems from its BRI project and other African projects. In addition to various financial and operational challenges encountered to BRI projects due to the COVID-19 disruption, a number of economic and political problems were revealed by the China-Africa collaboration including projects that were completed and delivered to host countries.

How can China continue its BRI and collaboration with African countries? What can Chinese companies do differently in RCEP agreements as a result of lessons learned from both BRI and China-Africa projects? First, let us start by understanding RCEP and the elements that distinguish this new agreement from others.

9.1. Regional Comprehensive Economic Partnership

Historically, international and regional economic agreements and partnership frameworks have been led by more developed countries, and most of the finished products resulting from these trade agreements have been shipped to more developed economies' markets due to their consumption demand and ability, and emerging markets countries' lack of efficient and effective trade rules and tariffs systems. That dilemma applied to most Asian trade agreements in the past, including the Comprehensive and Progressive Agreement for Trans-Pacific Partnership (CPTPP) that became effective in December 2018, and its predecessor, the Trans-Pacific Partnership (TPP) which became effective in February 2016. Because of CPTPP's structure with more developed countries taking leading roles, this Asia-Pacific regional trade agreement has not proceeded because of those countries' dissatisfaction with the agreement outcomes (eg the US withdrawal from TPP, and a tariff disagreement between Canada and major Asia-Pacific counties). If the effectiveness of a regional trade agreement is dominated by countries who are not part of the region, what does a regional trade agreement really mean to the region? Who are the ultimate beneficiaries from a regional agreement?

The answers to these questions may be a few of the motivating factors found in the initial Regional Comprehensive Economic Partnership (RCEP) framework that began in 2012. The RCEP was signed in November 2020 and contained two major differences from prior Asia-Pacific regional trade agreements: The RCEP is led by China, an emerging markets country; and the RCEP is a partnership trade agreement exclusively designed for Asian interests.

Since the worldwide business community is still engaged in post-pandemic economic recovery, what roles will the RCEP play in Asian and global economies? How will China help member countries recover from the pandemic and accelerate ESG adoption simultaneously? What opportunities will the RCEP create for China? Let us review the following highlights of the RCEP to seek answers:

9.1.1. What We Should Know About RCEP

RCEP is the world's largest trade bloc. According to World Bank's 2019 GDP data, RCEP member countries' total GDP is $25.84 trillion compared to $24.37 trillion from the US-Mexico-Canada North American Free Trade Agreement (NAFTA) and $18.85 trillion from the EU Economic Area. As of 2020, RCEP's fifteen-member countries represent 30% of world's GDP and population and its GDP percentage is expected to grow to 50% by 2030 according to an HSBC report. Since all member countries are from the Asia-Pacific region with complete cohesion anticipated by January 2022, the RCEP will create a regional supply chain ecosystem, introduce and encourage financial investment, and instill intellectual property protection rules to promote free trade in Asia.

RCEP member countries' diversity. Compared to previous Asian trade agreements, RCEP members are much more diverse in many aspects, including population sizes, wealth levels, geography (inland and archipelago countries), services and products trading, and types of imports and exports. Having smaller sized countries (eg Laos) and others with unstable political environments (eg Myanmar) will create more complications and less ambition to the RCEP. However, this diversity will also make the RCEP more influential for the region's sustainable economy development, peoples' livelihood improvement, regulatory practices, social responsibility, environmental protection, and perhaps political stability.

China's leading role in RCEP is essential for RCEP member countries' economic recovery. The COVID-19 crisis worsened the economic situation of many members countries such as Laos and Cambodia, who have been struggling, while Thailand has had to shut down, and the Philippines' infections numbers continue to increase. At the time of writing, most more developed countries in the world, including the US and UK, are also struggling to reopen their domestic economies despite the oncoming wave of COVID-19 variances. China's effective control of the COVID-19 crisis and the country's rapid economic recovery enabled it to be one of few countries with positive GDP growth in 2020 and promising expansion in 2021 and the coming years. China's stable economic growth and continued growth of the Chinese middle-class, and consumers' purchasing power and consumption of imported goods and services will create many opportunities to help member countries' economies recover once the RCEP becomes effective.

IP rights coverage is the most advanced improvement of the RCEP compared to any other Asian trade agreement. Unfortunately, Asia is well-known for its lack of commitment to IP rights protection and trade deals previously agreed upon neglected to acknowledge the seriousness of its application. Inserting IP rights coverage in the RCEP indicates the RCEP's intention to establish high-standard trade orders and a healthier ecosystem in the region. China has started to take serious action on IP protection since the beginning of 2019 with the establishment of a new IP Court of Appeals, new regulations on IP disputes, provisions in the 2019 Foreign Investment Law for IP transaction restrictions, and the most recent patent law amendment in June 2021. Due to an increasing number of IP ownership rights by Chinese companies and the proliferation of technology in China, Chinese IP protection regulations are needed not only to protect IP rights from more developed countries like the US, but also to protect Chinese companies' IP ownership rights. As discussed in Chapter 8, technology independence is one of the most important focuses of China's 14th FYP. As a result, further regulatory and funding support for research and development will occur, and the fostering of IP ownership rights by Chinese companies will further change the mentality and understanding of IP protection in China. With China's "dual circulation" strategy proposed from the 14th FYP, its IP protection improvement will undoubtedly encourage IP rights protection in its partner countries and other RCEP member countries.

The RCEP marks the first time an agreement has occurred between China, Japan and South Korea, three of the four largest economies in Asia. Will the RCEP help build economic co-operation among these three countries to create positive energy for development in the Asia-Pacific region? The predictions are two-fold at the moment. Signing the agreement is the first step and a positive sign of the three countries intention to work together, however substantial collaboration among them requires "win-win" strategies which need further discussion and exploration, as well as a global economic development scheme and progress from these three countries to stimulate economic collaboration to surpass historical problems between them.

9.1.2. Opportunities and Challenges for China as RCEP's Leading Country

Enhance products and services exchanges and capital market collaboration in the Asian market. It took China over thirty years to become the "The Factory of The World" with a comprehensive supply chain ecosystem that is essential to the chain's development. With the ongoing global supply chain relocation from China to other Asian countries, China's supply chain support system will continuously serve and benefit global supply chain development in other Asian countries toward the establishment of a regional supply chain system. In addition to the growing consumer demands from Chinese markets that will bring more manufacturers and export opportunities for member countries, China's perpetual technology development and growth requires a larger consumer market to absorb new products. The RCEP will create more win-win partnerships between China and other Asian countries for products, services and technology exchanges.

Due to the size of RCEP's member countries' collective GDP, successfully leading RCEP can also help China enhance its influence on the region's capital market and ESG movement.

Strengthen Chinese economic influence and currency usage. Although a nation's economic growth normally stirs wide acceptance and utilization of its currency in the global market, the pace of international usage of Chinese currency – the RMB - in both trade settlements and the countries' foreign currency reserve has been behind the pace of China's economic growth. (Details regarding the RMB internationalization will be discussed in Chapter 10). Despite the fact that the Chinese government's restricted currency control and the time needed for China to prove its stable economic growth are the major factors for the RMB's global utilization, establishing a solid "currency zone" is a pre-requisite condition for China to promote its currency within the global market. The potential increase of trade and capital market transactions among RCEP countries led by China could generate broader utilization of the Chinese RMB. If China can lead and contribute to the region's economic recovery and promote a subsequent increase in RMB usage along with other RCEP's members' continued collective GDP growth, the RCEP will become a great opportunity for China to establish its "economic zone" and "currency zone".

Accelerate ESG performance. ESG adoption is a big challenge for RCEP at the moment. The RCEP has received warranted criticism from more developed countries for its lack of labor rules, worker and human rights, and environmental protection, due to the fact that many RCEP member countries are under-developed, with a focus on key economic issues, and RCEP was launched in 2012, when ESG adoption was not widely accepted. However, the worldwide ESG movement (in part at least arising out of severe disasters from climate changes) requires the world – including RCEP countries - to commit to ESG integration, even though most RCEP countries are presently fighting for economic recovery and economic growth simultaneously. With China's active ESG movement driven by the country's top asset management firms and corporations, there is considerable likelihood and also ample opportunities to initiate and influence RCEP member countries' ESG awareness and compliance via ESG compliance requirements for investment projects by asset management firms (please see details in case study 7.1., Ping An Group's ESG adoption, in Chapter 7), or by supply chain ESG integration strategies initiated by Chinese companies (such as case study 7.2., Xiaomi ESG Integration, in Chapter 7).

Will China be able to accelerate RCEP member countries' economic growth? Can China have sufficient influence on other member countries who rely on China's rapid economic growth and quickly-evolving ESG revolution? Likewise with Japan and South Korea, would China be able to continue its unceasing momentum and develop successful collaborations with these two countries within the RCEP umbrella? Can China diplomatically manage the contemporary tension between itself and Australia without causing harm to the amicability within the RCEP?

The RCEP offers tremendous opportunities as well as challenges to China!

Fortunately, the RCEP is not the first regional partnership led by China. By virtue of the experiences and lessons learned from the BRI and China-Africa projects over the past few decades, the Chinese government and companies should become more sophisticated with their handling of economic and political matters, and more conscious of the development of sustainable strategies and other social and economic impacts on host countries. Next, let us review China's experiences from the BRI and African projects.

9.2. China's Belt and Road Initiative and Feedback

China's Belt and Road Initiative (BRI) is a global infrastructure development strategy launched by the Chinese government in 2013, with the initiative to increase China's economic links to Southeast Asia, Central Asia, Russia and Central and Eastern Europe. The BRI expanded to Latin American Countries in 2017 and has grown quickly since then. The most recent data in 2021 shows the BRI includes 139 countries (39 in Sub-Saharan Africa, 34 in Europe and Central Asia, 25 in East Asia and the Pacific, 18 in Latin America and Caribbean, 17 in Middle East and North Africa, and 6 in South Asia). These countries, including China, represent 63% of the world's population (the BRI covers 65 countries (including China), equivalent to 61.9% of the world's population, according to 2016 data).

Regardless of the debates regarding the BRI's political intention and diplomatic ambitions, the multibillion-dollar BRI investment platform has positively impacted the economic status of the developing world. Most BRI projects are in the infrastructure, energy, and transportation sectors. According to 2018 data, the BRI initiated projects to build 203 bridges, 199 powerplants, and 41 pipelines, and information from the China Global Television Network (CGTN) shows that China had signed 200 co-operation agreements with 138 countries and 30 international organizations using the BRI framework.

9.2.1. Positive Economic and Social Impacts

BRI has drawn considerable attention over the past several years and various discussions have been triggered. For the purpose of this book, I will only highlight BRI's major impacts on partner countries, ESG questions raised from these projects, and the challenges China is facing in the BRI's future.

Statistical data shows that the 82 overseas co-operation zones jointly built by China and countries under the BRI have created 300,000 local jobs and significantly contributed to local economic development and an improvement in peoples' livelihoods. Due to the increased dependence for external funding of African countries' infrastructure development of railways, roads, ports, and energy, BRI projects have contributed towards many African countries essential strategy for future economic development. Regardless of today's critics regarding China's motivation of these projects, the truth is that railways, bridges, pipelines, and powerplants are needed for these countries and their people. Statistics show that at least 39 African countries have been covered by BRI, and an unofficial study estimates that China's investment in Africa through the BRI is around $5 billion per year. Selected BRI projects include telecommunications in Ethiopia, Sudan, and Ghana and railroad projects in Nigeria, Gabon, and Mauritania that have made tremendous improvements in local peoples' lives. As a result, over time China became a source of hope for people from some African countries. During a recent interview with Lynda Kahari, an experienced African banking executive who moved to Port Moresby, Papua New Guinea for a new position in 2020, Ms. Kahari shared her concerns regarding Port Moresby's outdated telecom infrastructure system that prevented her and many others from working at home during the pandemic. She also shared her experiences in Africa detailing how China built infrastructure systems to improve local peoples' lives, and on a personal note, the gratefulness of her aged mother in Africa who had received a vaccination supported by the Chinese government while the vaccine shortages are still a big issue for many developing countries at the time of writing.

However, despite the positive impacts created by BRI projects, an increasing number of questions have been raised over the past few years concurrent with the COVID-19 crisis, and the escalation in ESG-related concerns of BRI projects.

9.2.2. Challenges for BRI's Future Development

Economic and Diplomatic Challenges. With the rise of debt-forgiveness requests and potential loan defaults due to the COVID-19 crisis, some BRI projects have been delayed as many African countries' debts are from BRI related projects. China has joined other G20 countries to agree to debt-service payments suspension from 73 countries until the end of 2021. How will the Chinese government manage the collateral assets of these default countries? Will China renegotiate new loan agreements with member countries and possibly risk or harm its reputation, or resolve to help these countries? Such are questions that will require sophisticated consideration and diplomatic responses that may incur economic consequences.

ESG-related challenges from BRI partner countries. The worldwide ESG movement has stirred an energy transformation trend as well as ESG concerns in BRI partner countries. Several impasses exist so a few are worth mentioning: Egypt postponed a coal-fired power plant construction project funded by China; Bangladesh cancelled a coal plant plan; and many African countries raised environmental questions for China's BRI projects. In addition, pressure has been mounting from partner countries' unions regarding labor rights considerations and controversies regarding local labor law, and workforce equality have recently been intensifying in Central Asian countries including Kazakhstan, Kyrgyzstan, Tajikistan, and Uzbekistan. The workforce related issues of BRI projects on host countries' local communities and working people will be further examined by various local and international organizations. Since addressing and improving these socially-related factors have become one of the priorities on the Chinese government's agenda, properly handling these questions with local organizations and governments may be challenging, but could also lead to increased opportunities for China to amplify its economic influence in partner countries through improving the ESG performance of BRI projects. On the other hand, because of various environmental and social issues related to China's BRI projects and a lack of transparency during the BRI projects' process, there may be potential for cancellation of unfavorable agreements. For example, Tanzania's new president requested the cancellation of a $10 billion port project, and Nigerian legislators voted to further review all loan agreements related to Chinese projects.

Competition from the Group of Seven industrialized countries (G7). During the most recent G7 summit that occurred in June 2021, a new infrastructure financing plan was agreed to by leaders of the G7 countries to counter China's BRI, in addition to offering "higher-quality" support to help developing countries in Latin America, the Caribbean, Africa, and the Indo-Pacific region with a broader range of services for them to recover from the COVID-19 pandemic by using G7 models and standards. The demand for high-quality physical, digital, and health infrastructure will cost approximately $40 trillion through to 2035, according to a World Bank estimation. Currently, there is no timeframe or pertinent details regarding the funding sources of G7's proposal.

Nevertheless, competition is always good for developing countries and the global economy, regardless from whom, which model, and what standards that will be applied for the infrastructure systems and other projects needed for the developing world for recovery and further development. Given the competition between the G7 and China, the world should expect better quality support (including collaboration terms, project quality, operation transparency) for developing countries. In addition, the competition from the G7 will also stimulate Chinese companies' ESG improvements in their overseas operations.

9.3. China-Africa Collaboration

China-Africa economic collaboration started in the 1970s marked by the 1,860 km Tazara Railway (from Tanzania to Zambia), a turnkey project financed and supported by China. Bilateral collaboration between China and Africa has been rapidly growing in recent decades based on African countries' economic development needs and China's well-known skills for building infrastructures. Infrastructure has been one of the most important China-Africa collaboration areas.

9.3.1. Impacts and Challenges

China-Africa collaboration has had a profound economic and social impact on African countries providing job opportunities, education assistance, and economic growth. Since the first FOCAC conference held in Beijing in 2000, China's direct investment in African countries has skyrocketed more than one hundred-fold, and bilateral trade volume has grown twenty-fold. According to a 2017 McKinsey survey of Chinese firms operating in Africa, 89% of employees of these Chinese firms are Africans (applying the percentage to over 10,000 Chinese-owned companies in Africa indicates several millions of Africans were hired by these companies at the time of the survey). In addition to Chinese direct investment in Africa that are mainly in infrastructure, resource-oriented mining, and agriculture sectors, the Chinese government, through its agencies, has become one of the major scholarship aid providers for Africa over the past few years. A 2020 UNESCO Global Education Monitoring Report referring to data provided by Education Sub-Saharan Africa (ESSA) shows that the Chinese government was the largest provider of that year with 12,000 scholarship opportunities for students in Sub-Saharan Africa, and China has increased its three-year scholarships for 2019-2022 to 50,000 (a 67% increase from 30,000 in the previous three-year period). Global scholarship aid (including those from China) created undergraduate, postgraduate and secondary education opportunities which were not otherwise available for local students in Sub-Saharan Africa countries.

However, China-Africa collaboration is facing serious economic and political challenges including environmental and social issues similar to those of the BRI projects. Due to the longer history of China-Africa collaboration compared to the BRI projects, business practices and culture conflict issues revealed by China-African projects have provided valuable learning opportunities for Chinese multinationals' global growth. The brief case study of Bui Dam Hydroelectricity Project in Ghana below highlights the workforce management challenges.

Case study 9.1. SinoHydro-Ghana Bui Dam Hydroelectricity Project – Calling for Regulation Improvements for Multinational Companies' Home and Host Countries

> Bui Dam is located in Bui National Park in Ghana. The Dam started operations in 2013, generates 400MW of power, provides water for irrigation to nearly 30,000 hectares of land, improved the local fishing industry, and attracts tourists to the region. However, due to the fact that the Dam's construction consumed a sizable land amount and caused resettlement of 1,216 people, fish and animals in the region, the project has been facing challenges from environmentalists.

The Bui Dam has been a controversy for almost one century because of political, environmental and local energy demand factors. The idea of building Bui Dam was initiated in 1925 when planning and discussions involving various experts and organizations from Great Britain and Australia occurred. The project construction started in the late 1970s with funding support from the World Bank, but stalled due to local military coups until restarting in the early 1990s. There were many economic and ecology debates and discussions from the 1990s to the 2000s regarding the necessity of completing the construction of the dam until the project was resumed in 2002.

In 2005, Ghana government authorities accepted a bid from Sino-hydro (the project's construction contractor) with funding support from the China Import-Export Bank. The construction started in 2007 and the dam began operations in 2013. The total project cost was $790 million and loans through the Chinese Export-Import bank totalled $562 million (71% of the total project cost). The size of the loan amount made the SinoHydro-Ghana Bui Dam Hydroelectricity (BUI) Project the largest Chinese investment in Ghana.

However, a complicated workforce situation of the construction project made workforce management quite challenging. During the project's duration from 2007 to 2013, a total of 7,000 employees were reported as having worked on the project that consisted of multiple tiers (direct-hire and contracted workers, workers with different skill levels, and workers of both genders). The workforce was comprised of employees from several countries (including China, Ghana, and Pakistan).

As a result, even after the project was completed. SinoHydro, a Chinese SOE hydropower engineering and construction multinational company, faced critics regarding labor-related matters due to various complications over the past several years. The dispute matters focused on:

- *Lack of education opportunity and job security*
- *Unfair compensation due to lack of pay transparency*
- *Insufficient consideration of workforce safety and work-related injury compensation*
- *Management's poor relationships with trade unions including its mishandling of a 2008 workers' strike*

Although the BUI project benefits both partner countries' economic and political needs in addition to an improvement in local peoples' livelihoods, its size and six-year duration (from 2007 to 2013) and the complications and challenges experienced during the project are probably incomprehensible. The BUI project has become study material for researchers regarding Chinese multinationals in Africa with key topics focusing on Chinese companies' compliance with local labor laws and their relationships with local labor unions, unfair competition, and the lack of environmental and local community considerations.

For the purpose of this book, let us focus on reviewing lessons that should be learned from the BUI project workforce related issues and how these lessons can help improve Chinese companies' ESG performance.

9.3.2. Major Problems of Chinese Multinationals' Overseas Operations

Lack of pressure for transparency, fair competition, and ESG compliance. As most Chinese multinationals' overseas projects in Africa are funded by Chinese financial institutions, the government's funding support provides these companies with better opportunities to win projects that are not funded by the international financial institutions (eg the World Bank) or local governments. However, the supervision and auditing mechanisms with funding and operational processes are not comparable to projects funded by the World Bank or other international organizations. As a result, these Chinese companies do not have the same pressure from Chinese financial institutions, contrary to international fund providers such as the World Bank who requires more restrictive compliance.

It is vitally important to understand that the BUI project was completed in 2013, when Chinese companies' overseas expansions were proliferating and most of these companies fixated on business development rather than CG practice and ESG performance. Today, transparency and fair competition are important criteria for good CG consideration, and ESG improvement, all of which require serious examination for Chinese multinationals' overseas operations not only in Africa, but in all host countries.

The key to solving this problem lies with closing the gap between

Chinese CG standards and international standards. Given China is on an ESG-revolution path to align its regulatory standards with countries which are leading on ESG considerations, Chinese financial institutions will implement strict funding requirements (such as those in the Ping An Insurance Group found in case study 7.1.) for bidding, investing, and operational information disclosure to encourage and help Chinese multinationals' CG development and ESG performance improvement.

Lack of effort to participate to local business communities. Most Chinese multinationals in Africa retain low profiles in host countries, similar to in other parts of the world. Other than business-related activities, Chinese companies traditionally do not get involved in local business affairs. Although the number of local employees of Chinese companies' African operations has been increasing over the years, the majority of Chinese executives assigned from China headquarters live in company provided housing facilities, that purposely isolate them from local communities mainly due to safety considerations, as well as language barriers.

This criticism echoes the injurious stories of Huawei and Tiktok, both of whom lacked efforts to build relationships with or contribute to local communities, which has been a historic weakness of Chinese multinationals regardless of the host countries' identities or locations. Perhaps the innovative approach and strategy of VIPKID as discussed in case study 7.3. can inspire Chinese companies to consider business mindset changes with new strategies for their future overseas development.

Lack of an independent voice of labor unions, fair job opportunities and labor law considerations. As discussed in Chapter 1, Chinese companies' unions are responsible for company events and certain employee benefits, which is a unique feature of Chinese companies' CG model. As a result, when Chinese multinationals operate in host countries, recognition of union independence and managing a beneficial relationship with a workplace's union becomes quite challenging for these companies. Chinese companies prefer to transfer employees from their headquarters to its overseas operations, which decreases job opportunities, especially management positions for the local workforce. In addition, many Chinese companies require longer working hours with or without providing compensation, and some overseas operations have reported hostile relationships between management and workplace unions.

These situations have revealed the requirement to understand and respect local business practices and compliance with local regulations. As we discussed in Chapter 5, multinationals' expansion strategies of imposing home country models to overseas operations that were employed by Western companies forty years ago are obsolete for modern multinational operations, including those from China. While the success of the "China model" has been embraced by many Chinese companies does not imply that foisting the "China model" on Chinese companies' overseas subsidiaries will lead to the same success. Furthermore, without understanding local practices and regulations, unilaterally implementing or enforcing the "China model" may cause unnecessary conflicts with local organizations, local governments, and international standards. In addition, remaining compliant with host countries' regulations is one of the most important CG functions for any organization. I trust that pointing out these issues and weaknesses will stir CG improvement.

Party Influence and government intervention. Since most Chinese multinationals similar to SinoHydro in Africa are SOEs, party influence is always a major concern within these multinationals, as are executives' dual roles in these companies. A case study from the Global Labor University summarized Chinese multinationals' successes in Africa as being based on five factors: cost advantage in overall project bidding; cheap capital offered by Chinese State-owned financial institutions; use of cheap local labor; access to cheap building materials; and political support from the Chinese government.

As discussed in earlier chapters of this book, the Chinese government's support is one of the key reasons for Chinese companies' successes, which also distinguishes Chinese multinationals from those of other emerging countries. After understanding this, perhaps the real concerns are the anticipated impact of party influence and government intervention on Chinese multinationals' CG practice, the transparency of information disclosure, checks and balances of a decision-making process, and the corporate culture regarding ESG matters.

9.3.3. Major Problems in Host Countries and Solutions in Home Countries

The research and studies of the SinoHydro-Ghana Bui Dam Project also revealed another element that contributes to these problems – the lack of a regulatory system in host countries. It is normal for multinationals to lower business operation standards in countries with loose regulatory controls and enforcement of environmental and workforce regulation compliance. Chinese multinationals are not the only corporations practicing bad business activities and performing unethical actions in developing countries. Multinationals from more developed countries share the same poor convention: for example, in 2020, the UK Supreme Court ruled against Shell Nigeria, Royal Dutch Shell's Nigerian subsidiary, in an oil-pollution lawsuit filed by Niger Delta communities who suffered from decades of pollution. The fact that the parent company - being a worldwide industry leader - follows international standards does not prohibit its subsidiary in developing countries from ignoring local environmental matters and the impact on local peoples' livelihoods.

Of course, there are many other factors in host countries that also allowed these countries to become victims of multinationals' careless behavior. Government corruption, lack of professional personnel, and educational resources are but a few. However, I believe that instead of blaming the poor for their poverty, the business world should focus on how parent companies and home countries of these multinationals can help improve business practices to avoid these problems.

I am convinced that the UK Supreme Court's ruling initiated one path in order to enforce multinationals' overseas operations: Multinationals will be held accountable for their overseas business activities and the resulting impact on host countries. To be fair, demands for improving home countries' regulation standards and an enforcement mechanism are essential to multinationals behavior in hosting countries. Thanks to the ESG movement, the Chinese government has been improving regulation standards to close the gap with international standards, and Chinese companies have been improving their operation standards resulting in an advanced position in the global ESG rating system. Consequently, the present time is appropriate for Chinese multinationals to seriously consider ESG compliance not only at home, but also in host countries.

As with many other international agreements and partnership frameworks, the success of these three collaborative agreements led by China were not singularly guaranteed by the intention of the participants, but by the behavior of partners and members who work together with mutual respect that benefits both them and the other members. I strongly believe that China and Chinese companies' success will be achieved by carefully executed role planning with predetermined goals that are tied to the demands of China's regulation standards and ESG performance improvement. Improving China's regulatory environment will also help reshape corporate culture which will positively influence a fresh business mindset of Chinese multinationals' leaders.

Of course, some critics questioning China's motivation in these regional initiatives allege political ambition over humanitarian and economic support, which adds another challenging layer to the complexity of these accusations and an accurate portrayal of China's true motive. Regardless of the myriad of critiques, an innocuous but challenging question for China's government's leaders to contemplate in order to attain global superpower status is: How will China handle these criticisms and improve its diplomatic approach with its global partners? The answer to this relevant question has the potential to positively persuade its adversaries.

Chapter 10
China's RMB Internationalization and the Future of Hong Kong

RMB's internationalization initiative started in 2003 and 2004 when RMB businesses for individuals were first established in Hong Kong and Macao, respectively. Hong Kong has been the largest RMB offshore center since then, and the first market for most of China's financial programmes promoting RMB's internationalization strategy. Therefore, it is impossible to talk about China's RMB internationalization without including Hong Kong as part of the discussion.

Over the past several decades, Hong Kong has been the first stop of most Chinese companies' "going global" strategy, and RMB internationalization is not only a mission to support the Chinese government's strategy, but also a great opportunity for these companies who have the capacity to capitalize on the regulator's incentives in an offshore RMB market in order to succeed, including the Hong Kong company for whom I worked. Please allow me to explain three important concepts before we start this chapter though – currency internationalization, the role of an offshore currency market, and the US dollar's dominant global currency position.

Currency internationalization is the process of one country's currency being used for international trade, investment and foreign currency reserves. Technically, currency internationalization should occur simultaneously with a countries' growing economic influence. The organic way to grow international use of a currency could happen from cross-border trading with three steps: First, the dominant party (usually the buyer) has the leverage to request trade settlement with its home country's currency due to considerations of exchange rate risk, exchange cost, and convenience; second, in order to set the payment amount of a foreign currency settlement, countries would have to either hedge on an exchange market to set the exchange rate at the time of payment, or reserve the foreign currency for payment on an agreed date; third, over time, if the dominant party's home currency has established a stable value, so countries may find the foreign currency reserve can not only help international trade settlement, but also help prevent local currencies' value fluctuation. These countries then will increase their reserve amount and tie their currencies to the reserved currency to stabilize their own currency's value and economy. Growing up in a southwest China province that shares a border with Myanmar, Laos, and Vietnam, I witnessed the first two steps of organic growth of RMB's use by these neighboring countries in the 1980s and 1990s.

However, a currency internationalization process is much more complicated as it involves a country's development strategies regarding monetary, financial, economic, and political policies, all of which vary depending on those countries. For the purpose of this book, I will only focus on China's RMB internationalization status and potential opportunities for its future development. For readers who are interested in learning more, I will list my research sources in the reference section. Hong Kong was the first and still is the largest offshore RMB center and will continue its role to accelerate RMB offshore market development for many years to come.

What, then, is the role of an offshore currency market? An offshore currency market is an economic function to promote the global use of a country's currency. The most important aspect of an offshore currency market's development is to help separate a country's risk from its currency risks and improve the financial stability of its onshore currency market. Using the US dollar as an example, after the 9/11 terrorist attacks in September 2001, US central banks were able to maintain normal operations of US dollar securities held in European countries. This example not only shows how its offshore dollar market helped the US during the crisis, but also demonstrates how it strengthened the US economy and its currency stability, which sustained the dollar as the dominant global currency over the past many decades. Over the following years, the US continued to increase its offshore vs onshore deposit ratio of 10.6% in 2004, 19.64% in 2007, and 25.5% in 2008, according to a 2010 Bank for International Settlements report.

The US dollar's dominant global currency position can be easily explained due to its strong position in the IMF's Special Drawing Rights (SDR) basket before and after RMB's joining. SDR basket currencies' assigned weights before the RMB joined were the US dollar (41.9%), the Euro (37.4%), the Japanese Yen (9.4%) and the British Pound (11.3%), while the assigned weights after it joined in November 2015 were the US dollar (41.73%), the Euro (30.93%), the RMB (10.92%), the Japanese Yen (8.33%), and the British Pound (8.09%). The US dollar's percentage did not change much, but other currencies had to forgo certain shares to the RMB. Therefore, promoting RMB internationalization is a "must-have" strategy for China to enhance its political and economic position in the world despite anticipated resistance from the US and other more developed economies.

Now, let us zoom into some highlights to understand China's RMB Internationalization and the future of Hong Kong.

10.1. China's RMB Internationalization

The rapidly-evolving and worldwide adoption of Chinese mobile payment platforms Alipay and WeChat made the RMB familiar to the rest of the world. Outside of China, though, the RMB is not yet easily found in currency exchanges, which simply indicates the limitation of the RMB's global use, in contrast to China's economic size and Chinese companies' global growth. Comparing the latest available statistics regarding the uses of RMB and the US dollar on two basic functions of an internationalized currency - trade settlement and foreign currency reserve - RMB internationalization is still in the embryonic stage. As of May 2021, the RMB accounted for only 4% of global trade transaction settlements, in contrast to 88% using US dollars, according to 2020 International Money Funds (IMF) data. Meanwhile, the share of RMB reserves held by central banks that year was 2%, while 59% used the US dollar. *Therefore, RMB internationalization still has a long way to go!*

Although joining the IMF's SDR basket in 2015 has been the most remarkable milestone for the RMB, minimal progress was made in the following years until the rise in urgency for RMB's internationalization as a consequence of the tension between the US and China started in 2018. Given an escalating concern about RMB's risks due to its dependence on the US dollar, focus on promoting RMB Internationalization has increased since then. As a result, international use of the RMB significantly progressed in 2019 in trading settlements (an 18.2% increase from 2018), capital transactions[1] (a 26.7% increase from 2018), and securities investments[2] (a 49.1% increase from 2018), while Chinese domestic RMB financial assets[3] held by foreign entities increased 30.3% from 2018, according to a 2020 PBOC report. This momentum will certainly continue in the coming years.

RMB Internationalization is important for China without doubt.

---

[1] Capital transaction includes Inward and Outward Direct Investment, Cross-Border RMB Cash Pooling transactions, and the issuing of RMB international bonds.

[2] Securities investment including Bond Investment, Shanghai-Hong Kong Stock Connect and Shenzhen-Hong Kong Stock Connect, RQGII.

[3] Domestic RMB financial assets include stocks, bonds, loans, and deposits.

What are the obstacles and the progress? What then is the impact on the world?

10.1.1. The Importance of RMB Internationalization

The 2008 global finance crisis highlighted the risks of the global financial system due to its reliance on one currency. With China becoming one of the largest trading countries as well as a major economy within emerging markets, increasing RMB Internationalization will benefit both China and the global business community.

For China. China's trading volume and increasing use of the RMB as trade settlements will reduce exchange rate risks and make Chinese trading companies more competitive in the global market. In addition, developing a strong offshore RMB market will make China's economy more resilient.

The slow progress of RMB internationalization indicates that China has not found the opportunity to break through the bottleneck created by the domination of the USD and EUR in international trade, investment settlement, and foreign currency reserves. Many improvements are still needed to leap forward such as: ascending the global value chain in order to acquire settlement currency leverage; establishing a China-centered economic zone with investment and trade opportunities to promote RMB use; having a system of strong financial institutions that includes offshore financial markets to provide services for Chinese companies and other multinationals; and building a stable economy with clear access channels to attract foreign investment in RMB assets.

For the global business community. China's neighboring countries and global partners will benefit from China's stable economic growth and currency value. Settling trade with the RMB can reduce the exchange rate cost and preserve transactional efficiency without using the US dollar or another global currency as the mediating currency. Because of lessons learned from the 2008 global financial crisis, member countries in an RMB-centered currency zone can be protected from the external currency risks of a dollar or Euro zone. Eventually, global currency diversity will provide global financial resilience. According to a 2018 study by Nomura Institute of Capital Market Research, a Japan-based research institution specializing in financial and capital market studies and policy proposals, currency competition will stabilize the international monetary system, and a "tripolar system centered on the dollar, euro and RMB would serve as a safety net for the global economy should the dollar regime collapse". However, establishing a "tripolar system" requires that a RMB currency zone be recognized and supported by Dollar- and Euro-zone dominated countries.

However, the resistance from the US and other countries cannot be underestimated, without analyzing the many reasons that led to the resistance. The simplest explanation for this is the amounts of US dollar debts and reserves held by countries during the US dollar's global expansion over the past several decades. Any potential for the US dollar to lose its stability and value could put these countries at significant currency and financial risk. Therefore, it is not likely to be possible to make significant progress in the RMB's internationalization without collaboration by the global community, and this process takes time.

10.1.2. The Progress of RMB Internationalization

The complexity of the RMB's internationalization during its early stages, despite much potential and some uncertainties, will continue to increase in strength. What has the Chinese government done to promote it? How will China measure its progress? I found that three currency internationalization prerequisites proposed in the same study by the Nomura Institute of Capital Market Research can be helpful to understand: *domestic regulation reform* to allow unencumbered capital transactions of the domestic financial market for both residents and non-residents; *economic and currency zone* establishment; and *international recognition and comparable positions* with other currency zones. Let us review a series of selected programmes launched chronologically since the 2000s by Chinese authorities with the purposes of opening financial markets, promoting offshore RMB markets, and liberalizing capital control regulations, then examine the RMB's internationalization progress from these three dimensions:

Qualified Foreign Institutional Investor (QFII)[4] *(launched in 2002), RQFII*[5]*(launched in 2011)*. QFII and RQFII are sibling programmes containing quotas, and the latter offers fewer restrictions for participants' qualification. Both QFII and RQFOO enable qualified foreign investors to invest directly in mainland China's stock markets (the SSE and SZSE). Although the Chinese government has initiated a copious number of reforms to simplify rules and remove restrictions of both programmes (including eliminating the quotas in 2019), the restrictions and barriers for investors to move money from China has offset the effectiveness of these two programmes. Further reforms to relax fund outflow restrictions will encourage more investments through both programs.

Dim Sum[6] *Bonds*. Dim Sum Bonds are RMB- designated bonds issued outside of China as a channel to allow foreign investors to buy RMB-designated assets. Dim Sum Bonds issuers can be either Chinese or non-Chinese institutions. The bonds programme was launched in 2007 and Hong Kong has been its primary market since then. Dim Sum Bonds emerged in 2010 and 2011 and their popularity has faded due to the RMB's volatility in 2015 and 2016, which indicates that investors' appetites for Dim Sum Bonds are heavily focused on the stability of the RMB's value.

Pilot programs and Free Trade Zones. To enable RMB international settlements, the Chinese government introduced a pilot program in four cities in 2008, then extended the program throughout the country a couple of years later. Today, all trade and investment transactions with other parts of the world can be conducted in RMB. In addition, free trade zones have been established in nearly 20 provinces in China (including Shanghai, Guangdong, Tianjing, Fujian and Hainan) since 2013 to stimulate the RMB's flow between free trade accounts and foreign companies' onshore and offshore accounts.

---

[4] Qualified Foreign Institutional Investor (QFII) is the first programme to allow qualified foreign investors to invest in both SSE and SZSE. Although the QFII has operated using specific quotas and certain prerequisites mandated for qualified investors, the programme is China's first step to relax capital control and open its capital market.

[5] The RMB Qualified Foreign Institutional Investor (RQFII) programme was established to allow foreign institutional investors' RMB investment funds to be set up in Hong Kong and invested directly in the Chinese capital market.

[6] Dim Sum is a popular cuisine from southern China.

Offshore RMB markets and bilateral swap agreements. In 2009, the PBOC launched offshore RMB clearing houses to encourage offshore RMB business. The establishment of offshore RMB markets accelerated the RMB's use as a trade settlement currency and also enabled direct currency trade between participating countries without using the USD as a mediating currency. Hong Kong has been the major offshore RMB hub since then, followed by Singapore. In addition, China has engaged in currency swap agreements with 39 countries since 2009 to accelerate the development of offshore RMB markets. At the end of 2019, the total offshore RMB deposit amount was RMB3.7 trillion (three percent of onshore RMB totaled approximately RMB109 trillion). Compared to the ratio of the USD's offshore versus onshore deposit amounts listed in the early part of this chapter, there is a long way to go for RMB offshore market development.

Cross-border RMB cash pooling. A two-way, cross-border RMB cash pooling programme was launched in 2014 to enable channels for qualified Chinese and foreign multinationals to move RMB across borders, providing the amount is within the quota's restrictions. The programme also enabled RMB loan-granting abroad. The cross-border cash pooling programme was extended to multiple currencies in 2019. Feedback about the programme has been quite positive. However, there are potential international tax issues (such as interest deductibility, transfer pricing, withholding tax and value added tax) if the tax body country differs from the cash location countries with cash pooling programmes, so participants need to understand possible tax repercussions. While cash pooling programmes were offered by Chinese banks as loan arrangements with no specific regulations at national levels, addressing these tax issues has become challenging without having unified regulatory guidance.

Interbank Payment System (CIPS). CIPS is the Chinese alternative to the Society for Worldwide Interbank Financial Telecommunication (SWIFT), the main international financial transaction network based in Belgium. CIPS was launched in 2015 under the supervision of the PBOC and is becoming the main channel of RMB cross-border transactions, allowing barriers to RMB's overseas use to be gradually removed. In 2019, CIPS processed RMB transactions across 96 countries and regions in Asia,

Europe, Africa, and Oceania totaling RMB135.7 billion ($19.4 billion) per day (SWIFT covers over 200 countries with $5 trillion daily transactions).

Panda Bonds. In contrast to Dim Sum Bonds which are RMB-designated bonds issued outside of China (mainly in Hong Kong) by Chinese or foreign issuers, Panda Bonds are RMB-designated bonds issued in the Chinese market by non-Chinese issuers. The issuing of Panda Bonds in 2015 was an important step in promoting RMB's international bond market's development providing low risk and stable returns. The amounts of Panda Bonds issued and the geographic area of issuers have not yet seen significant changes, but issuers have become more diversified. In 2019, a total of forty Panda Bonds were issued totaling RMB59.8 billion, of which twenty-three were issued by twelve non-Chinese-owned foreign entities, while over half were new issuers.

Removing the Cap for Foreign Ownership in Certain Financial Sectors. A remarkable milestone in China's financial market opening is the removal of the requirement for foreign financial institutions to have a local partner for certain financial sectors (eg mutual fund operations) in China. In July 2021, BlackRock submitted an application with the CSRC to launch its mutual fund product "BlackRock China New Horizon Mixed Securities Investment Fund" as the first foreign wholly-owned mutual fund enterprise in China. JPMorgan Chase and Morgan Stanley are currently planning to buy out their Chinese partners. Allowing sole foreign ownership in the financial sector will motivate more global funds to invest directly in the Chinese market.

Further opening of the financial markets will also stimulate the improvement of Chinese financial regulation standards and Chinese companies' ESG performance. For example, the wholly-owned Chinese subsidiaries of influential financial institutions such as BlackRock will be likely to stir more ESG momentum of shareholder engagement in the Chinese market, coinciding with shareholder interest protection actions as discussed in case study 8.1. Although the practice of shareholder engagements and shareholder interest protection is still very new in the Chinese market, further regulatory support from the Chinese authorities and practical guidance from these international advocates will accelerate the movement and help establish a trustworthy investment environment in China, and eventually support RMB internationalization.

In addition to the low percentage of RMB use in trade settlement and foreign currency reserve today that suggests a lack of these programmes' effectiveness, feedback from participants also revealed the fundamental challenges that these programmes face: a complicated processing procedure that includes less efficiency (eg the offshore RMB clearing process); a demand for further regulation reform (eg QFII and RQFII investors' concerns regarding barriers on moving money from China); and the concern regarding the RMB exchange rate stability (eg Dim Sum Bonds' marketability fading out in 2015). Further reforms to simplify application and operation procedures and improve regulatory guidance will enhance the effectiveness of these programmes. At the same time, discussions regarding transforming from a controlled-RMB exchange rate system to a market-oriented RMB exchange rate system were initiated in 2019 by the PBOC, but well-structured reforms to move the RMB to a floating exchange rate system and its interest rate liberalization are needed to free capital transactions and flow.

On the other hand, it is worth mentioning that the question regarding to what extent is *liberating capital control* necessary for a currency's internationalization has been a topic for ongoing debate and research. Research and study of the USD's boost in the international monetary market of the 1960s and 1970s combined with the US government's authorities' significant control of capital during the same period, further supports the argument that fully liberalizing capital control is not a necessary condition for a country's offshore currency market expansion, as long as the country establishes regulatory support to balance the potential risks of its offshore currency markets. However, I believe further study or practical experimenting are needed before any final conclusions are reached on this topic. RMB internationalization may also become another testimonial in the coming decades. For the time being, most cross-border fund transfers in and out from China still need approval by the State Administration for Foreign Exchange.

Although the above programmes did not significantly move RMB's internationalization forward, they made tremendous improvements toward enhancing China's financial regulation system while bettering CG standards in financial and other sectors in China's domestic market, both of which have become important parts of the foundation for

China's future economic growth and the promotion of RMB's global use. Compared to the progress on domestic market, RMB's internationalization status in the establishment of a regional currency zone and international recognition are still at very early stages. One important role of a regional currency zone is to protect member countries from exchange rate fluctuations from external influences. Japan previously led the Asia-Pacific region's economy for over four decades until China surpassed it in 2010. However, the Asia-Pacific regional currency zone has never, as of yet, been formed.

The BRI has created a platform for China to promote RMB Internationalization and build a RMB-centered currency zone. With institutions such as the Asian Infrastructure Investment Bank and Silk Road Fund - both of which were created to support the BRI - China has been trying to incentivize debt settlements using RMB and to develop RMB reserves for settlements of future accounts. Since its launching in 2013, the BRI has successfully helped spread China's influence and offered the RMB as a currency choice option, but the progress of RMB use on BRI projects is relatively slow. At the moment, a majority of BRI investments are still using USD rather than RMB. However, BRI projects' estimated completion dates are in 2049, so will China be able to accelerate the use of the RMB in future BRI projects? Given the ESG issues raised from BRI partner countries and the challenges and competitions from the west as discussed in Chapter 9, perhaps putting together a comprehensive strategy is necessary and urgent for China to better utilize the platform to improve social and economic impacts, enhance its financial institutions' supports, and leverage capital provider's power to promote the use of the RMB.

RCEP is another opportunity for China to build a regional economic and currency zone due to the influential size of RCEP member countries' collective GDP, although most Asian countries today still tie their currency to the USD in order to acquire stable exchange rates. Will China be able to capitalize on opportunities from large-scale trading agreements with its RCEP partners to stimulate RMB's internationalization? The "seed has been planted" and China needs to demonstrate the stability of its economic growth and continuous improvement of the country's institutions, which are the two fundamental elements needed to become the pre-eminent power in the region and build trust with RCEP member countries.

In the end, the RMB's wide acceptance as a trade settlement and foreign reserve currency requires *trust* – the *trust* in the stability of China's economic growth and the *trust* in a stable Chinese monetary policy and RMB exchange rate. Realistically the Chinese government's short-term goals should focus on building trust and escalating the RMB in the international currency hierarchy.

10.1.3. Chinese Digital Currency

Distinguished from bitcoin, which is not regulated, digital RMB, China's central bank digital currency (CBDC), is issued by China's central bank, the PBOC. The Chinese government's strategy involving digital RMB is identical to most other strategies, and takes a "gradualist approach". The development of digital RMB started in 2014; pilot programs in Shenzhen and Chengdu started in 2019, and another trial program in 2021 is to release RMB40 million ($6.2 million) to citizens in Beijing as a lottery to prepare for that currency's use by foreign visitors at the 2022 Beijing Winter Olympics.

Although digital RMB is still in its trial period, a cross-border CBDC trading platform has been initiated by the Hong Kong Monetary Authority (HKMA) and the Bank of Thailand, eight Thai banks and two Hong Kong banks have joined the platform to test digital currency-based cross-border transactions between Thailand and Hong Kong. The PBOC and Central Bank of the United Arab Emirates (UAS) also joined the platform during its second phase. Presently, the CBDC trading platform is exploring potential businesses with a desire to become a cross-border network for large financial institutions. In addition to the CBDC trading platform, Indonesia and China formed a partnership in September 2020 that allows direct exchange rates and interbank trading between Chinese RMB and the Indonesian rupiah instead of using the USD as a reserved currency for transaction settlements. Direct exchange rates and interbank trading are essential and symbolic steps for the CBDC trading platform to work efficiently.

Digital RMB can make foreign exchange transactions faster and less expensive, but the exchange rate will not be different between traditional and digital RMB. The CBDC trading platform might offer competitive foreign exchange rates and convenient options such as short-term, cross-border borrowing and transaction settling liquidity to attract more central banks to join. However, global adoption of CBDC trading platform requires interrelated international legal and regulatory standards in digital currency, digital taxes, and anti-money laundering. Therefore, digital RMB is an advanced function that improves the efficiency of cross-border RMB transactions at the moment, but is not a driver for RMB's internationalization.

10.1.4. What's Next?

Explore more opportunities through the BRI and RCEP. The BRI has created many opportunities for RMB internationalization in investing, financing, and trading. The Chinese government could encourage Chinese financial institutions to set up overseas branches and provide policy support for these overseas branches to extend their offshore RMB business; Also, opportunities with partner countries to increase the use of the RMB in investment and financing, and encouraging innovation regarding financial products to enhance the promotion of RMB internationalization should be considered. China is now the leading country of RCEP so exploring opportunities with partner countries will undoubtedly make better use of sizable trade agreements.

Explore more opportunities through global green economy transformation. The Chinese government's commitment to green energy, green infrastructure and green economy transformation will hopefully capitalize on opportunities through the country's emboldened green finance system. Will China be able to extend its economic influence in the transformation towards a global green economy? Will China's global partners collaborate?

As one of the Chinese government's long-term strategies, RMB's internationalization is time-sensitive, and its pace will be affected by the above conditions relative to domestic, regional, and international implications. RMB's internationalization can help build a healthier global financial system and will need support and acceptance from global partners and dominant countries from other currency zones. The long-term goal for China's RMB internationalization should not be the replacement of the USD or euro, but to become one of the designated currencies in the "tripolar system".

10.2. The Future of Hong Kong

As one of the international financial centers and a world tax haven, Hong Kong has been considered the window to and from China that attracted many foreign banks, financial institutions and corporations to establish regional headquarters and branches there over the past several decades.

However, political climate changes in Hong Kong in recent years, combined with the unpredicted COVID-19 pandemic, meant that many expats from Western countries returned to their home countries, while a number of Hong Kongers migrated to Singapore or other countries. Moreover, thousands of street shops and luxury stores have closed down due to the absence of mainland Chinese shoppers and a significant reduction of international tourists during the pandemic, Hong Kong's economy was negatively impacted. As the same time, Shanghai has grown strongly on financial functions and Shenzhen has gained a reputation as China's innovation center, Therefore, the future of Hong Kong now becomes a concern for the entire world.

At the 14th Asian Financial Forum on January 18th, 2021, Guo Shuqing, Party Secretary and Deputy Governor of the PBOC, clearly defined Hong Kong's supporting roles in China's 14th FYP "Dual Circulation" strategy, and Hong Kong's important roles as an international financial center, major offshore RMB market for RMB internationalization, and part of GBA development. This section will focus on reviewing Hong Kong's three important functions in the future.

10.2.1. International Financial Center Roles

In May 2021, the CSRC officially confirmed its plan to promote both Hong Kong and Shanghai as international financial centers by 2035, with expectations of future reciprocal openings, improved international financial services, and further international alignment. CSRC officials also confirmed the "high-quality" development strategy for both Shanghai and Shenzhen Stock Exchanges, consistent with China's 14th FYP.

Hong Kong has been known for decades as an international financial center due to its sound legal system, effective financial regulations, and mature capital market. Shanghai's financial status has been accelerating quickly within recent years due to the opening of the city's free trade zone, the launch of a STAR market, the recent opening of a Climate Bonds office (the Shanghai Office of the Climate Bonds Initiative) and a Chinese national carbon trading market. The Chinese authority's decision to promote two international financial centers will stir competition between these two cities focusing on legal and supervisory system improvements, investor interest protections, and systematic financial risk mitigation.

With market capitalization sized at $6.1 trillion, the HKEX was the third-largest in Asia and the fifth-largest in the world by the end of 2020, following the SSE, which currently ranks second in Asia and fourth in the world. Although the HKEX was ranked below the SSE, there are some advanced features of the HKEX that will take some time for the SSE to develop and equal:

An effective and trustworthy financial regulation system. In addition to its registration-based IPO system, broader international exposure, sound financial infrastructure, and effective regulatory system, the HKEX has built a trustworthy investment environment over the past several decades which has been vitally important for HKEX's international reputation. The continuous regulation reform of the HKEX, including the creation of the Hang Seng Tech Index, has made the exchange more attractive for high-tech and biotech companies. In 2020, 154 companies raised USD51.28 billion at the HKEX through IPO offerings - that included nine US-listed Chinese companies secondarily listed in Hong Kong with funds totaling $16.9 billion – nearly 30% of the total amount on the HKEX - which put the HKEX second in global ranking in 2020 (NASDAQ was first with $57.3 billion, while the SSE was third with $49.42 billion). HKEX estimates for 2021 is strong with over 120 IPOs anticipated to raise over HKD400 billion ($51.5 billion) with a trend shifting from traditional real estate and financial services to technology, e-commerce, and biotech.

First choice of Chinese companies "homecoming wave". HKEX reform in 2018 allowed dual-class shares structure that enabled Alibaba's secondary listing in 2019 to raise $11 billion with a 6.6.% share price increase on the first trading date (Alibaba was not able to list on the HKEX before the 2018 reform due to restrictions on Alibaba's dual-class share structure). Alibaba's HKEX IPO was the world's largest listing in 2019, surpassing Uber who raised $8 billion through an IPO in that year. Increased scrutiny and regulatory uncertainty from US stock markets by default, permitted Alibaba's successful experience that made the HKEX the first-choice location among Chinese companies' secondary listing. Chinese technology companies led by JD.com, Baidu, and Bilibili chose Hong Kong as their secondary listing in 2020 and 2021. More companies will follow.

Leading ESG regulation reforms. As we discussed in Chapter 3, the HKEX was the first Chinese Stock Exchange to issue ESG reporting guidance in 2012 with several updates afterwards, the latest updates being in 2020 including climate-related disclosure requirements to align with TCFD international standards. The HKEX also plays a role to facilitate ESG-reporting education by offering training courses and various consultation services.

Parallel to HKEX's advantages, high expectations exist for the SSE to become the world's largest exchange for IPOs by the end of 2020. A remarkable reform of the SSE was the launch of a new "NASDAQ-style" STAR Market overseen by the Exchange in the second half of 2019. In 2020, a total of 104 companies successfully issued IPOs on STAR's board, raising funds amounting to 52.5% of total SSE IPO amounts that year. A flagship IPO on STAR's board was the secondary listing of HK-listed chip maker Semiconductor Manufacturing International Corp. demonstrated major effects of SSE's reforms through its STAR board, such as a registration-based listing system allowing for dual-class share issuance; and more importantly, the higher valuation potential on the STAR's board for high-tech companies. Moreover, compared to the SSE's regular IPO application processing time which averages six months, STAR's board showcased its twenty-six-day, fast-track approval with Ant's expedited IPO application in September 2020, despite the fact that the Ant IPO was suspended by Chinese regulators late that year.

In addition to the SSE's great potential led by its STAR board,

Shanghai's international financial center's lead role in green finance transformation will become more evident in 2021 due to some of the latest developments: *Climate Bonds Office in Shanghai* - In March 2021, CBI[7] Shanghai office was launched in Shanghai Lujiazui Financial City that confirms Lujiazui's role as a green financial center to promote green bonds, green standards, and green transition finance, together with the establishment of a Sino-British "two-city linkage" platform between Lujiazui Financial City and London. *China's National Carbon Market based in Shanghai* - The launch of a national carbon market in Shanghai with plans to have the city administer all carbon trading transactions occurring in eight regional pilot exchanges will make Shanghai the center of China's carbon market.

Meanwhile, the CBI released a report in June 2021 to address a GBA green infrastructure investment opportunity report, highlighting a significant amount of $299 billion green infrastructure investment in Guangdong province out of a total budget of $777 billion for the major infrastructure projects that were planned in China's 14th Five-Year-Plan for the province. The report also emphasized GBA's important roles in green finance development such as promoting green asset-backed securities and the issuance of local government green bonds, and discussed the role of the Hong Kong capital market to support GBA's green infrastructure development. In the same month, Guangdong province also launched a renewable energy trading platform that will eventually contribute to GBA green economic transformation. As an important part of GBA, Hong Kong will play an important leading role in the regulatory development needed for economic transformation due to its relatively mature capital market.

Both Shanghai and Hong Kong are important players in China's green finance transition and further economic growth in the coming decades. The next steps will depend on actual action to capitalize on opportunities and plans.

---

[7] CBI - Climate Bonds Initiative is a not-for-profit international organization launched in 2012. By providing annual studies on the evolution of the green bonds market and standards and guidance on green bonds, CBI advocates climate change considerations through financial institutions' investment and lending activities.

10.2.2. An Important RMB Offshore Center

Hong Kong has been the largest RMB offshore center since 2003 and the largest market of RMB international bonds (both Dim Sum bonds and Panda bonds). According to Hong Kong Monetary Authority 2019 information, over 70% of world RMB settlements have been resolved through Hong Kong; Hong Kong held the biggest RMB liquidity pool of over RMB632.2 billion outside of China ending in 2019, (that number decreased from its peak of RMB1,003 billion in 2014). The HKEX had already identified the reasons for Hong Kong's offshore RMB deposit amount reduction from 2014 to 2019, and provided options to increase its offshore RMB liquidity pool in a HKEX 2019 report.

Over the past many decades, the sales of H Shares on the HKEX have been one of the most important channels for Chinese equities to access offshore capital. As the largest RMB offshore center subservient to Chinese capital controls, Hong Kong has been instrumental in its support of the authorities to guide the direction of offshore RMB exchange rates and interest rates. With its broad exposure to the international financial system, Hong Kong is the best measurement tool regarding monetary demand trend in the international market.

Although the amount of RMB cross-border transactions handled in Shanghai has been increasing according to a 2020 PBOC report, the know-how and financial market supporting system developed in Hong Kong has placed Hong Kong ahead of the game in the offshore RMB markets' future growth. In addition, Hong Kong's lead role in a digital RMB cross-border trading platform also anchors the city's important position in RMB's internationalization.

10.2.3. Potential of Guangdong-Hong Kong-Macau GBA

The concept of the Guangdong-Hong Kong-Macau GBA was established in China's 13th FYP in 2016. The GBA covers nine cities in Guangdong (including Shenzhen and Guangzhou, the capital city of Guangdong province) together with Hong Kong and Macau, that comprises 5% of China's total population and 12% of the country's GDP. With many well-known Chinese tech companies (eg Huawei and Tencent) headquartered in Shenzhen and the comprehensive supply chain system in other Guangdong cities in the GBA, the concept has become the primary platform for the world's fast prototyping systems and low-cost engineering processes, by which it ostensibly gained its Asian "Silicon Valley" name. In addition, the GBA is part of China's BRI encompassing a well-developed infrastructure system, with rich features from Cantonese culture that includes the official language, Cantonese, spoken in both Hong Kong and Macau. Therefore, the GBA is a national plan to integrate the Special Administrative Regions (SAR) of Hong Kong and Macau and the nine Guangdong cities across the Pearl River Delta.

The 2019 Outline Development Plan for the Guangdong-Hong Kong-Macau GBA developed by the Chinese government lays out two milestones for the GBA's development: to establish the framework for an first-class international bay area (consisting of Guangzhou, Shenzhen, Hong Kong, and Macau) by 2022; and to attain that status by 2035.

Historically, Hong Kong's economy has been chiefly centered on four sectors (supply chain, financial, professional service, and tourism), which can no longer support Hong Kong's economic condition due to global economic landscape changes in the past couple decades. Hong Kong's GDP has slowed since the early 2000s, consequently, Hong Kong's economic restructuring will happen one way or another. Being part of the GBA opens broader industrial opportunities for Hong Kong, offers diversified job opportunities for Hong Kongers, and will accelerate Hong Kong's economic restructuring. At the same time, Hong Kong can leverage its advanced financial and supply chain system to help achieve GBA's potential.

Because of recent political environmental changes in Hong Kong, many people there are worried about Hong Kong's future. Despite those concerns, having been well-known as an international financial hub and the world's top tax haven, together with its reputable legal and financial systems, Hong Kong has earned trust from global investors, businesses, and wealthy individuals. Fear, then, may be illusory. Given that, it's hard to separate the true reasons between the COVID-19 pandemic and Hong Kong's political climate changes with regards to the recent trend of foreign expats' returning to home countries and the other immigration trend of Hong Kongers moving abroad.

Without diving into the complicated relationship between Hong Kong and the mainland, it is worth considering that the problems between Hong Kong and China did not happen overnight. The gaps separating Hong Kong and mainland China are the results of century-long system differences, external influences, and lifestyles, all of which cannot be easily bridged merely because Hong Kong is a somewhat integral part of China. Additionally, decades of distinct developments particular to Hong Kong that were required to build its effective and lucrative financial system as the Asian financial center has benefitted the global community. Although recent trends indicate the Chinese government's commitment and determination to improve the country's regulatory standards to align with international benchmarks, building a trustworthy society including a credible nationwide social credit system may take decades to construct in order to achieve these goals.

Therefore, it makes little sense to lose Hong Kong's global financial hub's position to spite China's long-term interest. Understanding it will take decades to overcome significant differences in order to unify Hong Kong and mainland China, the Chinese government will need to measure and balance the sufficiency of Hong Kong's political and economic autonomy in order to retain Hong Kong's role as an international financial center.

In the end, Hong Kong's future will be written by Hong Kong and China, with the understanding and support of the rest of the world.

Chapter 11

Conclusion

2021 was meant to be the "year of action" for the world!

Climate change is a global risk- worldwide natural disasters caused by extreme weather came one after another. Taking serious action on climate change has become a top priority for every country, organization, and human being. Green economies and transformation-centered regulation reforms are being introduced in every part of the world.

Fighting the pandemic will be a long-term battle. Global vaccine development and the vaccination progress are racing to conquer the fast-changing nature and spreading of COVID-19 variations. The gradual reopening of economies from many countries has taken a much slower pace than had originally been thought and online education and remote work are becoming the norm. Business model transformations are taking place in different industries with various new formal processes being created as a result of the pandemic.

These enormous social and economic reforms were initiated in China at the beginning of 2021. In March: banking regulators warned of potential risks ("gray rhino")[2] to Chinese real estate values, which will probably lead to regulation reform in the real estate industry to prevent a potential property "bubble"; new education regulations were released in July banning for-profit tutoring companies as the high tutoring fees became a burden for Chinese parents, additional education reforms will

---

[2] "Gray rhino" means that obvious risks that are often being ignored, while leaders and organizations that face up to these risks have a competitive advantage. The term "gray rhino" was introduced to the World Economic Forum Annual meeting by American author Michele Wucker in 2013. Ms. Wucker later published a book *The Gray Rhino in 2016*. The concept of "gray rhino" was adopted by the Chinese government in 2017 and has been applied to various Chinese financial and risk management policies since then.

probably follow to improve the equality and inclusivity of China's education system; also, eye-catching news regarding the Chinese regulators' actions of placing Didi Global Inc (China's "Uber") under cybersecurity review to block Didi apps from Apple-compatible devices - two days after Didi went public on the NYSE on June 30th - is revealing. These regulatory reforms will impact future prospective Chinese companies' CG developments.

"Stay low profile, work high profile"

Similar to the ESG and green transformation reforms discussed in this book, Chinese regulations will take proactive and aggressive approaches toward social and economic reforms in 2021, echoing the Chinese government's new diplomatic strategy of defending itself due to the public opinion crisis promulgated by tensions with the US. The "stay low profile" maxim repeatedly appears in the Chinese media regarding the government's previous global image, and many Chinese multinational companies' business behaviors within the global marketplace that are accused of having a lack of consideration for stakeholders. Is there, then, a quandary with the "stay low profile"?

China's culture, which is thousands of years old, is well-known for its ancient philosophies of Confucianism, Taoism and Buddhism, all of which have recorded erudite quotes from great thinkers, such as Confucius (the founder of Confucianism) and Lao Tzu (the founder of Taoism). The first part of Lao Tzu's philosophical mantra "stay low profile, work high profile" has been taught in school and at home as being a virtue for individuals. The "stay low profile" which embodies strategic thinking without controversy, begets respect for the inner law of things, and reflects human behavior as being humble, not showing off and having peace of mind. This virtue could be translated into good business behavior, ie to focus on one's own business developments, but not to flaunt them. The original meaning of the latter, "work high profile", is taking effective action and working hard. The "stay low profile, work high profile" is the perfect portrayal of China's previous appearance to the global community, and the manner in which many Chinese companies have been conducting their businesses, including businesses overseas.

However, in today's business world, corporations are required to take seriously their social responsibilities and to attend to stakeholders, including all segments of the business community. The original meaning of the "work high profile" will not necessarily qualify a company to become a good global citizen or industry leader. Moreover, the "stay low profile, work high profile" merely "focuses on one's own business development" without consideration of stakeholders and has become an obstacle to Chinese companies' further global growth. To become good global citizens, some Chinese companies have started to participate in the global community, for example, VIPKID decided to proactively engage with local communities as their strategy (see case study 7.3.), while other Chinese companies (eg Tiktok and Alipay) have chosen to join other world-class companies (eg FedEx, Coca-Cola) to sponsor global sport events such as the UEFA European Championship Games in order to participate in the global community. For China to succeed and attain superpower status, perhaps now is an ideal time for the country to consider Lao Tzu's "work high profile" mantra and re-interpret it to mean proactively helping others and contributing to business communities, strategically pioneering global ESG movements and green transformation, and diplomatically influencing global collaboration by demonstrating its own efforts of collaborating with global partners.

Mutual Understanding

During my five years working for Chinese companies, I often found myself overthinking these companies' motivations when particular situations arose. For example, accounting reconciliation became a nightmare when cash transactions between Chinese parent companies and their overseas subsidiaries were randomly deposited in different bank accounts. Given my Western business mindset, I initially questioned if a unique cash management strategy was being utilized until I reconsidered and had a chance to speak with the individuals who handled the bank transfers. I then realized it was simply different individuals' preferences when processing transactions without them understanding how they would effect the subsidiaries' companies' business practices. Of course, the absence of knowledge was due to insufficient guidance. After a few incidents, I realized that internationalization is a long journey and time is needed for multinationals to understand the business practices of their overseas operations and to establish policies and procedures to guide daily transactions. Before standard practices are enacted in a multinational company, establishing mutual understanding is a key to avoiding confusion, which means making considerable effort to empathize and understand local practices is crucial.

With the relationship between China and the US changing from strategic partners to strategic competitors, tension between these two countries is reasonable and only to be expected, but the consequential pressures across the world, exacerbated by the pandemic, have not been healthy or helpful to solve present global crises. However, accolades are warranted and should be given to the burgeoning ESG movement, which has been addressing global interdependence awareness and the likely changing business, and possibly political, mindsets internationally. Regardless of any economic growth ambitions or political agendas, improving peoples' livelihoods and protecting the environment of our shared planet are common goals that require mutual understanding and co-operation among global superpowers.

While most parts of the world are still struggling to recover economically from the COVID-19 crisis, deadly virus variances have created additional pandemic surges in different parts of the world, and fatal flooding in Germany and central China have taken hundreds of lives and further disrupted the pandemic's recovery. Despite that, China's continuous growth has benefitted everyone. According to a July 13, 2021, Reuters news article, China's economy experienced a 18.3% GDP increase in the first quarter of 2021 and an 8.1% increase in the second quarter. The country's estimated 2021 annual growth is on track to reach 8.6% (US had a 6.4% GDP increase in the first quarter and an estimated growth of 6.6% according to a US economic outlook report in July 2021). China's ascending domestic output will provide more opportunities for its neighboring countries and other global partners' recovery and growth and increased contributions will help the global economy recover from the COVID-19 pandemic. China's sizable and stable domestic market has been the most powerful foundation for Chinese companies' growth in the past, and that momentum will continue.

China's increasing international influence will make the country a stronger player within the new international business order and enhance the global presentation of the "China model". However, in order to gain worldwide recognition and to become a moral influencer in the global business world, China and Chinese companies need to understand international expectations in addition to striving for improvement of China's regulatory system for global business growth. If the country truly wants to procure superpower status, it will need to actively help others and contribute more to global society, and it's time to make a new interpretation of the "work high profile" part of the "China model's" characteristics, without losing the virtue of the "stay low profile".

Simultaneously, in the Western world, the demand to recognize the "China model" has been increasing, and moreover, successful stories of the "China model" confirm that what has worked for the West may not work for emerging markets. Twenty years ago, headlines such as "China is twenty years behind the US", "China is still ten to twenty years from matching the US economy", etc. were popular in newspapers and other media. At that time, it was a common understanding and it was expected that China would follow the Western model and eventually catch up with more developed countries of the West. We don't see these kind of headlines very often now as China's economy has evolved, and the country has taken its own path and proved its success over the past decade. The establishment of the "China model" also indicates the demand and necessity of diversified models for emerging markets as far as economic growth, regulation reform, and their evaluation systems. As a result, measurement systems and factors developed in the West may not be proper to evaluate emerging markets economic and social performances as well. Given that the worldwide ESG movement is positioned to help solve global risks such as climate change, different strategies, approaches, and measurements will be needed for the evaluation of ESG performance of emerging market countries including China, although the advanced world has been driving the movement.

A Mindset Change of Regulation Compliance and Social Impact

Most developing countries' regulation systems have been known for their ineffectiveness mainly due to lagging economic growth, a lack of practical guidance, and an absence of an enforcement mechanism. Laggard institutional system norms create huge gray areas in compliance, and nourish negligence, irresponsibility, and government corruption. The Chinese regulatory system is now past its early stage after forty years of reforms and is heading toward higher standards, but instilling a mindset change regarding compliance will most likely take another few decades if an effective enforcement mechanism is not present.

Over the past several decades, the Chinese regulatory system's flexibility has offered freedom for the creativity that enabled many Chinese companies to grow globally but also caused these companies to misunderstand what compliance with regulations meant. This miscalculation resulted in detrimental business opportunities and strategies, such as Ant Group's approach of cutting corners when it positioned itself as a high-tech company and ignored regulatory requirements (see case study 5.3.). After suspending Ant Group's highly anticipated IPO and disciplining the ride-hailing giant Didi for ignoring warnings of data security infractions, tightened anti-trust enforcement rules made apparent the Chinese government's message of its clear determination to boldly proclaim that the **Chinese government has "zero" tolerance for compliance violations!**

In order to quickly build a trustworthy society allowing for a high-quality livelihood for its citizens, the Chinese government also wants quick results toward mindset changes on social impact. The rewards and punishments mechanism designed to promote behavior changes for individuals and businesses quickly (as discussed in Chapter 8), and future reforms in real estate and education in response to China's 14th FPY's high-quality new development strategy, are resetting the tone for future CG development.

Some media outlets may refer to the Didi story as another example of uncertainty involving the Chinese regulatory system, or blame "the system for causing another victim" due to the tussle between China and the US, similar to the criticism regarding China's new social credit system. Because of China's different social and economic conditions, these scrutinizing mechanisms may seem excessive by Western standards, but in order to stimulate business and social mindset changes, and to prevent multinationals from becoming uncontrollable, these standards are crucial.

Whether or not these measures are "extreme" or "effective", the jury will decide in the coming years!

Continuous Evolving of Chinese Companies' CG Models

The gap between China's influential economic growth and the mediocre standards of its traditionally lagging institutional systems are a few of the many reasons that have caused China's current public opinion crisis. The lack of mature regulatory guidance and reluctance to enforce behavior violations, slow alignment with international standards, and substandard requirements for transparency in operational processes have been reflected by various social and environmental controversies in both China and partner countries during Chinese companies' global growth. In addition, turning its global position from a follower to a pioneer and pacesetter requires both the Chinese government and Chinese companies to become more responsible and proactive in pursuing a higher-quality economic and social system and a higher-standard of ESG performance and demonstrate their ability to make them real!

In order to bridge the gap, China can benefit by collaborating with more developed countries and international organizations since it has been working on improving regulatory alignments to coincide with international standards or even those of advanced countries. China's recently-amended IP law regarding manufacturing design started when it joined the internationally-recognized Hague Agreement; the Green Bond regulation reform protocol began at the beginning of 2021 (before the first "carbon neutrality" bond's issuance); and the unified domestic criteria for "green projects" to align with EU standards, are all signs of the new strategy for China's future reform and growth. Equally important are the increased international use of RMB, the establishment of an Asian economic zone, and careful handling of the tenuous relationship between Hong Kong and China to minimize the disruption of Hong Kong's economy and Hong Kongers' lives.

Accomplishing these delicate tasks requires continuous innovation with economic reforms such as encouraging new programmes for green transformation and creative financial products to accelerate international use of the RMB. These reforms will certainly stimulate the development of creative CG models in Chinese companies. For instance, VIPKID is exploring a new CG model with its proactive social impact strategy, mounting social entrepreneurship demonstrated by Pinduoduo's founder (case study 2.3.), and ByteDance's CEO's leadership example (case study 8.2.) are signs of the continuous evolving of CG in Chinese companies.

In *Understanding Corporate Governance in China*, co-authored by Bob Tricker and Gregg Li, the authors point out that "China has developed a unique approach to corporate governance. Although initially building on Western experience, the Chinese see corporate governance as a means of improving the economy and building society in the interests of the people, the party, and the State."

A few years have passed since their book was published in 2019. Some Chinese companies have proved the success of their CG models, while some have failed; however, significant reforms have improved the Chinese regulatory system and economic environment. Upcoming mindset changes and extensive global collaboration will most likely lead to continuing evolution in Chinese corporate governance to better serve the interests of the people, party, State, and global community.

Appendix 1 – List of Further Reading

Casanova, Lourdes, Fernanda Cahen, and Anne Miroux, *Innovation from Emerging Markets: From Copycats to Leaders*, Oxford University Press, 2021.

Casanova, Lourdes, and Anne Miroux, *The Era of Chinese Multinationals – Competing for Global Dominance*, Elsevier Academic Press, 2019.

Clarke, Thomas, *International Corporate Governance – A Comparative Approach* (2nd Edition), Routledge Press, 2019.

Hu, Yong, and Yazhou Hao, *Haier Purpose: The Real Story of China's First Global Super Company*, Infinite Ideas, 2017

Kakabadse, Andrew, and Nada Kakabadse, *Leading the Board – The Six Disciplines of World-Class Chairmen*, Palgrave Macmillan, 2008

Larcker, David, and Brian Tayan, *Corporate Governance Matters*, Pearson Education, 2016.

Leng, Jing, *Corporate Governance and Financial Reform in China's Transition Economy*, Hong Kong University Press, 2009.

Jawad, Ali Qassim, and Andrew Kakabadse, *Leadership Intelligence – The 5Qs for Thriving as a Leader*, Bloomsbury, 2019.

Tian, Tao, and Chunbo Wu, *The Huawei Story*, Sage Publications Pvt. Lmt.; First Edition, 2015.

Tricker, Bob, *Corporate Governance* (4th Edition), Oxford University Press, 2019.

Tricker, Bob, *The Evolution of Corporate Governance*, Cambridge University Press, 2021.

Tricker, Bob, and Gregg Li, *Understanding Corporate Governance in China*, Hong Kong University Press, 2019.

Wucker, Michelle, *The Gray Rhino*, St. Martin's Press, 2016.

Wucker, Michelle, *You Are What You Risk*, Pegasus Books, 2021.

Yi. Jeannie J. and Shawn X. Ye, *The Haier Way: The Making of a Chinese Business Leader and a Global Brand*, Homa and Sekey Books, March 3, 2003.

Appendix 2 – List of Acronyms

Introduction

CG	Corporate Governance
SOEs	State-Owned Enterprises
RMB	Renminbi
CSR	Corporate Social Responsibility
VIE	Variable Interest Entity
M&A	Mergers and Acquisitions

Chapter 1

SSE	The Shanghai Stock Exchange
SZSE	The Shenzhen Stock Exchange
HKD	Hong Kong Dollar
HKEX	Hong Kong Stock Exchange
CSRC	The China Securities Regulatory Commission
SEC	Securities and Exchange Commission
IPO	Initial Public Offering
ESG	Environmental, Social and Governance
NYSE	New York Stock Exchange
OECD	Organization for Economic Cooperation and Development
SASAC	State-Owned Assets Supervision and Administration Commission

Chapter 2

AGM	Annual General Meetings
OLOE	The Overseas Listed Offshore Entity
WFOE	The Wholly Foreign Owned Enterprise
SAMR	State Administration for Market Regulation

Chapter 3

RQFII	Renminbi Qualified Foreign Institutional Investors
CSCS	Corporate Social Credit System
STAGE	Sustainable and Green Exchange
CRS	Contract Responsibility System
BRI	Belt and Road Initiative
HKICPA	Hong Kong Institute of Certified Public Accountants
TCFD	Task Force on Climate-Related Financial Disclosures
SoCS	China's Social Credit System

Chapter 4

SEC	The Securities Exchange Commission
ISS	Institutional Shareholder Services
PCAOB	Public Company Accounting Oversight Board

Chapter 5

WHH	Wahaha Group
Ant	Ant Group
SMEs	Small and Medium-sized Enterprises
PBOC	The People's Bank of China
TAL	Tomorrow Advancing Life

Appendix 2 – List of Acronyms

Chapter 6

GMI	Governance Metrics International
SRI	Socially Responsible Investing
STGF	SynTao Green Finance
ESG-ECV	ESG Epidemic Control Valuation model
CSI	Chinese Securities Index Co., LTD
DM	Developed Markets
EM	Emerging Markets
AMAC	he Asset Management Association of China
CASVI	The China Alliance of Social Value Investment

Chapter 7

SDG	Sustainability development goals
DNSH	Do No Significant Harm
CBI	Climate Bonds Initiative
GBA	Greater Bay Area
CDB	China Development Bank
CICC	China International Capital Corporation
STAR	Shanghai Stock Exchange's Science and Technology Innovation Board
PRI	Principles for Responsible Investment
KPI	Key Performance Indicators
NSSF	National Council of Social Security Fund
PBOC	People's Bank of China

Chapter 8

SoCS	China's social credit system
FYP	China's 14th Five-Year Plan
CSCS	China's Corporate Social Credit System
EPR	Enterprise Resource Planning
IP	Intellectual Property
WIPO	World Intellectual Property Organization
SPC	The Supreme People's Court
FEILO	Feilo Acoustics Co., Ltd.

Chapter 9

RCEP	Regional Comprehensive Economic Partnership
FOCAC	Forum on China-Africa Cooperation
CPTPP	Progressive Agreement for Trans-Pacific Partnership
TPP	Trans-Pacific Partnership
NAFTA	North American Free Trade Agreement
CGTN	China Global Television Network
G7	Group of Seven industrialized countries
ESSA	Education Sub-Saharan Africa
BUI	Bui Dam Hydroelectricity

Chapter 10

SDR	Special Drawing Rights
IMF	International Monetary Funds
QFII	Qualified Foreign Institutional Investor
CIPS	Interbank Payment System
SWIFT	Society for Worldwide Interbank Financial Telecommunication
CBDC	China's central bank digital currency
HKMA	Hong Kong Monetary Authority
UAS	United Arab Emirates
SAR	Special Administrative Regions

Appendix 3 – References by Chapter

Chapter 1 References:

A. De la Cruz, A. Medina, and Y. Tang, "Owners of the World's Listed Companies". *OECD Capital Market Series, Paris, March 21, 2021*, https://bit.ly/3n0Bf8u

Alibaba Group, "Alibaba's 2019 Annual Report", Alibaba Group, May, 2019, https://www.alibaba.com.

Alibaba Group, "Alibaba's Sustainability," April 18, 2020, https://alibabagroup.com/en/about/sustainability.

Alibaba IPO Prospectus, US Government publication, May 6, 2014. https://www.sec.gov.

Alibaba Report, "Alibaba's and Ant's Financial Restructuring in 2015", Alibaba Group, February 15, 2015, https://www.alibaba.com.

Alibaba's SEC Filing, US Government publication, Washington, DC, 2017, May 25, 2020, https://www.sec.gov.

Ashley Feng, "We Can't Tell if Chinese Firms Work for the Party" *Foreign Policy*, February 7, 2019, https://bit.ly/309mnM2.

B. Joseph, "The Company that Apple is Frightened by: Huawei" *The Startup*, August 12, 2018, https://bit.ly/3qoziF3

Corporate Governance of Listed Companies in China, Chinese Central Government report, OECD, OECD Publishing, 2011, http://dx.doi.org/10.1787/9789264119208-en.

Debra Holley, "China Allows Foreigners to Trade its Stock and Securities: The Shanghai Exchange is the Setting for the First Such Action Since Investors Were Thrown Out in 1949" 1992, https://lat.ms/3oi4eUO

Eric Jhonsa, "Alibaba's Singles Day Event: 4 Trends That Helped Drive Growth" *Real Money*, November 11, 2019, https://bit.ly/3D4PbE3 .

Eustance Huang, "Alibaba Shares Surge in Hong Kong Debut, World's Largest Listing so Far in 2019" *CNBC*, November 25, 2019, https://www.cnbc.com/2019/11/26/alibaba-shares-jump-more-than-6percent-in-hong-kong-debut.html.

Federica Russo, "Politics in the Boardroom: The Role of Chinese Communist Party Committee" *The Diplomat*, December 24, 2019, https://bit.ly/30agIWM

"GPIF Has Become a Signatory to the UN-PRI" Government Pension Investment Fund, 2015, June 28, 2021, https://www.gpif.go.jp/en/investment/pdf/signatory_UN_PRI_en.pdf.

Hendrik Laubscher, "What Jack Ma Taught Us About Good Corporate Governance This Week" *Forbes*, 2018, https://bit.ly/30agG0o

James McRitchie, "Corporate Governance Defined" *Navigation*, May 29, 2021, https://www.corpgov.net/library/corporate-governance-defined/.

Juro Osawa, "Alibaba Founder's Recent Deals Raise Flags" *The Wall Street Journal*, July 7, 2014, https://www.wsj.com/articles/alibaba-founder-jack-mas-recent-deals-raise-flags-1404760656.

Karen Jingrong. Lin, et al., "State-Owned Enterprises in China: A Review of 40 years of Research and Practice" February 15, 2020, https://bit.ly/3bOaeii

Krystal Hu, "Jack Ma's Departure Spurs Debate over Alibaba's Governance Structure" *Yahoo Finance*, September 11, 2018, https://finance.yahoo.com/news/jack-mas-departure-spurs-debate-alibabas-governance-structure-145137075.html.

Lakshna Rathod, "Huawei – GDPR Corporate Governance Challenges to Business" *Diligent*, February 19, 2020, https://diligent.com/en-gb/blog/huawei-gdpr-corporate-governance-challenges-to-businesses/.

Lawrence Loh, "Is Huawei's Rise Due to its Corporate Governance Style?" *The Business Times*, March 12, 2019, https://www.businesstimes.com.sg/opinion/is-huaweis-rise-due-to-its-corporate-governance-style.

Li Na, "Huawei Switches to Rotating Chairman System with Ren Zhengfei Retaining CEO" *Yi Cai*, March 26, 2018, https://bit.ly/3F2yqdl

Michael J. Mol, Jedrzej George Frynas, and Kamel Mellahi, "Management Innovation Made in China: Haier's Rendanheyi" University of California Berkeley, July, 2018, April 19, 2020, https://researchgate.net/publication/326725496.

Ming Zeng, "Alibaba and the Future of Business" *Harvard Business Review*, September – October, 2018, https://hbr.org/2018/09/alibaba-and-the-future-of-business.

News Wire Feed, "Huawei Wins Vodafone Deal" *Light Reading*, June 29, 2007, https://www.lightreading.com/mobile/3g-hspa/huawei-wins-vodafone-deal/d/d-id/643846.

"New Code of CG for Listed Companies in China", ACGA, 2018, https://www.acga-asia.org/advocacy-detail.php?id=149&sk=&sa= .

Nie Qing Ping, "Historical Recollections of Some Important Events in My Country's Stock Market" (translated), 2010, http://news.cnstock.com/news,yw-201901-4321157.htm ok .

"One of the Destructions of Old Stock Investors: Opening an Account for the First Time Investing in the Sea" (translated) Tencent News, September, 2020, https://new.qq.com/omn/20200905/20200905A0G8W500.html?pc

Peter Gourevitch, "Political Power and Corporate Control: The New Global Politics of Corporate Governance" *Foreign Affairs (Council on Foreign Relations),* Princeton University, January, 2006, https://researchgate.net/publication/24117949.

Peter J. Williamson, Xiaobo Wu, and Eden Yin, "Learning from Huawei's Superfluidity" *Ivey Business Journal,* May/June, 2019, https://iveybusinessjournal.com/learning-from-huaweis-superfluidity/.

Platform Governance Department, "Alibaba's 2016 Annual Report" Alibaba Group, April 10, 2020, https://bit.ly/3F4Ab9S

Qingping Nie, "Historical Memories of Some Important Events in China's Stock Market" (translated), *Shanghai Securities News,* January 8, 2019, http://news.cnstock.com/news.yw.-201901-4321157.htm.

Rebecca Smith, "Why Huawei Swaps CEO Every Six Months" *Management Today,* April 7, 2016, https://www.managementtoday.co.uk/why-huawei-swaps-ceo-every-six-months/article/1389976.

Reuters Staff, "Alibaba Names Partnership Members in New IPO Prospectus" *Reuters,* June 16, 2014, https://www.cnbc.com/2014/06/16/alibaba-names-partnership-members-in-new-ipo-prospectus.html.

Reuters Staff, "Timeline: China's Intervention in the Stock Market" *Reuters,* July 7, 2010, https://www.reuters.com/article/us-markets-china-stocks-timeline/timeline-chinas-intervention-in-the-stock-market-idUSTRE6670PO20100708.

Rita Liao, "Meet Daniel Zhang, the New Face of Alibaba" *Tech In Asia*, September 10, 2019, https://www.techinasia.com/daniel-zhang-alibaba.

Ryan Mac, "Alibaba Claims Title for Largest Global IPO Ever with Extra Share Sales" *Forbes*, November 22, 2014, https://bit.ly/31EFCOo

Sean Ross, "What Are Some Examples of Different Corporate Governance Systems" *Investopedia*, 2021, https://www.investopedia.com/ask/answers/051115/what-are-some-examples-different-corporate-governance-systems-across-world.asp.

Shanghai Vacuum Electronic Devices Co., Ltd. RMB Special Stock (B Stock) Listing Report, (translated), 1991, March 21, 2021, https://bit.ly/3EXOFZ8

Shujle Leng, "'Be in Love with Them, but Don't Marry Them'– How Jack Ma Partnered with Local Government to Make E-Commerce Giant Alibaba, and Hangzhou, a Success," *Foreign Policy*, October 31, 2014, https://foreignpolicy.com/2014/10/31/be-in-love-with-them-but-dont-marry-them/.

Simon Luk, "Exploring the Alternatives to VIE Structures" *Market Watch*, June 26, 2014, March 14, 2021 China Business Law Journal, https://law.asia/zh-hans/vie/

Staff Report, "China Corporate Governance Code," R and A Associates, August 4, 2014, https://www.rns-cs.com.

Staff Report, "New Code of CG for Listed Companies in China,", ACGA, 2018, July 13, 2021, https://www.acga-asia.org/advocacy-detail.php?id=149&sk=&sa=.

Tian Tao and David De Cremer, "Leadership Innovation: Huawei's Rotating CEO System" *The European Business Review*, November 20, 2015, https://www.europeanbusinessreview.com/leadership-innovation-huaweis-rotating-ceo-system.

Yu-Hsin Lin and Thomas Mehaffy, "Open Sesame: The Myth of Alibaba's Extreme Corporate Governance and Control," https://brooklynworks.brooklaw.edu/cgi/viewcontent.cgi?article=1219&context=bjcfcl.

Chapter 2 References:

A. De La Cruz, A. Medina, and Y. Tang, Owners of the World's Listed Companies, OECD Capital Market Series, Paris, 2019, https://www.oecd.org/corporate/Owners-of-the-Worlds-Listed-Companies.pdf.

Alison Durkee, "Investors Begin to Revolt Against Mark Zuckerberg," Vanity Fair, 2019, https://www.vanityfair.com/news/2019/06/facebook-investors-revolt-against-mark-zuckerberg.

Eva Mathews and Sophie Yu, "Pinduoduo's Founder Steps Down as Chairman as Quarterly Revenue Surges," Yahoo News, 2021, https://finance.yahoo.com/news/chinas-pinduoduo-quarterly-revenue-more-122846087.html.

Herbert Kwok, "A Side Story About Sina.com," Hong Kong Lawyer, 2021, http://www.hk-lawyer.org/content/sidestory-about-sina-com.

Jon Russell, "Yahoo Spin-Out Altaba is Selling its Entire Alibaba Stake and Closing Down" 2019, https://tcrn.ch/308V454

Karen Jingrong, et al., "State-Owned Enterprises in China: A Review of 40 years of Research and Practice," Elsevier, February 15, 2020, https://bit.ly/3bOaeii

Matthew Johnson, "Top 5 Shareholders of Facebook" Investopedia, December 9, 2020, https://www.investopedia.com/articles/insights/082216/top-9-shareholders-facebook-fb.asp.

Staff Report, "Ownership and Governance of State-Owned Enterprises" OECD, 2018, https://bit.ly/30ak63e

W. Raphael Lam, Markus Rodlauer, and Alfred Schipke, *Modernizing China: Investing in Soft Infrastructure*, 2016, March 27, 2021, https://www.elibrary.imf.org/view/books/071/23209-9781513539942-en/23209-9781513539942-en-book.xml

Wang Xi and Liu Yang, "A Study on the Dual-Class Share Structures of Overseas-Listed Companies – Taking Alibaba Group as an Example" *European Journal of Business, Economics and Accountancy*, 2018, Progressive Academic Publishing, www.idpublications.org.

Wei Jiang, "Alibaba: A Dictatorship" 2016, https://www8.gsb.columbia.edu/articles/chazen-global-insights/alibaba-dictatorship

Wen Wen and JianboSong, "Can Returnee Managers Promote CSR Performance?", *Evidence from China*, 2017, https://journal.hep.com.cn/fbr/EN/10.1186/s11782-017-0012-8.

Yu-Hsin Lin and Thomas Mehaffy, "Open Sesame: The Myth of Alibaba's Extreme Corporate Governance and Control" 2016, https://brooklynworks.brooklaw.edu/cgi/viewcontent.cgi?article=1219&context=bjcfcl.

Yujie Xue and Jane Zhang, "Colin Huang Takes Another Step Back from Pinduoduo Just When Things are Starting to Take Off" 2021, https://bit.ly/31OtACi

Chapter 3 References:

"Guidelines for the Content and Format of Information Disclosure by Companies Offering Securities to the Public No. 2_-Content and Format of Annual Reports" 2017, (translated), *CSRC*, May 13, 2021, http://www.csrc.gov.cn/pub/newsite/flb/flfg/bmgf/xxpl/xxplnr/201805/P020180520760024848296.pdf.

"Behind the Scenes: How GE Appliances Became Part of Haier" May 10, 2020," *State Council*, Trans, June 14, 2014.

Alexander Chipman Koty, "China's Corporate Social Credit System: What Businesses Need to Know" *China Briefing,* November 5, 2019, https://www.china-briefing.com/news/chinas-corporate-social-credit-system-how-it-works/.

Amena Saiyid, "Chinese Regulators Set ESG Disclosure Rules as Financiers Eye Investment Opportunities" *HIS Markit*, July, 2021, https://bit.ly/3klZhcE

Archived article/author unknown "Two Years Since Haier Acquisition, GE Appliances Highlights Major Investment Plans" May 10, 2020,

Chinese Central Government publication, "Labor Contract Law of the People's Republic of China (pdf)" April 20, 2021, https://www.ilo.org/dyn/natlex/docs/ELECTRONIC/76384/108021/F755819546/CHN76384%20Eng.pdf.

Corporate press release, "Haier Delivers First Order in Just 20 Minutes During 11.11 Shopping Carnival" November 26, 2014, May 10, 2020, https://www.haier.com/in/about-haier/news/20190816_97656.shtml.

Corporate press release, "Haier the Only Chinese Brand to Take Home Prestigious German Plus X Innovation Award" CISION PR Newswire, June 25, 2015, May 10, 2020, https://www.prnewswire.com/news-releases/haier-the-only-chinese-brand-to-take-home-prestigious-german-plus-x-innovation-award-300104743.html.

David Liu, "HKEX ESG New Reporting Regimes Effective on July 1, 2020" *Kroll*, March 24, 2020, https://bit.ly/3wGze4Q

Hu Yong and Hao Yazhou, "The Inside Story of the Rise of Haier, China's First Super-Company" *Thinkers 50*, May 10, 2020, https://thinkers50.com/media/inside-story-rise-haier-chinas-first-super-company/.

Jedrez George Frynas, Michael J. Mol, and Kamel Mellahi, "Management Innovation Made in China: Haier's Rendanheyi" *California Management Review*, July 31, 2018, https://journals.sagepub.com/doi/pdf/10.1177/0008125618790244..

Jeffrey Towson, "Foreign Acquisitions and What Everyone Got Wrong About Haier's Purchase of GE Appliances" July 24, 2017, https://bit.ly/3C6x9jq

Joel Backaler, "Haier: A Chinese Company That Innovates" *Forbes*, June 17, 2010, https://bit.ly/3qtwVB6

Jun Zhao, "Haier's Acquisition of GE Appliances" (PDF), May 10, 2020, https://articlegateway.com/index.php/JBD/article/view/2364/2252.

K. Palepu, T. Khanna, and Ingrid Vargas "Haier: Taking a Chinese Company Global", Harvard Business School, August 25, 2006.

Kendra Schaefer, "China's Corporate Social Credit System: Context, Competition, Technology and Geopolitics. US-China Economic and Security Review Commission" *Trivium*, 2020, https://www.uscc.gov/sites/default/files/2020-12/Chinas_Corporate_Social_Credit_System.pdf.

Lenovo Corporate report, "2020 Corporate Governance Report" Lenovo, March 3, 2020.

Lourdes Casanova and Anne Miroux, "Emerging Markets Multinationals Report (EMR)", Emerging Markets Institute, Johnson School of Management, Cornell University, 2018, 2019, 2020, https://bit.ly/3om5o1w

Michael Ng and Iris Leung, "Haier D-Share IPO Breaks New Ground" *China Business Law Journal*, December, 2018, https://www.vantageasia.com/haier-d-share-ipo-breaks-new-ground/.

Richard Haigh, "500 2018 Ranking", *Brand Finance*, 2018, May 21, 2021, https://brandirectory.com/rankings/global/2018/table.

Staff report, "Haier Accelerates Innovation by Making Everyone a CEO" February 5, 2020, https://bit.ly/3c6o0Ne

Tim Bajarin "How a Chinese Company Became a Global PC Powerhouse" *Time Magazine*, May 2, 2015, May 5, 2020, https://time.com/3845674/lenovo-ibm/.

Wharton Business School staff report, "Beyond China: Can a New Acquisition Help Haier Crack Japan?" Wharton University of Pennsylvania, November 9, 2011, https://whr.tn/3HerJXJ

Zhang Jun, "China's 40 years of Reform and Development: 1978 – 2018" Australian National University, April 20, 2021, https://bit.ly/3ojP9Cf

Chapter 4 References:

"Big Four Auditors Squeezed Between US and China" *Financial Times*, April 29, 2021, https://on.ft.com/3qt2c7g

"Deloitte Chinese Companies Independent Board Director Study 2019" (translated), February 17, 2020, https://bit.ly/3oiLxsc (in Chinese).

Aish Sinha, "How Alibaba Took on eBay in China (and a Few Lessons for Indian Entrepreneurs)" 2018, https://medium.com/@aishsinhaindia/how-alibaba-took-on-ebay-in-china-and-a-few-lessons-for-indian-entrepreneurs-4f5ae9709089.

Anbound report "Luckin Case may Damage Other US-Listed Firms" *Global Times*, April 7, 2020, https://www.globaltimes.cn/content/1184939.shtml.

Barbara Powell "WorldCom, Ex-CEO Ebbers in Loan Dispute" May 18, 2003, *Midland Daily News*, https://bit.ly/3CapHUt

Appendix 3 – References by Chapter

Billy Duberstein "Another Luckin Scandal Gives Investors Yet Another Reason to Sell" *The Motley Fool*, June 8, 2020, https://www.fool.com/investing/2020/06/08/another-luckin-scandal-gives-investors-yet-another.aspx.

Bob Pisani "Luckin Coffee is a Painful Reminder of 'the Extreme Fraud Risk' of Some China-Based Companies" *CNBC*, April 3, 2020, https://www.cnbc.com/2020/04/03/luckin-coffee-debacle-is-a-painful-reminder-of-fraud-risk.html.

Emma Lee "Luckin Coffee Admits to Sales Fraud" *TechNode*, April 3, 2020.

Evelyn Cheng "China Talks up the Stock Market Lurking Concerns About Share-Backed Loans" *CNBC*, 2018, https://www.cnbc.com/2018/10/24/china-stocks-share-pledge-loans-pose-risk-to-equity-markets.html

Fang Zhou and Brett Zhang, "VIE Structure – a Long Untold Story" Financierworldwide.com 2018.

Francine McKenna, "The US-China Audit Showdown, and the Decision the Big Four Don't Want to Make" December 9, 2020, https://bit.ly/3C2IDod

Gregory J. Millman "Alibaba's IPO Puts VIE Structure in the Spotlight" *The Wall Street Journal*, September 22, 2014, https://on.wsj.com/3F96jsT

Jihun Bae and Ruishen Zhang "Do Anti-Pledging Policies Have Unintended Consequences for Corporate Governance?" The CLS Blue Sky Blog, 2019, https://bit.ly/3C5bMiO

Jing Yang "Behind the Fall of China's Luckin Coffee: A Network of Fake Buyers and a Fictitious Employee" 2020, https://on.wsj.com/3HcyKYY

Jing Yang, "Ernest & Young Says it Isn't Responsible for Luckin Coffee's Accounting Misconduct" *WSJ*, 2020, https://on.wsj.com/3olVBIS

John Biotnott, "7 Business Risks Every Business Should Plan For" 2019.

Joshua Franklin, Harry Brumpton, and Julie Zhu "Starbucks' China Challenger Luckin Raises $561 Million in US IPO" *Reuters*, May 16, 2019.

Kare Jingron et al., "State-Owned Enterprises in China: A Review of 40 years of Research and Practice" February 15, 2020, https://bit.ly/3bOaeii

Kornelia Fabisik, "Why Do US CEOs Pledge Their Own Company's Stock?" November 11, 2019.

Maurice Sanchez "Alibaba-: Case B: Jack Ma Takes Alipay" *Yahoo!*, 2011, https://www.readkong.com/page/alibaba-yahoo-case-b-1303530.

Paul Clarke "Big Luckin Coffee Investor Sells Entire Stake", *Barrons*, April 29, 2021.

Paul Hastings, "The SEC's Proposed Disclosure Rules for Hedging Transactions by Directors, Officers, and Employees" 2015, https://bit.ly/3kriI3Q

Pymnts.com staff report "Luckin's Jolt and Echoes of WeWork's Governance Debacle" *Pymnts.com*, April 7, 2020, https://bit.ly/3krtNlr

Reuters staff report "JD.com Chief Liu QiangDong Will Not Face Rape Charges" *BBC News*, 2018, https://www.bbc.com/news/world-asia-china-46652347.

Siqi Wei, "Inside Share Pledging, Managerial Risk-Taking, and Corporate Policies" May 1, 2021. https://bit.ly/3krGEnx

Sofia Baruzzi "China Releases Anti-Monopoly Guidelines for its Platform Economy" *China Briefing*, 2020, https://bit.ly/3qrlfP7

US Government publication "Luckin Coffee 2018 Annual Report with SEC" September 15, 2020, https://bit.ly/3n4ZkLF

Ying Dou, Ronald W. Masulis, and Jason Zein, "Shareholder Wealth Consequences of Insider Pledging of Company Stock as Collateral for Personal Loans" *ECGI*, January, 2019, www.ecgi.global/content/working-papers.

Chapter 5 References:

Cheng Leng and Ryan Woo, "Ant to Change How It Makes Loans with New Consumer-Finance Company" *The Wall Street Journal*" 2021, https://bit.ly/3qwzUZl

Cheng Leng, "China's Ant Group to Restructure Under Central Bank Agreement" *Reuters*, 2021, https://reut.rs/3F44Cx1

Emerging Markets Institute, Johnson School of Management, Cornell University, https://bit.ly/3Dbn9XG

Hua Liu, "Zong Qinghou Counter-Controlled Danone Path Investigation" (translated), *Sina.com*, 2017, https://bit.ly/3wzb24l
iNEWS staff report "When Can Zong Fuli Be in Charge of Wahaha Independently?", *INEWS*, 2021, https://bit.ly/3n4kdXe

James T. Areddy, "Trademark Ruling Favors Wahaha" *The Wall Street Journal*" 2007, https://on.wsj.com/3wzDH9c

John Sheehy, "It's An Unfair Deal and There's Nothing You Can Do About It" SINA Privatization Proxy, 2020, https://bit.ly/3wBLOlB

Julie Zhu, et al. "Ant Group Reaches Deal with China Regulators on Restructuring – Source" 2021, *Channel News Asia*, 2021, https://www.channelnewsasia.com/news/business/ant-group-reaches-deal-with-china-regulators-on-restructuring-14104434.

Lin Lingyi "What is Driving the Privatization Trend for Chinese-Listed Companies?" *KR Asia*, 2020, https://bit.ly/3om04n1

Liza L.S. Mark, "US Listed Chinese Companies: Regulatory Scrutiny and Strategic Options", *Lexology*, 2020, https://www.lexology.com/library/detail.aspx?g=8260378c-4b0a-4b55-8f1c-4f508ef49469.

Lourdes Casanova and Anne Miroux, "Emerging Markets Multinationals Report (EMR)", 2018-2020, https://bit.ly/3om5o1w

Maarten-Jan Bakkum and Ken Dijkstra "China's Bid to Attract Capital Creates New Opportunities in Bond and Equity Markets" *NN Investment Partners*, 2021, https://bit.ly/3n449Vi

Maria Angeles Alcaide, Elena de la Poza and Natividad Guadalajara, "Assessing the Sustainability of High-Value Brands in the IT Sector" *Sustainability, Vol. 11, Issue 6,* March 15, 2019, https://www.mdpi.com/2071-1050/11/6/1598/htm

Megan Cattel, "Sina Goes Private After 21 years on Nasdaq" *SupChina*, May 9, 2021, https://supchina.com/2021/03/24/sina-goes-private-after-21-years-on-nasdaq/.

Meghan Davies "A Wave of Chinese Companies Seek US IPOs as Delisting Concerns Ease" *Asia Financial Times*, 2021, https://bit.ly/3omG8YW

Michael Schumann, "The Electric-Car Lesson That China Is Serving Up for America" *The Atlantic*, 2021, https://bit.ly/3krpbvE

Nancy A. Fischer, et al. "Senate Bill Could Result in De-Listing of Certain Chinese Companies and Non-Chinese State-Owned Enterprises from US Securities Exchanges" *Pillsbury*, 2020, https://www.pillsburylaw.com/en/news-and-insights/HFCAA-holding-foreign-companies-accountable-act.html.

Nicholas R. Lardy and Tianlei Huang, "Rising Foreign Investment in China's Onshore Stocks and Bonds Shows Accelerating Financial Integration" *PIIE*, 2021, https://bit.ly/3n7g4la

Report "Global 500 2018 Ranking" *Brand Finance*, 2018.

Reuters report "What's Next for Jack Ma's Ant Group After China Orders Revamp?" *Channel News Asia*, 2021, https://www.channelnewsasia.com/news/business/china-ant-group-jack-ma-restructure-capital-valuation-credit-14652192.

Ross Kerber, "Three Chinese Telecom Companies to Be Delisted by NYSE" *Reuters*, 2021, https://reut.rs/3oiZ233

Russell Flannery, "How to Lose in China?" *Forbes*, 2007.

US Government publication "Chinese Companies Listed on Major US Stock Exchanges", 2020, https://bit.ly/3H5qCcy

Chapter 6 References:

CFI Staff report "Socially Responsible Investments (SRI)" *CFI* (n.d.), June 28, 2021, https://bit.ly/3F7hToE

Ying Chen "Corporate Social Responsibility from the Chinese Perspective" 2011, *Indiana International and Comparative Law Review,* 21(3), p.419-433, October 4, 2020, https://bit.ly/3quDinA

Shujle Leng, "'Be in Love With Them, but Don't Marry Them': How Jack Ma Partnered with Local Government to Make E-Commerce Giant Alibaba, and Hangzhou, a Success" *Foreign Policy*, October, 2014, , https://foreignpolicy.com/2014/10/31/be-in-love-with-them-but-dont-marry-them/.

MSCI report "MSCI Global Sustainability Indexes Methodology" *MSCI*, November, 2014, https://bit.ly/30eQXoe

MSCI report "China Through an ESG Lens" *MSCI ESG Research LLC*, September, 2019, https://www.msci.com/documents/10199/78514cc5-a16d-493a-9774-af1012aa0420.

MSCI report "ESG Ratings Corporate Search Tool" *MSCI ESG Research LLC* (n.d.), July 2, 2021 https://www.msci.com/our-solutions/esg-investing/esg-ratings/esg-ratings-corporate-search-tool .

Philippe Gugler, "Multinational Corporates: Lost War in Pertaining Global Competitiveness?" *Journal of Business Ethics*, 87, 3-24. https://bit.ly/3khczqE

OECD report, "Corporate Social Responsibility: Partners for Progress" *OECD*, October, 2001, https://bit.ly/3Ha6DJP

Ninjing Liu, "Ping An, CEIS Launch China-Specific ESG Rating System" *Seneca ESG*, December, 2020, https://bit.ly/3krIPYp

"Country Garden Beautiful China ESG 100 Index Report," [Translated title], *Sina Finance*, June, 2021, https://bit.ly/3HeLqP9

Standard and Poor's report, "Standard & Poor's Corporate Governance Scores and Evaluations: Criteria, Methodology and Definitions" *Standard & Poor's Governance Services*, McGraw-Hill Companies Inc., January, 2004, https://bit.ly/3F4la8d

Guo Peiyuan, Chairman, "Decennial Report on the Responsible Investment in China" *SynTao Green Finance and Aegon Industrial Fund*, 2019, https://bit.ly/2Yt8rMu

Milton Friedman, "The Social Responsibility of Business Is to Increase Its Profits" *The New York Times*, September, 1970, https://www.nytimes.com/1970/09/13/archives/a-friedman-doctrine-the-social-responsibility-of-business-is-to.html.

Jianyu Wang, "An Overview of China's Corporate Law Regime" *SSRN Electronic Journal*, August, 2008, https://www.researchgate.net/publication/228204574.

RBC Wealth Management report, "ESG Versus SRI: Successfully Aligning Your Investments and Values" *Wealth Management* (n.d.), June 28, 2021, https://bit.ly/3kryHyS

Meng Liu, "Is Corporate Social Responsibility China's Secret Weapon?" World Economic Forum, 2015, https://www.weforum.org/agenda/2015/03/is-corporate-social-responsibility-chinas-secret-weapon.

MSCI report "Corporate Governance in China" *MSCI*, September, 2017, https://www.msci.com/documents/10199/1d443a3d-0437-4af7-aa27-ada3a2655f6d

Chapter 7 References:

"China's Carbon Market Set to Miss Target to Start Trading", *Bloomberg Green*, 2021, https://www.bloomberg.com/news/articles/2021-06-28/china-s-carbon-market-set-to-miss-target-for-start-of-trading.

"China's Former Grid Chief Sees Emissions Peaking Early in 2028" *Caixin*, 2021, https://bit.ly/3n2JRf2

"China's Carbon Emissions Trading Market will be Launched Soon" (translated), *China News Network*, June 2021, https://www.chinanews.com/gn/2021/06-23/9505780.shtml.

"Energy Insider: Carbon Market to Expend to Eight Industries" *Caixin*, June, 2021, https://bit.ly/3H4tl6l

"The Full List of Listed Companies in China, How Many are Listed in China," *Ultimate Time in Space*, 2021, (translated), http://www.wl-mould.net/gupiao/5146.html

CISION staff article, "CICC Underwrites the First Financial Green Bond Issued by China Development Bank" *CISION,* March, 2021, https://prn.to/3koDBwq

Climate Bonds Initiative press release, "Notice on Issuing the Green Bond Endorsed Projects Catalogue" *Climate Bonds Initiative* (2021 Edition), April, 2021, https://bit.ly/3bXkAMP

Corporate conference report "Asian Business Dialogue on Corporate Governance 2020" ACGA Conference Report, November 25, 2020, https://bit.ly/3qoYprp

Dan Murtaugh, "The Chinese Government Needs to Become a Clean Energy Supermajor" *Bloomberg Green,* 2021, https://bloom.bg/3wz7y1N

Deepti Sri, "Report: China to Launch National Carbon Trading Market by June" *Tech In Asia,* March 30, 2021, https://bit.ly/3ocUon7

Enoch Yiu, "China's Carbon Neutral Goal: Shanghai's New National Carbon Emissions Trading Platform Unveils Trading Rules, Sets Stage for Launch" *South China Morning Post,* June, 2021. https://bit.ly/30bj1bG

Guandi Xia, Zhihu. (n.d.), "Quantitative Analysis of State-Owned Enterprises in Listed Companies" (translated), 2021, https://zhuanlan.zhihu.com/p/138181140?jdyscene=chat

Iain Mills, "China's NSSF Takes More Active Social Role" *IPE,* 2011, https://bit.ly/3kqq1bI

Jeremy Goldkorn, et al. "A Brief Guide to China's Stock Markets and Indices" *SupChina,* 2021, https://bit.ly/308rWLn

Jiang Simin, "CGTN: Leading With Action: China in the Fight for Carbon-Neutral Future" *Business Wire,* April, 2021, https://bwnews.pr/3C1AAYT

Jolie Ho, "NCSSF Invites Bids for Landmark Overseas Equity Mandates" *Asian Investor*, 2020, https://bit.ly/3ohd3y5

Ori Ben-Akiva, Michael Nouvellon, and Ziang Fang, "The Value in China's SOEs" *Man Institute*, 2019, https://www.man.com/maninstitute/the-value-in-chinas-soes

Wang Liwei and Luo Meihan, "China, EU Set to Agree on Green Finance Definitions by Year-End, Official Says" *Caixin*, June, 2021, https://bit.ly/3HjAq35

Wang Liwei and Luo Meihan, "Weekend Long Read: Views on China's Green Transformation From Inside the Central Bank" *Caixin*, May, 2021, https://bit.ly/3HjAq35

Wenchi Yu, "Risk Mitigation and Creating Social Impact: Chinese Technology Companies in the United States" Harvard Kennedy School, April 2021, https://bit.ly/3bZGr6f

Witold Henisz, Tim Koller, and Robin Nuttall "Five Ways that ESG Creates Value" *McKinsey Quarterly*, November, 2019, https://mck.co/3kmXwvH

World Economic Forum press release "A Leapfrog Moment for China in ESG Reporting", World Economic Forum, 2021, https://bit.ly/3D43CZg

Chapter 8 References:

"The Country's First Representative Litigation Case was Judged: Feilo Acoustics was Sentenced to 123 Million Shareholders in Compensation and an Average of 390,000 Compensation was Awarded, East" *Money*, 2021, (translated), http://finance.eastmoney.com/a/202105111917575671.html

"Xi Jinping: We Must Focus on Improving the System Environment and Strengthening the Construction of a Social Credit System" (translated), *Sohu*, February, 2019, https://www.sohu.com/a/298187739_100013182

Alexander Chipman Koty, "China's Corporate Social Credit System: What Businesses Need to Know" *China Briefing*, 2019, https://bit.ly/31HbphD

Alexandra Ma, "China's Controversial Social Credit System Isn't Just About Punishing People – Here's What You Can Do to Get Rewards, from Special Discounts to Better Hotel Rooms" *Insider*, February, 2019, https://bit.ly/3knXtQ8

Cheng Ting-Fang and Lauly Li, "US-China Tech War: Beijing's Secret Chipmaking Champions" *Nikkei Asia*, 2021, https://s.nikkei.com/3ocQomF

Coco Liu and Zenping Huang, "ByteDance Eyes a New $185 Billion Business Ahead of Mega IPO", *Bloomberg*, May, 2021, https://bloom.bg/30aJQgy

CPI staff article, "Chinese Tech Giants Pledge to End Unfair Competition" *Competition Policy International*, April, 2021, https://bit.ly/3bXlOaT

Drew Donnelly, "An Introduction to the China Social Credit System" *New Horizons*, April 15, https://nhglobalpartners.com

Echo Wang and Yingzhi Yang, "'I'm Not Very Social'. ByteDance Founder to Hand CEO Reins to College Roommate" *Reuters*, 2021, https://reut.rs/3kn5AN5

Fan Li, "Amendment to China Patent Law Offer PTA, PTE and Patent Linkage" *Foley*, June, 2021, https://bit.ly/3n1bRjd

"Feilo Acoustics" Case Demonstrates the Important Role of Specialization in Investor Rights Protection" (translated), *Sina*, May, 2021, https://bit.ly/3H7UDbI

"Feilo Audio: Regain the Sorrows of the Past" (translated), *China Economic Net*, May, 2021, https://bit.ly/3wBk4xM

GT staff reporters, "China's 5-year Plan to Lead Global Recovery" *Global Times*, 2021, https://www.globaltimes.cn/page/202103/1217749.shtml

Jack B. Hicks, "China Announces Long-Awaited and Significant Updates to Intellectual Property Protections" *The National Law Review,* December, 2020, https://bit.ly/3bVDH9Z

Jinghan Xu and Lauren Zelin, "China's 14th Five-Year Plan Sets Foundation for Climate Action, But Important Details Are Still Needed" *World Resources Institute,* May 22, 2021, https://bit.ly/3Hb8spS

Jinghan Xu and Lauren Zelin, "China's 14th Five-Year Plan Sets Foundation for Climate Action, But Important Details Are Still Needed" *World Resources Institute*, March 12, 2021, https://www.wri.org.news

Katja Drinhausen and Vincent Brussee, "China's Social Credit System in 2021: From Fragmentation Towards Integration" *MERICS,* March 3, 2021, https://merics.org.en

Kendra Schaefer, "China's Corporate Social Credit System: Context, Competition, Technology and Geopolitics. US-China Economic and Security Review Commission" *Trivium,* November, 2020, https://bit.ly/3D7KMjS

Kenji Kawase, "Inside China's Secret Plans" *Nikkei Asia*, 2021, https://s.nikkei.com/3wuenl6

KPMG report, "The 14th Five-Year Plan: Sector Impact Outlook" *KPMG*, 2021, https://bit.ly/3kqp03D

Michael Gu, "Merger Control Review 2020" *International Law Office*, 2021, https://bit.ly/3qplgmS

Michal Meidan, Philip Andrews-Speed, and Yan Qin, "Key Issues for China's 14th Five Year Plan", *Oxford Energy Comment*, March, 2021, https://www.oxfordenergy.org/wpcms

NikkeiAsia staff article, "ByteDance CEO Zhang Yiming's Resignation Letter – Full Text," NikkeiAsia 2021, https://s.nikkei.com/3kpjtdp

Qian Yu, "Fourteenth Five-Year" Governance Has "Number" to Open a New Chapter" (translated), *People*, 2020, http://theory.people.com.cn/n1/2020/1028/c40531-31908612.html

Sofia Baruzzi, "China Releases Anti-Monopoly Guidelines for its Platform Economy" *China Briefing*, 2020, https://bit.ly/3wBf2Bo

Stephen Yang, "China: Review of the 4th Amendments of China's Patent Law" *Mondaq*, January, 2021, https://bit.ly/3wuVajf

"Ten Key Research Directions for the Construction of the Social Credit System in 2015" (translated), *Sohu*, March, 2020, https://www.sohu.com/a/378101732_777813

WIPO staff article, "China Becomes Top Filer of International Patents in 2019 Amid Robust Growth for WIPO's IP Services, Treaties and Finances" *WIPO*, April 2020, https://www.wipo.int/pressroom/en/articles/2020/article_0005.html

WIPO staff article, "Innovation Perseveres: International Patent Filings via WIPO Continues to Grow in 2020 Despite COVID-19 Pandemic" *WIPO*, March, 2021, https://www.wipo.int/pressroom/en/articles/2021/article_0002.html

Yukon Huang, "China's Record on Intellectual Property Rights is Getting Better and Better" *PF*, October, 2019, https://foreignpolicy.com/2019/10/16/china-intellectual-property-theft-progress/

Zhang Yiming, "A Letter from Yiming" ByteDance official website, May, 2021, https://www.bytedance.com/en/news/60a526af053cc102d640c061

Chapter 9 References:

Bora Ly, "The Nexis of BRI and Internationalization of Renminbi (RMB)," *Cogent Business and Management*, 2020, https://doi.org.10.1080/23311975.2020.1808399

BRI staff article, "Workshops in Africa to Build Skills by China" *Belt and Road News*, May 8, 2021, https://www.beltandroad.news

BRN staff report, "Is the Pandemic Really Hurting China's Belt and Road Initiative?" *Belt and Road News*, May 17, 2021, https://www.beltandroad.news

Business Reporting Desk, "China-Africa Partnership Seen Rapid Growth in Bilateral Collaboration" *Belt and Road News*, May, 2021, https://bit.ly/3qqIf0G

Business Reporting Desk, "New Opportunities in South Caucasus After the 44-days War and China's Belt & Road" *Belt and Road News*, 2021, https://bit.ly/3qn4nsM

Clare Connellan, et al. "Okpavi v Royal Dutch Shell Plc: UK Supreme Court Allows Nigerian Citizens' Environmental Damage Claim to Proceed Against UK Parent Company", *White and Case*, February 19, 2021, https://www.whitecase.com

Daniel J. Ikenson, "NAFTA 2.9: The Best Trade Agreement Ever Negotiated (Except for all of the Others)," *Cato Institute*, October, 2018, https://bit.ly/31D4Nkm

David Sacks, "Countries in China's Belt and Road Initiative: Who's in and Who's Out" Council on Foreign Relations, March, 2021, https://on.cfr.org/2YCF0b6

Harri Taliga, "Belt and Road Initiative in Central Asia" *ITUC*, 2021, www.ituc-csi.org

Ian Lewis and Eileen Wang, "New Free Trade Zones Declared Open in Tianjin, Fujian and Guangdong: How Attractive Will They Be to Foreign Investors?" *Mayer Brown JSM*, May, 2015, https://bit.ly/3bTsua2

John Gong, "If RCEP Comes, Can CPTPP be Far Behind for China?" *CGTN*, November, 2020, https://bit.ly/3H2gmSB

Kate Whiting, "An Expert Explains: What Is RCEP, the World's Biggest Trade Deal?" World Economic Forum, May, 2021, https://www.weforum.org/agenda/2021/05/rcep-world-biggest-trade-deal/

Kyodo News staff article, "China OKs World's Largest Free Trade Deal Including Japan, ASEAN" *Kyodo News*, March, 2021, https://bit.ly/3D2qIiZ

Kyodo News staff article, "G7 to Launch Infrastructure Plan to Counter China's Belt and Road" *The Jakarta Post*, June, 2021, https://bit.ly/3obPvST

Kyodo News staff article, "Japan Approves World's Largest Trade Deal Including China, ASEAN" *Kyodo News*, April, 2021, https://bit.ly/3D400Xc

Ledger Insights staff report, "Foreign Firms More Keen to Use China's Digital Renminbi CBDC Than Domestic Firms" *Ledger Insights*, July, 2020, https://bit.ly/3oiq7Do

Lyndsey Zhang, "Manufacturing Is on the Move in Asia" *Global Finance*, June, 2020, https://www.gfmag.com/magazine/june-2020/manufacturing-move-asia

Lyndsey Zhang, "People's Bank of China Tightens Cryptocurrency Regulations" *Global Finance*, June, 2021, https://www.gfmag.com/magazine/june-2021/china-tightens-crypto-regulations

Appendix 3 – References by Chapter

Mathee Supapongse, "Leveraging Distributed Ledger Technology to Increase Efficiency in Cross-Border Payments" Project Inthanon-LionRock, Hong Kong Monetary Authority, January 22, 2020, https://hkma.gov.hk/media/eng/

Matteo Giovannini, "Why RCEP Deal Is a Crucial Milestone in China's Multilateralism Push" *CGTN*, November 17, 2020, https://www.cgtn.com

Michael Corder, "Dutch Court Orders Shell Nigeria to Compensate Farmers" *AP News*, January, 2019, https://bit.ly/3DeDYAQ

Payal Bhattacharya, "Why India Opted Out of World's Biggest Trade Deal Signed Today" *Times of India*, November, 2020, https://bit.ly/3oi9rMf

Pearl Risberg, "The Give-And-Take of BRI in Africa" Center for Strategic and International Studies (n.d.), July 2, 2021, https://www.csis.org/give-and-take-bri-africa

Project report, "Bui Dam Hydroelectricity Project, Ghana" *Water Technology* (n.d.), July 7, 2021, https://www.water-technology.net/projects/bui-dam-hydro-power-ghana/

Rebecca Fang, "China Reforms QFII, RQFII but Leaves Critical Problems Untouched" *Global Capital China*, September, 2019, https://bit.ly/3qlhCdy

Robin Ganguly and Cedric Sam, "China's Ambitious Plan to Make the Yuan the World's Go-To Currency" *Bloomberg*, September 26, 2016, https://bloomberg.org

Sofia Horta e Casta and Tian Chen, "China Takes Its Most Visible Measure Yet to Curb Yuan's Gain" *Bloomberg*, May, 2021, https://bloom.bg/3n0GPYD

UNESCO staff report, "Global Education Monitoring Report 2020" UNESCO, 2020, https://resourcecentre.savethechildren.net/node/17803/pdf/373718eng.pdf

Chapter 10 References

Anthea Wong, Linjun Shen, and Bo Yu, "Cross-Border RMB Cash Pooling Made Possible for Multinational Corporations in China" *PWC*, February, 2015, https://pwc.to/3c02w4F

Asset report, "Guide to the Chinese Fixed Income Markets" *J.P. Morgan Asset Management,* December 12, 2019, https://www.jpmorgan.com/commercial

Blog article, "Renminbi internationalization: China's Path to a World Currency?" *iBanFirst Blog*, April, 2020, https://bit.ly/3qp5NmD

Bloomberg News, "China Mulls Turning Tutoring Companies into Non-Profits" *Al-Jazeera*, July, 2021, https://bit.ly/3HbfomU

Bruno De Conti. "The Internationalization of the Chinese Renminbi: Firm Steps, but a Long Road Ahead" November 24, 2020, https://www.e-ir.info/pdf/88662

CBN Editor, "Bank of China Report Calls for Shift from SWIFT to CIPS for Cross-Border Settlement Due to Concern over US Sanctions" *China Banking News*, July 15, 2021, https://bit.ly/3H4GpIV

Chi Hung Kwan, "Issues Facing Renminbi Internationalization: Observations from Chinese, Regional and Global Perspectives" *IDEAS*, September, 2018, https://ideas.repec.org/a/mof/journl/ppr14_05_03.html

Chi Hung Kwan, "Issues Facing Renminbi Internationalization: Observations from Chinese, Regional, and Global Perspectives" Nomura Institute of Capital Markets Research, Public Policy Review, September, 2018, https://www.mof.go.jp/english/pri

Appendix 3 – References by Chapter

Chris Brummer, "Institute of International Economic Law, Georgetown University Law Center (IIEL) Issue Brief. Renminbi Internationalization and Systematic Risk," February, 2017, https://bit.ly/31SmRY9

Climate Bonds Initiative report, "Green Infrastructure Investment Opportunities – Guangdong-Hong Kong-Macao Greater Bay Area 2021 report" Climate Bonds Initiative, July 15, 2021, https://bit.ly/3og8ELZ

David Pan, "How China's Digital Yuan Could Go Global" *Coin Desk*, March 17, 2021, https://www.coindesk.com

Dong He and Robert Neil Mccauley, "Offshore Markets for the Domestic Currency: Monetary and Financial Stability Issues, *Bank of International Settlements*, September, 2010, https://bit.ly/3ocYxHH

Dorcas Wong, "China's Six New Free Trade Zones: Where Are They Located?" *China Briefing*, September, 2019, https://www.china-briefing.com/news/china-free-trade-zones-six-provinces/

Duan Jin-Chuan, "Will China's Digital Currency Accelerate the Internationalization of the RMB?" (translated), *Think China*, November 18, 2020, https://thinkchina.sg

Edwin L. -C. Lai, "Renminbi Internationalization: The Prospects of China's Yuan as the Next Global Currency" *HKUST IEMS* (n.d.), July 7, 2021, https://bit.ly/3F5roEy

Evelyn Cheng, "China's Yuan Could Become the World's Third-Largest Reserve Currency in 10 years, Morgan Stanley Predicts" *CNBC*, September 4, 2020, https://cnb.cx/31NnjH0

Gang Meng, "China's Belt and Road Initiative and RMB Internationalization" *World Scientific* (n.d.), July 27, 2021, https://www.worldscientific.com/worldscibooks/10.1142/11230

Glynne Williams, et al., "Chinese Multinationals: Threat to, or Opportunity for, Trade Unions? The Case of Sinohydro in Ghana" 2017, June 2, 2021, https://bit.ly/3C1IxNJ

Guo Shuqing, "China's New Development Stage and Hong Kong SAR's New Opportunities" *BIS*, January, 2021, https://www.bis.org/review/r210127j.pdf

Heather Zeiger, "Will China's Digital Yuan Displace the US Dollar in Global Trade," *Mind Matters*, May 12, 2021, https://mindmatters.ai

HKMA staff report, "International Use of the Renminbi - A New Era" *HKMA*, January, 2016, www.hkma.gov.hk

Hongbin Cai, "The Path of Economic Restructuring of Hong Kong" HKU Business School, July 17, 2021, https://bit.ly/3koIVQq

Jacob Kurien and Bernard Yudkin Geoxavier, "The Political Economy of International Finance: A Revised Roadmap for Renminbi Internationalization" *Yale Journal of International Affairs*, December, 2020, https://bit.ly/3n1RKRL

James Chen, "Qualified Foreign Institutional Investor (QFII)" *Investopedia*, May, 2020, https://bit.ly/30aQRxU

Jing Yang, Keith Zhai, and Corrie Driebusch, "Didi Tried Balancing Pressure from China and Investors. It Satisfied Neither" *WSJ*, 2021, https://on.wsj.com/3n8YZrr

John Xie, "EU-China Relations Enter Downward Spiral" *Voice of America*, April 2, 2021, https://www.voanews.com

Jonathan Cheng, "China Banking Regulator Sees Risk From "Bubble" in Real-Estate Price" *WSJ*, March, 2021, https://on.wsj.com/3qpcF3e

Kathy Chu, "Shaken Investors Losing Appetite for China's 'Dim Sum Bonds" *ABC News*, October, 2011, https://abcn.ws/3F3nZ9y

Appendix 3 – References by Chapter

Kenji Kawase and Michelle Chan, "How the National Security Law Transformed Hong Kong in One Year" *Nikkei Asia*, June, 2021, https://s.nikkei.com/3C1g9eG

Leena Fatin, "Climate Bonds Opens Shanghai Office: Signs MoU with Luijiazui Financial City" Climate Bonds Initiative, March 29, 2021, https://bit.ly/3qn7HEg

Liao Qianyun, Sheng Xiaohong, and Sun Ruoyang, "Indexed Investment – A New Perspective on Investing in China's Bond Market" *Market Axess*, October, 2020, https://bit.ly/3F1tvJQ

Lindsey Marie Thill, "RMB Internationalization and the BRI: Reality or Fantasy?" *Elcano Blog*, July 7, 2021.

Muneeb Jan, "The Rise of the Renminbi: Hong Kong's Role as an Offshore RMB Hub" *The China Guys*, April, 2021, https://bit.ly/3c4jChL

Nathan Chow, "Understanding China: RMB Internationalization 2.0" *DBS Corporate Banking*, January 22, 2021, https://bit.ly/3HafThe

NikkeiAsia staff report, "West Wants to Defend International Order, Not Contain China: Blinken" *Nikkei Asia*, May, 2021, https://s.nikkei.com/3F0BBlH

Norton Rose Fulbright, "Chinese Central Bank Calls for Public Comments on New Anti-Money Laundering and Counter-Terrorism Financing Measures" February, 2021, https://bit.ly/2YyiO1D

Nosmot Ghadamosi, "Ghana's Bauxite Boom "*Africa Brief*, January, 2020, https://bit.ly/3bVINTM

Quentin Webb, "BlackRock Gets Green Lights to Start Offering Mutual Funds in China" *WSJ*, June, 2021, https://on.wsj.com/3wwhokR

Research report, "Leveraging Hong Kong as an Offshore Renminbi Centre for Advancing Renminbi Internationalization" *HKEX*, March, 2021, https://bit.ly/3bValss

Robin Ganguly and Cedric Sam, "China's Ambitious Plan to Make the Yuan the World's Go-To Currency, *Bloomberg*, September 28, 2016.

Sarah Chan, "Assessing China's Recent Capital Outflows: Policy Challenges and Implications" *China Finance and Economic Review*, 2017, https://chinafinanceandeconomicreview.com

SCMP Events, "Can Hong Kong Become a Global Hub for Green Finance" *South China Morning Post*, June 1, 2021, https://www.scmp.com/events/business

Serkan Arslanalp and Chima Simpson-Bell, "US Dollar Share of Global Foreign Exchange Reserves Drops to 25-Year Low" *IMF Blog*, May, 2021, https://bit.ly/3bXqFsD

Staff report, "2020 RMB Internationalization Report" *PBOC*, 2020, https://bit.ly/3oivYbQ

Staff report, "China to Lift HK, Shanghai's Roles as Global Financial Hubs in Broad Plan for Capital Market" *Global Times*, May 9, 2021, https://www.globaltimes.cn/index.html

Staff report, "Dominant Gateway to China" Hong Kong Monetary Authority (n.d.), July 17, 2021, https://bit.ly/3F3p4hC

Staff report, "Hong Kong Ranks as 2nd Largest IPO Market in 2020" *Sovereign Resources*, March, 2021, https://bit.ly/3H6YgyI

Staff report, "IMF adds Chinese Renminbi to Special Drawing Rights Basket" *IMF News*, September, 2016, https://bit.ly/2YyrBAP

Staff report, "The Conference Board Economic Forecast for the US Economy" *The Conference Board*, July, 2021, https://www.conference-board.org/research/us-forecast

Susie Chen, "US Offshore RMB Accounts Open the Door to Growth Opportunities in China" *J.P. Morgan* (n.d.), July 7, 2021, https://bit.ly/3n3uuCQ

Ulrike Glueck, "An Overview on Cash Pooling in China" *CMS*, December, 2020, https://cms.law/en/chn/publication/an-overview-on-cash-pooling-in-china

Venus Feng, "China Education Tycoon Loses $15 Billion as Shares Tumble" *Bloomberg Wealth*, July, 2021, https://bloom.bg/3kmahX8

William Bratton, "China Reboots the Internationalization of its Currency" *Nikkei Asia*, April 29, 2021, https://s.nikkei.com/3083c5B

Witold Henisz, Tim Koller, and Robin Nuttall, "Five Ways That ESG Creates Value" *McKinsey Quarterly*, November, 2019, https://mck.co/3C2KTvF

Xintong Wan, "China's National Carbon Market Makes its First Trade" Caixin, July, 2021, https://bit.ly/3c0VuwJ

Yang Chengxi and Matteo Giovannini, "Shanghai Bourse Could be World's Biggest IPO Market as it Turns 30" *CGTN*, November, 2020, https://bit.ly/3cdY7LT

Yang Sheng and Xie Jun, "Biden Appears More Positive Toward China, but Still Lacks Clarity on Policy" *China/Politics*, February, 2021, https://www.globaltimes.cn/page/202102/1215079.shtml

Appendix 4 – List of Interviewees

This list includes brief biographies of individuals who have participated in interviews and shared their opinions and experiences of various topics. While some of interviewees have respectfully requested they remain anonymous, their contributions are nonetheless genuinely appreciated.

Professor Andrew Kakabadse – Professor Kakabadse is Professor of Governance & Leadership, Programme Director of The Board Director's Programme, and Chairman of the Henley Directors' Forum. Professor Kakabadse has undertaken global studies spanning over 20,000 organizations in the private, public, and third sectors encompassing 41 countries. His research focuses on board performance, governance, leadership and policy. Professor Kakabadse is listed in Who's Who and is a life member of the Thinkers 50 Hall of Fame.

Professor Lourdes Casanova – Professor Casanova is a Senior Lecturer and Gail and Rob Cañizares Director of Emerging Markets Institute, S.C. Johnson School of Management, Cornell University. An accomplished researcher and author of many books, in 2014 and 2015, Professor Casanova was selected as one of 50 of the most influential Iberoamerican intellectuals by ES Global, an influential Hispanic executive training organization. Then in 2017, Professor Casanova was named as one of only 30 Iberoamerican intellectuals by the same organization.

Professor Edward Freeman – Dr Freeman is a philosopher and professor of business administration at the Darden School at the

University of Virginia. Dr Freeman has been recognized since the 1980s for his stakeholder theory and his work on business ethics.

Christine Raynaud - Ms Raynaud is a former board director of the European Chamber of Commerce in Hong Kong and a senior executive with various world-class talent management consulting firms. Ms Raynaud has advised Western and Asian companies with their global talent strategies since the 1980s and lived in Hong Kong for ten years.

Thomas Estines - Mr Estines is the Co-CEO of Groupe Investissement Responsible Inc., a Canadian-based global firm specializing in sustainable development, responsible investment, and finance. As the Co-CEO, Mr Estines ensures that the votes cast on behalf of GIR clients comply with their proxy voting policies, and the quality of the analyses produced by the team. Mr. Estines is also in charge of client relations, business development and the creation of partnerships with other members of the industry.

Vivian Lin Thurston, CFA – Ms Thurston is a partner and portfolio manager at William Blair Investment Management, co-managing various Emerging Markets and Chinese equity strategies. Previously, she worked at UBS Global Asset Management and Calamos Investments as a consumer analyst specializing in investment research and stock selection in the global consumer sector. She is also the founder and Chairman of the Board of Chinese Finance Association of America. Vivian received a BL in Sociology from Peking University and an MA in Sociology and MS in Finance from the University of Illinois at Urbana-Champaign.

Agnes K Y Tai – Ms Tai is the Director of Great Glory Investment Corporation (a family-owned firm) and a responsibility officer for an Asian asset management company.

Fedor Heijl – Mr Heijl, a native of The Netherlands, transformed his family's automotive business into an international success, sold his company to a leading US corporation, then established a consulting firm specializing in advising family-owned business entrepreneurs with their long-term business strategies. He also serves as a board member for numerous family-owned businesses.

Ernst Gylfe – Mr Gylfe is the owner and Vice Chairman of Novita Ltd., a family-owned yarn manufacturer founded in Finland in 1928, and is one of the largest of its kind in Europe. Mr Gylfe is also the Chair of Board of Directors of a Zurich-based boutique investment company that manages wealth for UHNWi, and the founding partner of EMC Advisors Ltd. in Zurich. Mr Gylfe has a Master's Degree in Business and Finance.

Lynda Kahari – Ms Kahari is a business executive with extensive banking experience in large and start-up banks in Africa and the Pacific. Ms Kahari holds a Master's degree in Finance & Investments and a Master's in Business Administration She is a graduate of the Australian Institute of Company Directors program and is also a Balanced Scorecard Professional.

Index

[All references are to paragraph numbers and appendices]

Acronyms
    list of App 2
Alibaba case studies
    controlling structure 1.2.3; 2.2.1, 2.2.3
    succession planning 1.2.3
    VIE structure 4.2.2
Ant Group
    IPO incident case study 5.2.3
Anti-trust law enforcement 8.3.2
    consumer data collaboration and protection 8.3.2
    M&A transactions involving VIE structures 8.3.2
    new legal framework with severe penalties for violations 8.3.2
    regulatory reforms, and 5.2.3; 8.3.2
Asset management firms
    ESG revolution, and 7.2.2
    Ping An Insurance Group ESG adoption case study 7.2.2
Audit
    quality and information transparency 4.5

Belt and Road Initiative (BRI) 9.2
    challenges for future development 9.2.2
    RMB internationalization, and 10.1.2, 10.1.4
    positive economic and social impacts 9.2.1
Boards
    function independency and objectivity 4.5
    ineffective independence and functions, SOEs and 2.1.2
Business mindset change trend
    ESG revolution, and 7.3.2
ByteDance Ltd
    founder's resignation case study 8.4

Index

Carbon neutrality
    bonds 7.1.2
    goals 7.1, 7.1.3; 8.1.2
Central bank digital currency (CBDC) 10.1.3
    trading platform 10.1.3
CEO share pledging risks
    Chinese companies 4.1.4
    landscape in US 4.1.3
    motivations 4.1.1
CG Code 1.1.4
CG development
    comparisons *see* Comparisons between China and Japan; Comparisons between China and US
    governance models and practices *see* CG practices; Governance models
    "gradualist approach" 2.3.3
    key factors driving *see* Key domestic drivers of CG practices; Major international drivers of CG practices
    reform *see* CG reform
    status *see* Status of CG development
CG models *see* Governance models
CG practices
    creativity and quick reaction capacity 5.1.2
    evolving, domestic and international drivers *see* Key domestic drivers of CG practices; Major international drivers of CG practices
    government's influence 5.1.1
    pros and cons 5.1
    vernal years 5.1.3
CG reform 3.3
    companies' improvement parallels regulatory development 3.3.1
    Lenovo's CG model, case study 3.3.1
    trends 3.3.2
Challenges
    BRI's future development 9.2.2
    China-Africa collaboration 9.3.1
    China as RCEP's leading country 9.1.2
    ESG revolution 7.3
Chief Executive Officers (CEOs)
    nomination, succession planning and compensation 1.3.3
China-Africa collaboration 9.3
    impacts and challenges 9.3.1
    lack of regulatory system in host countries 9.3.1; 9.3.3
    major problems of Chinese multinationals' overseas operations 9.3.2, 9.3.3
    SinoHydro-Ghana Bui Dam Hydroelectricity Project case study 9.3.1

China Development Bank (CDB)
    "carbon neutrality" bonds 7.1.2
China International Capital Corporation (CICC)
    underwriter of green bonds 7.1.2
"China Model"
    Chinese multinationals' overseas operations, and 9.3.2
    mutual understanding 11
"China Puzzle" phenomenon 2.1.1
China Securities Regulatory Commission (CSRC) 1.1.2
    establishment 1.1, 1.1.2; 3.3
    issue of CG Code 1.1.4; 3.3
    issue of new ESG reporting rules 7.1.1
    plan to promote Hong Kong and Shanghai as international financial centers 10.2.1
    suspension of IPOs 1.1.3
China's Belt and Road Initiative *see* Belt and Road Initiative (BRI)
China's 14th Five-Year-Plan (FYP) 7.3.1; 8.1
    international financial center roles, and 10.2.1
    reshaping of ESG landscape, and 8.1.2
    three development features 8.1.1
Chinese companies' unions
    Chinese multinationals' overseas operations, and 9.3.2
    "owned by the people" concept, and 1.2.2
Chinese corporations
    ESG revolution, and 7.2.3
    Xiaomi Corporation ESG integration case study 7.2.3
Chinese currency *see* Digital currency; RMB internationalization
Climate Bonds Initiative (CBI) 7.1.2; 10.2.1
    GBA green infrastructure investment opportunities report 7.1.2; 10.2.1
Comparisons between China and Japan 1.4
    controlling structure 1.4.1
    stakeholder relationships 1.4.2
Comparisons between China and US 1.3
    CEO nomination, succession planning and compensation 1.3.3
    government's influence 1.3.1
    power of SOEs 1.3.2
Compensation
    CEOs 1.3.3; 5.1.1
Comprehensive and Progressive Agreement for Trans-Pacific Partnership (CPTPP) 9.1
Conflicts of interest
    SOEs controlling ownership, and 2.1.2
Controlling structure
    Alibaba, case studies 1.2.3; 2.2.1, 2.2.3

Index

    comparisons between China and Japan 1.4.1
    founder *see* Founder controlling structure
    SOEs *see* Key CG matters of SOEs
Corporate Governance Code *see* CG Code
Corporate repurpose
    revolution 4.1.2
Corporate Social Credit System (CSCS)
    Social Credit System (SoCS), and 8.2.1, 8.2.2
Corporate Social Responsibility (CSR) 6.1
    evaluation systems 6.2, 6.2.1
    government's influence in development 6.1.2
    history and development 6.1.1
    introduction of concept 3.3
COVID-19 pandemic
    BRI's future development, and 9.2.2
    concluding comments 11
    quick reaction capacity, and 5.1.2
    recovery from 1.3.1; 9.2.2
    Regional Comprehensive Economic Partnership (RCEP), and 9.1
    Social Credit System (SoCS), and 8.2, 8.2.2
Creativity 5.1.2
    governance models and business practices 5.1.2
Currency *see* Digital currency; RMB internationalization

Digital currency 10.1.3
    Hong Kong's cross-border trading platform 10.2.2
Domestic asset owners
    ESG revolution, and 7.2.2

Economic environment
    improving quality of 5.2.3
Economic reform
    concluding comments 11
    "gradualist approach" 2.3.3; 3.1
    regulation reform, and 3.3
    SOE reform, and 3.1, 3.2.5
    Status of CG development, and 1.1.1-1.1.4
    VIE structure, and 2.3.3
Enterprise Resource Planning (EPR) system 8.2.3
Environmental, Social and Governance (ESG)
    adoption a challenge for RCEP 9.1.2
    CG reform, and 3.3
    challenges from BRI partner countries 9.2.2

China's 14th Five-Year-Plan, and 7.3.1; 8.1.2
   Chinese multinationals' overseas operations, and 9.3.2
   establishing 1.1.4
   movement *see* ESG movement
   new reporting rules 7.1.1
   rating systems *see* ESG rating systems
   regulation reforms 7.1.1; 10.2.1
   revolution *see* ESG revolution
ESG evaluation system's development
   context for 6.4.3
   necessity 6.4.2
   non-government advocate organizations 6.4.1
   unique factors 6.4.3
ESG movement 7.1
   carbon emission control 7.1.3
   concluding comments 11
   major drivers 7.2.1
   mutual understanding 11
   regulation reforms 7.1.1
   transforming to green finance 7.1.2
ESG rating systems 6.2, 6.2.2
   future development *see* ESG evaluation system's development
   MSCI *see* MSCI ESG ratings systems and indexes
ESG revolution 3.3.2
   challenges and opportunities 7.3
   major drivers *see* Major drivers of ESG revolution
   moving up value chain 7.3.1
   Social Credit System (SoCS) impact on 8.2.3
   trend of business mindset change 7.3.2
   VIPkid's social impact strategy case study 7.3.2

Fair competition
   Chinese multinationals' overseas operations, and 9.3.2
Fair job opportunities
   Chinese multinationals' overseas operations, and 9.3.2
Feilo Acoustics Co Ltd
   minority shareholders' interest protection case study 8.3.3
Foreign investments
   increasing amounts in Chinese companies 5.3.2
   Founder controlling structure 2.2
   Alibaba case studies 2.2.1, 2.2.3
   dictatorship and voting rights 2.2.1
   founder's commitment 2.2.3

Index

    leadership transfers 2.2.4
    long-term value creation 2.2.2
    share structure contrasts with Alibaba and Facebook 2.2
    sustainability concerns 2.2.4
Founders
    Chinese companies' share pledging risks 4.1.4
    controlling structure *see* Founder controlling structure
    resignation, ByteDance case study 8.4
    retirement and leadership transfer 2.2.4; 5.2.2; 8.4
Further reading
    list of App 1

Generational leadership transfer 2.2.4
Global branding
    challenges 5.2.1
Governance models 1.2
    Alibaba and Huawei case studies 1.2.3
    creativity 1.2.3; 5.1.2
    evolving 11
    Lenovo, case study 3.3.1
    "owned by the people" 1.2.2
    two-tier boards (German vs China) 1.2.1
Government's influence 1.3.1
    CG practices, and 5.1.1
    CSR development 6.1.2
Government's interventions 1.1.3
    Chinese multinationals' overseas operations 9.3.2
"Gradualist approach"
    CG development 2.3.3
    digital RMB 10.1.3
    economic reform 2.3.3; 3.1
Greater Bay Area (GBA) *see* Guangdong-Hong Kong-Macau GBA
Green finance transformation
    collaborating with international climate bonds organizations 7.1.2
    ESG movement, and 7.1.2
    Hong Kong and Shanghai's international financial centers' roles 10.2.1
    promoting "green" finance movements 7.1.2
    RMB internationalization, and 10.1.4
Group of Seven industrialized countries (G7)
    BRI and competition from 9.2.2
Guangdong-Hong Kong-Macau GBA
    concept and development of 10.2.3
    green infrastructure investment opportunities report 7.1.2; 10.2.1
    potential of 10.2.3

Haier Group Corporation
    CG weaknesses of Rendanheyi model, case study 5.2.1
    SOE reform, case studies 3.2.1, 3.2.3, 3.2.5
Hangzhou Wahaha Group (WHH)
    founder's retirement case study 5.2.2
High-standard regulation system
    anti-trust law enforcement 8.3.2
    commitment to 8.3
    intellectual property (IP) rights protection 8.3.1
    minority shareholders' interest protection 8.3.3
Hong Kong
    future of 10.2
    Guangdong-Hong Kong-Macau GBA see Guangdong-Hong Kong-Macau GBA
    important RMB offshore center 10.2.2
    international financial center roles 10.2.1
Huawei
    governance model, case studies 1.2.3

Independent board directors
    share pledging risk mitigation, and 4.1.2
Information transparency
    audit 4.5
    Chinese multinationals' overseas operations, and 9.3.2
    SOEs and concerns 2.1.2
Initial Public Offerings (IPOs) 1.1.2
    Chinese companies seeking in US stock market 5.3.1
    Hong Kong and Shanghai as international financial centers, and 10.2.1
    incident, Ant Group case study 5.2.3
    suspension 1.1.3
    VIE structures, and 4.2.1
Insider share pledging 4.1
    CEO share pledging landscape in US 4.1.3
    CEO share pledging motivations 4.1.1
    Chinese companies' founders and CEOs 4.1.4
    risk mitigation 4.1.2
Intellectual property (IP) rights protection 8.3.1
    establishment of new IP Court of Appeals at national level 8.3.1
    IP applications to WIPO 8.3.1
    Patent Law Amendment enacted in 2021 8.3.1
    Regional Comprehensive Economic Partnership (RCEP), and 9.1.1
Interviewees
    list of App 4

Index

Japan
    major CG contrasts with China *see* Comparisons between China and Japan
JD.com
    impact of founder's reputation, risk case study 4.3

Key CG matters of SOEs 2.1
    "China Puzzle" 2.1.1
    conflicts of interest due to controlling ownership 2.1.2
    ineffective boards independence and board functions 2.1.2
    information transparency issue 2.1.2
Key domestic drivers of CG practices 5.2
    CG weaknesses, case studies 5.2.1, 5.2.2
    continuous regulatory reform and enhancement of regulation enforcement 5.2.3
    global branding challenges 5.2.1
    leadership transfer challenges 5.2.2

Labor law considerations
    ESG-related challenges from BRI partner countries 9.2.2
    major problems of Chinese multinationals' overseas operations 9.3.2
Labor unions *see* Chinese companies' unions
Leadership transfers
    founder's retirement and succession planning 2.2.4; 5.2.2; 8.4
Legal uncertainty
    VIE structure 4.2.1
Lenovo
    CG model, case study 3.3.1
Lists
    acronyms App 2
    further reading App 1
    interviewees App 4
Long-term value creation
    founder controlling structure, and 2.2.2
Luckin Coffee
    share pledging risks, case study 4.1.4

"Made in China 2025" strategy 7.3.1
Major drivers of ESG revolution 7.2
    asset management firms 7.2.2
    Chinese corporations 7.2.3
    domestic asset owners 7.2.2
    policy makers and regulators 7.2.1
    Xiaomi Corporation ESG integration case study 7.2.3

Major international drivers of CG practices 5.3
    increase of foreign investments in Chinese companies 5.3.2
    US scrutiny of US-listed Chinese companies 5.3.1
Minority shareholders' interest protection 8.3.3
    Feilo Acoustics Co Ltd case study 8.3.3
Mobile payment
    regulatory reform 5.2.3
Moving up the value chain
    ESG revolution, and 7.3.1
MSCI ESG ratings systems and indexes 6.3
    MSCI China ESG Leader Index 6.3.2
    MSCI Global Sustainability Indexes 6.3.1
Mutual understanding 11

Nominations
    CEOs 1.3.3

Offshore holding companies *see* Overseas Listed Off-shore Entities (OLOEs)
Online payment
    regulatory reform 5.2.3
Opportunities
    China as RCEP's leading country 9.1.2
    ESG revolution 7.3
Organizational structure *see* Governance models
Overseas Listed Off-shore Entities (OLOEs)
    VIE structure, and 2.3.1; 4.2, 4.2.1, 4.2.2
"Owned by the people"
    concept 1.2.2

Party Committee
    CG practices, and 5.1.1
    involvement in Chinese companies, risk or support 4.4
    SOE reform, and 3.2.5
Party influence *see also* Government's influence
    Chinese multinationals' overseas operations 9.3.2
Pinduoduo
    leadership transfer and succession planning, case study 2.2.4; 5.2.2; 8.4
Ping An Insurance Group
    ESG adoption case study 7.2.2
Policy makers
    ESG revolution, and 7.2.1
"Principles for Responsible Investment" (PRI)
    signatories and ESG revolution 7.2.2

Index

Public Company Accounting Oversight Board (PCAOB)
    audit quality and audit information transparency 4.5
    scrutiny of US-listed Chinese companies, and 5.3.1

Quick reaction capacity
    CG practices, and 5.1.2

Regional Comprehensive Economic Partnership (RCEP) 9.1
    agreement between China, Japan and South Korea 9.1.1
    China's leading role 9.1.1
    IP rights coverage 9.1.1
    member countries' diversity 9.1.1
    opportunities and challenges for China as leading country 9.1.2
    overview 9.1.1
    RMB internationalization, and 9.1.2; 10.1.2, 10.1.4
Regulation compliance
    alignment with government strategy reducing risks 5.1.1
    mindset changes 11
Regulation enforcement
    Ant Group IPO incident, case study 5.2.3
    continuous reform and enhancement 5.2.3
Regulation reforms 2.2.4
    anti-trust law enforcement 5.2.3; 8.3.2
    ESG, and 7.1.1; 10.2.1
    higher standard regulation system *see* High-standard regulation system
    online/mobile payment 5.2.3
    regulation enforcement 5.2.3
    timetable and milestones 3.1
    VIE structure *see* Variable Interest Entity (VIE) structure
Regulators
    Ant Group IPO incident, case study 5.2.3
    ESG revolution, and 7.2.1
    reform and enhancement of regulation enforcement 5.2.3
    VIE structure issues, and 2.3.3; 4.2.1
Risks
    audit quality and audit information transparency 4.5
    board function independency and objectivity 4.5
    founder controlling company's key person 4.3
    impact of JD.com founder's reputation, case study 4.3
    insider share pledging *see* Insider share pledging
    Party Committee involvement in Chinese companies 4.4
    related transactions 4.5
    VIE structure *see* VIE structure risks

RMB internationalization 9.1.2; 10.1
    bilateral swap agreements 10.1.2
    cross-border cash pooling 10.1.2
    digital RMB 10.1.3, 10.2.2
    Dim Sum Bonds 10.1.2
    Free Trade Zones 10.1.2
    Hong Kong largest RMB offshore center 10.2.2
    importance of 10.1.1
    Interbank Payment System (CIPS) 10.1.2
    offshore markets 10.1.2
    opportunities to explore 10.1.4
    Panda Bonds 10.1.2
    pilot programs 10.1.2
    progress of 10.1.2
    Qualified Foreign Institutional Investor (QFII) and (RQFII) 10.1.2
    removing cap for foreign ownership in certain financial sectors 10.1.2

Securities Exchange Commission (SEC)
    scrutiny of US-listed Chinese companies, and 5.3.1
    share pledging disclosure requirement 4.1.3
    VIE structure risks, and 4.2, 4.2.3
Shanghai Environment and Energy Exchange (SEEE)
    overseeing function 7.1.3
Shanghai Stock Exchange (SSE) 1.1.1, 1.1.2
    ESG movement, and 7.2.1
    history 1.1.1
    Hong Kong and Shanghai as international financial centers, and 10.2.1
    official operations 1.1.2
    reopening 1.1; 3.3
    ten percent cap system 1.1.3
Shanghai Stock Exchange's Science and Technology Innovation Board (STAR) 7.2.1
    international financial center roles, and 10.2.1
Shanghai United Asset and Equity Exchange (SUAEE)
    overseeing function 7.1.3
Shareholder engagement
    share pledging risk mitigation 4.1.2
Share pledging *see* Insider share pledging
Shenzhen Stock Exchange (SZSE) 1.1.1, 1.1.2
    ESG movement, and 7.2.1
    founding 1.1; 3.3
    official operations 1.1.2
    "Social Responsibility Instruction to Listed Companies" 6.1.2
    ten percent cap system 1.1.3

Sina-com
    VIE structure, case study 2.3.2
SinoHydro-Ghana Bui Dam Hydroelectricity Project
    workforce management challenges, case study 9.3.1
Social Credit System (SoCS) 3.3.2; 8.2
    Corporate Social Credit System (CSCS), and 8.2.1, 8.2.2
    COVID-19 pandemic, and 8.2, 8.2.2
    impact on ESG revolution 8.2.3
    punishments and rewards 8.2.2
    transitional version 8.2.1
Social entrepreneurship
    Bytedance founder's resignation, case study 8.4
    rise of 2.2.4; 8.4
Social impact
    mindset changes 11
Socially Responsible Investing (SRI) 6.2
    establishment 6.1.2
    origins 6.2
SOE reform
    autonomy and incentive 3.2.1
    corporatization 3.2.3
    establishment of Contract Responsibility System (CRS) 3.2.2
    extensive 3.2.5
    history 3.2, 3.2.2
    stages of, and Haier case studies 3.2.1- 3.2.5
    State-Owned Asset Management System Reform 3.2.4
    timetable and milestones 3.1
STAGE
    ESG, and 7.2.1
Stakeholder relationships
    major differences between China and Japan 1.4.2
State Administration for Market Regulation (SAMR)
    VIE structure, and 2.3.3
State-Owned Asset Management System Reform 3.2.4
State-Owned Assets Supervision and Administration Commission (SASAC)
    CSR, and 6.1.2
    establishment 3.2.4
    governance models, and 1.2
    government's influence, and 1.3.1; 5.1.1
    SOE reform, and 3.2.4
State-Owned Enterprises (SOEs)
    board structure *see* Governance models
    CEO nomination, succession planning and compensation 1.3.3; 5.1.1

    CG practices and government's influence 5.1.1
    ESG revolution, and 7.2.3
    key CG matters *see* Key CG matters of SOEs
    power of 1.3.2
    reform *see* SOE reform
    strengths 2.1.1
    weaknesses 2.1.1
Status of CG development 1.1
    CG Code 1.1.4
    CSRC 1.1.2
    government's intervention 1.1.3
    SSE and SZSE 1.1.1
"Stay low profile" 11
Stock subscription rights 1.1.2
Succession planning
    Alibaba case study 1.2.3
    CEOs 1.3.3
    leadership transfers 2.2.4; 5.2.2; 8.4
Sustainability considerations
    founder controlling structure, and 2.2.4

Trans-Pacific Partnership (TPP) 9.1
Transparency *see* Information transparency

United States (US)
    audit of all listed foreign companies 4.5
    CEO share pledging landscape 4.1.3
    major CG contrasts with China *see* Comparisons between China and US
    narrowing anti-trust enforcement gap with China 4.2.3
    Public Company Accounting Oversight Board (PCAOB) 4.5; 5.3.1
    scrutiny of US-listed Chinese companies 5.3.1
    Securities Exchange Commission *see* Securities Exchange Commission (SEC)

Value creation
    Founder controlling structure, and 2.2.2
Variable Interest Entity (VIE) structure
    brief history 2.3.2; 4.2
    loophole and government's approach to fixing 2.3; 4.2.1
    M&A transactions under anti-trust review 8.3.2
    Overseas Listed Off-shore Entities (OLOEs) 2.3.1; 4.2, 4.2.1, 4.2.2
    regulator's oversight 2.3.3
    regulatory improvements 4.2.1
    risks *see* VIE structure risks

Index

    simplified 2.3.1
    Sina-com case study 2.3.2
    unique business structure 2.3.1
    Wholly Foreign Owned Enterprise (WFOE) 2.3.1; 4.2
VIE structure risks 4.2
    Alibaba Alipay ownership transfer, case study 4.2.2
    investors' fragile ownership 4.2.2
    legal uncertainty 4.2.1
    managing 4.2.3
VIPkid
    social impact strategy case study 7.3.2
Voting rights
    founder controlling structure, and 2.2.1

Wholly Foreign Owned Enterprise (WFOE) 2.3.1; 4.2
"Work high profile" 11
Workplace unions *see* Chinese companies' unions
World Intellectual Property Organization (WIPO) 8.3.1
    IP applications, and 8.3.1

Xiaomi Corporation

Notes

Notes

Notes

Notes

Notes

Notes